RELIGION, MARRIAGE, AND FAMILY

Series Editors

Don S. Browning
John Wall

More Lasting Unions

CHRISTIANITY, THE FAMILY, AND SOCIETY

Stephen G. Post

William B. Eerdmans Publishing Company
Grand Rapids, Michigan / Cambridge, U.K.

Published 2000 by Wm. B. Eerdmans Publishing Co.

255 Jefferson Ave. S.E., Grand Rapids, Michigan 49503 /

P.O. Box 163, Cambridge CB3 9PU U.K.

Printed in the United States of America

04 03 02 01 00   7 6 5 4 3 2 1

Library of Congress Cataloging-in-Publication Data

Post, Stephen Garrard, 1951–

More lasting unions : Christianity, the family,

and society / Stephen G. Post.

p.   cm.

Includes bibliographical references.

ISBN 0-8028-4707-2 (pbk. : alk. paper)

1. Family — Religious aspects — Christianity.   I. Title.

BT707.7.P67 2000

261.8′358 — dc21   99-086147

Acknowledgments

A good portion of Chapter 5 first appeared in the *Journal of Religious Ethics,* vol. 25, no. 1 (Spring 1997): 149-68.

Certain parts of Chapter 7 are revised from *Spheres of Love: Toward a New Ethics of the Family.* Dallas: Southern Methodist University Press, 1994.

Certain parts of Chapter 3 are revised from Chapter 16, "Marriage and Family," in *Christian Ethics: Problems and Prospects.* Edited by Lisa Sowle Cahill and James F. Childress Cleveland: Pilgrim Press, 1996.

Contents

Series Foreword

The Religion, Marriage, and Family series evolves out of a research project located at the University of Chicago and financed by a generous grant from the Division of Religion of the Lilly Endowment, Inc. The first phase of the project lasted from 1991 to 1997 and produced eleven books on religion and family. In late 1997, the Lilly Endowment gave the project an additional major grant that supports a second phase of research and publication. The books in the Eerdmans Religion, Marriage, and Family series come directly or indirectly from the initiatives of this second phase.

In some cases, the books will evolve directly from the University of Chicago project. In other cases, they will be books written in response to that project or in some way stimulated by it. In all cases, they will be books probing the depth of resources in Judaism and Christianity for understanding, renewing, and in some respects redefining current expressions of marriage and family. The series will investigate issues of parenthood and children, work and family, responsible fatherhood, and equality in the family; the responsibility of the major professions in promoting and protecting sound marriages and families; the biblical, legal, and philosophical grounds of Western family systems; selected classics of these traditions; and the respective roles of church, market, and state in supporting marriages, families, parents, and children.

The Religion, Marriage, and Family series intends to go beyond the sentimentality, political manipulation, and ungrounded assertions that characterize so much of the contemporary debate over marriage and family. It plans to develop an intelligent and accessible new literature for colleges and seminaries, churches and other religious institutions, questing individuals and families. Marriage and family issues are not just preoccupations of the United States; they have become worldwide concerns as modernization, globalization, changing values, emerging poverty, and changing gender roles disrupt families and challenge the very idea of marriage throughout the world. It has been predicted that the emerging marriage and family crisis will be the central issue of the twenty-first century. The Religion, Marriage, and Family series hopes to contribute to more balanced and well-informed public debate on this issue, both in the United States and around the globe.

*   *   *

We are pleased to open the series with Professor Stephen Post's excellent *More Lasting Unions: Christianity, the Family, and Society*. In this multifaceted work, Post develops unique theological perspectives on the American debate over the family. He is also in a profound dialogue with the earlier volumes of the University of Chicago project. Post develops a theology of marital equality but without sacrificing the unique contributions of both husbands and wives, fathers and mothers. He continues his insightful reflections on parental love first opened in his earlier *Spheres of Love: Toward a New Ethics of the Family* (1994). He not only brings both theology and the social sciences to the assessment of the meaning and consequences of divorce, nonmarital births, fatherlessness, and single parenthood; he also advances the most powerful theological justification for adoption available in the current literature. Nor has Professor Post, an expert on aging, forgotten the plight of the elderly and how it affects caretaking spouses and families. He concludes by issuing a powerful call to Christian families to resist the temptations of insularity and self-serving consumerism and to reach out in love to the neighbor.

In short, Stephen Post has made a powerful new contribution to serious theological thought about marriage and family. He also has done what relevant scholarship should always do — help continue and enrich an important new cultural and religious conversation, in this case the dialogue about the present health and possible future of marriages and families.

DON S. BROWNING and JOHN WALL, series editors

Preface

This is one of those books that took shape over four years and finally came together during two months of uninterrupted writing in the summer of 1998 at the Becket Institute, located at St. Hugh's College, Oxford University. The Institute was established by the Becket Fund for Religious Liberty, located in Washington, D.C. I owe a great deal to Kevin J. Hasson, President and General Counsel of the Becket Fund.

The quiet green landscape between Oxford City Center and Summertown provided a change from my usual environment at Case Western Reserve University in Cleveland, Ohio — where I conceived and drafted these chapters in an effort to say something useful on the topic of basic Christian ethics, marriage, and the family. My work at the Becket Institute was supported by the John Templeton Foundation, to which I am very grateful.

The impressive chapels of Oxford reminded me of my student days at the University of Chicago Divinity School (1978-1983), where I studied the history of Christian social thought and ethics with James M. Gustafson, Robin W. Lovin, and Don S. Browning, who has since then contributed in remarkable ways to the discussion of marriage, family, and society.

This book is a sequel to an earlier one, entitled *Spheres of Love: Toward a New Ethics of the Family.* I wish to express gratitude to Lonnie D. Kliever of Southern Methodist University for his encouragement of that project. My earlier work is an effort in pure constructive theology. This new book, by contrast, covers the history of Christian social thought and practice, applied to a number of contemporary issues of social importance in an age of divorce. Much of the content of *More Lasting Unions* was initially determined in July of 1995, when I was invited by Tom Needham and Cameron Lee to present a week of lectures in a course offered at Fuller Theological Seminary, focusing on new topics left uncovered in my previous work and of likely interest to their students studying family therapy. Thus, this new book is by necessity more grounded in social-science data than my earlier writings are. I wish to thank everyone at Fuller for being helpful.

This book is certainly my fullest theological and ethical statement on the institutions of marriage and the family, on the importance of parental and filial responsibility, and on Christian responsibility for culture and society. It is a book nurtured by the splendid editorial efforts of Mary Hietbrink of William B. Eerdmans. To her I offer my appreciation and thanks.

STEPHEN G. POST
Cleveland, 1999

Introduction

In a time when social science points to how important marriage and family are for the health of society, how can a culture lacking any clear affirmation of more lasting marital unions ever contribute to that health? This book examines the deeper spiritual foundations of lasting unions in the context of Western culture as it was shaped by Christianity, and shows the continuing need for a spirituality of marriage and family life that encourages us all to see the tremendous value in a deeper form of commitment than contemporary culture appears able to encourage.

Chapter One, "Marriage, Family, and Society: A Social-Scientific Perspective," establishes a general interpretation of data on the adverse consequences of the divorce culture, and also establishes a framework for thinking about marriage, family, and society that is Christian, rational, and part of the public discourse. Chapter Two, "Marriage and Family in the Teachings of Jesus," emphasizes the Judaic context of Jesus of Nazareth's teachings on marriage, summarizes the most relevant New Testament passages affirming marriage, and makes the argument that, with respect to his affirmation of the ideal of marital permanence, Jesus must be understood as a part of the tradition of the Jewish Prophets. Not an exegete by training, I must rely heavily on the work of others, especially Geza Vermes and E. P. Sanders, both of whom are highly regarded scholars who have highlighted the teachings of Jesus on marriage and family. I place Jesus' criticisms of the family in proper context:

he was critical of the family only when it became an obstacle to his mission.

Chapter Three, "The Spiritual Value of the Family," provides a perspective on the spiritual and moral meaning of the family within the Christian tradition. The spiritual emergence of marriage and the family occurred over centuries. An excellent history of this emergence and its impact on Western law is John Witte's masterful *From Sacrament to Covenant;* those readers seeking a full review replete with detailed analysis of primary sources should consult that volume.[1] My purpose is therefore not to repeat Witte's excellent work but to provide a spiritual and theological perspective on the value of marriage and the family that draws on historical sources without being uncritical of the past.

These initial chapters establish a framework for Chapter Four, "Toward a Contemporary Theology of the Family," in which the current literature of Christian ethicists and pastoral care is discussed quite critically. Pastoral care, for example, stresses unconditional love for persons regardless of the particular form of their family. In a culture as pluralistic, economically complex, and morally privatized as our own, Christians engaged in family counseling should not allow the historical teachings of Christianity with regard to marriage and family to obstruct their immediate response to those in need. Yet the wisdom in those teachings on the value of more lasting unions should still be applied in creative ways that are sensitive and caring. The tradition of marriage that is entered into with a serious vow, followed by the birth and raising of children, is biblically, theologically, and socially essential. It is wrong for any Christian to think that formlessness in marriage and family is perfectly reasonable or theologically sound. The present actuality of those in need must be understood, but the principle of more lasting unions must also be retained.

Chapter Five, "Adoption, Love, and Justice," is probably the most innovative chapter in the book because Christian ethics pays so little attention to this time-honored practice. Too many books on marriage and family do not discuss adoption, a gap that leaves adoptive families unattended to. There are no good studies, historical or otherwise, on adop-

1. John Witte Jr., *From Sacrament to Contract: Marriage, Religion, and Law in the Western Tradition* (Louisville, Ky.: Westminster/John Knox Press, 1997).

2

tion as a social practice within Christian culture. I attempt to underscore how relinquishment and adoption resonate with Christian social thought, and to stress the extent to which Western culture has approved the practice of adoption. Adoption, however, is at odds with the norm of the biological family and is approved as an alternative under less than ideal conditions.

Chapter Six, "The Challenge of Intensive Family Caregiving," is also devoted to an aspect of family life that deserves more attention: the challenge of caring for loved ones with severe, disabling conditions. As an example, I focus on the care of spouses and parents with dementia against the background of an aging society and its implications. The demographic reality is that we have extended the human life span in unprecedented ways. Thus, the vow of permanence in marriage usually requires more of us than of any preceding generations, especially when a loved one suffers from a chronic, long-term illness. Filial obligations are also changing. The commandment "Honor thy father and thy mother" remains fully valid in today's world, but it requires much more of us now than it did when parents died much younger, usually long before the age of onset for most chronic illnesses of the elderly. I've become acutely aware of this fact through my own work. Although I was trained in theological ethics, I have for the last ten years been a faculty member at an academic medical center. I have drawn from the model of the diaconate, in which an identifiable at-risk constituency is served; most of my work has been focused on families dealing with dementia, often of the Alzheimer's type. Thus, I have never lost sight of my theological interests in love, marriage, and the family.[2]

Chapter Seven, "Familial Bonds and Love for All of Humanity," takes up the question of the ordering of priorities in Christian ethics. Specifically, it considers the inevitable moral tension between love for those near and dear and neighborly love for all of humanity. Given the radical universal demands of *agape,* this tension cannot be easily negotiated. *Agape,* which includes love even for enemies, is the work of an adventurous God who builds on natural solicitude for the near and dear

---

2. See Stephen G. Post, *The Moral Challenge of Alzheimer Disease* (Baltimore, Md.: The Johns Hopkins University Press, 1995).

and then calls for a radical expansion of moral priorities. This is a difficult topic but one that ultimately must be addressed to avoid the inward-turning tendencies of familial concern, which often lead to the abandonment of wider moral spheres and to a rampant consumerism.

I view this book in part as a sequel to my earlier work, *Spheres of Love,* which developed broad constructive theological interpretations of Christian love that centered on the parent-child axis;[3] it also took up at length the question of balancing self-denial and self-concern in Christian love. This second work on the theme of Christian love and the family is distinguished by its degree of attention to contemporary social issues and controversies, and by its appeal to aspects of traditional Christian social thought. I would not wish to be considered either a liberal or a conservative on matters of marriage and family. I do try, however, to conserve that which is, I think, of great importance to Christianity.

3. Post, *Spheres of Love: Toward a New Ethics of the Family* (Dallas: Southern Methodist University Press, 1994).

1

Marriage, Family, and Society: A Social-Scientific Perspective

When men and women marry and bring children into the world, they migrate into new spheres of mature love that will both challenge and change them. Conjugal love and subsequent parental love form the basis of the "family" as I consider it here, however extended it might be beyond this essential biological core. The high moral expectations connoted by the term "family" are often best fulfilled in the context of the surrounding extended family, of which the nucleus is frequently our last remnant. If this domestic window to the sacred is to succeed, it must inevitably be shaped by patience, kindness, forgiveness, trust, hope, perseverance, and other features that Christians associate with *agape,* after the words of Saint Paul (1 Cor. 13:4-7).

Marriage and Family at a Crossroads

What is a family? In the modern Western world, the term "family" most commonly refers to a group of kinship-related persons who share a home. In this context, the family consists of a kinship system whose members belong to it by marriage, birth, or adoption. Some persons consider themselves to be a family because they live communally and have caring relationships, and this metaphorical notion of the family is certainly to be respected and appreciated. My focus, however, is on the family as a biological community within nature that is defined by sexual differentiation, procreation, and kinship descent; it is the social unit in which children are born, protected, supported both economically and emotionally, and socialized. This entity is termed "nuclear" when parents and children live in an independent household, and "extended" if the household includes grandparents and/or other relatives. Parental, filial, conjugal, and sibling responsibilities define the biological family. As Lisa Sowle Cahill writes, the family "has a basic and constitutive relation to biological relationship (including reproductive partnership to produce the next generation), for which other relations, however valid, are analogues, not replacements."[1]

Marriage is widely understood in the Western world and, for the most part, cross-culturally as the stabilizing foundation for responsible procreation. Certainly the monotheistic religions of the Western world have clothed marriage with the garb of sacred vows. It is only very recently that the concept of marriage as being merely optional prior to procreation has become thinkable. From a Christian perspective, however, the emerging advocacy groups for optional marriage in the United States and Great Britain must be viewed critically. Optional marriage is a very different phenomenon than either justified divorce or single-mother parenthood due to the death of a husband because it creates fatherlessness by choice rather than by undesired contingencies. (A child who has lost his or her father due to untimely death will not feel abandoned by choice or neglect.) Recent studies show that more than half of American children and growing numbers of European children now spend significant periods of their childhoods without fathers.[2] An unmarried woman who chooses to have a child without a social father does form a biological family in the sense of a mother-child bond; this arrangement does not, however, provide the child with the usually enhancing dyadic husband-wife foundation. There is much sensible wis-

1. Lisa Sowle Cahill, *Sex, Gender, and Christian Ethics* (Cambridge: Cambridge University Press, 1996), p. 106.

2. David Blankenhorn, *Fatherless America: Confronting Our Most Urgent Social Problem* (New York: Basic Books, 1995).

dom in the old rhyme "First comes love, then comes marriage, then comes junior in the baby carriage."

Optional marriage is unlikely to overwhelm traditional common sense — if only for the practical reason that having four hands is better than just two. But there is far more than tradition and practicality at stake here. I will argue throughout this book that Christians, for both theological and empirical reasons, must view cultural challenges to the norm of marriage as the necessary foundation for procreation as a high-stakes issue worthy of their full attention.

While optional marriage remains a somewhat marginal practice, it could not have arisen as a socially acceptable possibility without the increasing moral and theological minimization of the time-honored importance of lasting marriage. This minimization began in the 1960s in both American and European societies. The law, which was historically allied with Christian expectations for the family, has now much diminished its previously robust statements about responsibility and accountability in marriage and parenthood. Political philosopher Michael J. Sandel points to the radical deflation of moral expectations in these spheres, both in the United States and in Europe, and to the steep rise of the self unencumbered by moral judgments or concerned with the family's stakeholders.[3] Legal diminishment and the privatization of conscience work hand in hand, and one of the consequences is a rising divorce rate. Nine out of ten Americans eventually marry, and half of the marriages entered into since 1970 have ended in divorce; thus, an estimated 45 percent of American adults will experience the breakup of at least one marriage.[4] Institutionalized monogamy has mutated into serial monogamy. The question, then, is not whether monogamy can be saved; the question is whether it can be restored in a manner most fully respectful of human dignity, equality, and love.

Since the 1969 Divorce Reform Act in Great Britain, the divorce rate has risen above 40 percent, the highest in the European Union.[5]

---

3. Michael J. Sandel, *Democracy's Discontent: America in Search of a Public Philosophy* (Cambridge: Harvard University Press, 1996), p. 111.

4. Andrew J. Cherlin, *Marriage, Divorce, and Remarriage,* rev. ed. (Cambridge: Harvard University Press, 1992).

5. Office for National Statistics, *Social Trends* 27 (London: HMSO, 1997).

Many British Christians are concerned about the new confusion that strips meaning from the trinity of mother, father, and child — a trinity beautifully sanctified in late medieval paintings of the "holy family." Prompted by a desire to bring spirituality into the home so that families might be better sustained, European Christian thinkers have established the International Academy for Marital Spirituality (INTAMS).[6] Marriage Resource, a Christian charity in Britain, was responsible for the launch of the first National Marriage Week in February 1997; this event involved 600 churches and 45,000 individuals, and captured great media attention. But the struggle to influence the wider culture and law with regard to marriage and family is difficult; scarcely any residual dignity remains when marriage is entered into without high purpose and lightly dissolved without justification.

Christianity and the Public Square

Most people are somewhat ambivalent about their familial experiences. Families can be oppressive or abusive at worst, and even at best they will surely be imperfect. Even in harmonious families, the adolescent may well have a heightened ambivalence about the family as he or she breaks free of the parent-child axis in order to assert an independent identity. Jesus of Nazareth himself broke free of his family in order to begin his ministry. Christianity is not naive about the imperfections of family life, including the problems of myopic insularity, consumerism, and overindulgence that ignore wider spheres of moral and spiritual commitment. Yet Christianity nevertheless powerfully endorses the overall value of the family as the human context for faithful marriage and procreation shaped by equality of the partners and covenant love for children. As I shall argue, this endorsement is a profoundly essential one to Christianity and must inform its endeavor to positively affect culture and society.

There are certain moments when the Christian must speak as a Christian to address a high-stakes public issue about which the tradi-

---

6. See the scholarly journal *INTAMS Review* (Review of the International Academy for Marital Spirituality).

tion is clear. The Christian must choose these moments carefully if his or her voice is to be taken seriously. Precisely the same caution should be exercised by feminists, deconstructionists, African-Americans, Marxists, and many others who have meaningful voices in a pluralistic and liberal polity. A liberal polity enables those different voices to create alliances when they happen to agree practically (though worldviews and epistemic priorities may vary). Any voice that lacks intellectual rigor or that displays imperialistic arrogance, incivility in discourse, or lack of attentive listening to other voices will ultimately have no impact. In the words of George M. Marsden, all religious perspectives should be welcome in the academy and in the public square "so long as their proponents are willing to support the rules necessary for constructive exchange of ideas in a pluralistic setting."[7] Without this pluralistic mix of voices, public discourse becomes dreary and uniform rather than creative, challenging, and tolerant. The value of democratic pluralistic discourse is that it does not require participants to privatize their core convictions.

Critics of the religious voice insist on the single language of secular monism in addressing matters of the commonweal. While the believer can address many issues in the purely secular, rational language necessary for public policy, there are times when he or she should use specifically religious language in public. Abraham Lincoln, for example, was deeply theological in many of his public utterances; Martin Luther King Jr. built his "I Have a Dream" speech around scriptural references to the prophet Amos. Surely both Protestants and Catholics should have spoken out against Nazism from their theological traditions much earlier than they did; Dietrich Bonhoeffer was an eloquent exception whose voice was silenced only by death in a Nazi prison. Often the religious voice plays a constructive role without which public dialogue would be impoverished.

With regard to the current extraordinary circumstances of cultural, political, and legal trivialization of lasting marriage and responsible motherhood and fatherhood, the Christian must enter the public

---

7. George M. Marsden, *The Outrageous Idea of Christian Scholarship* (New York: Oxford University Press, 1997), p. 45.

9

square armed with rigorous rational arguments, informed appeal to established empirical fact, and specific religious reasoning. A robust pluralism imposes no silence in modern nations and universities who have long been committed to pluralism and disestablishment, and for whom fears of religious establishment at this point in history are no longer grounded in reality.

Indeed, it would be impossible to replace the distinctive themes of Christian thought in the public debate. One distinctive theme, for example, is the impassioned prophetic critique of the bourgeois or aristocratic family that serves as the local and national agent of class hierarchies, unacceptable economic disparities, and racism. Latin American liberation theologians have criticized the family that contributes to political and social oligarchy. Such ruthless control of wealth and power was precisely the object of prophetic criticism in the Hebrew Bible. Prophetic social analysis must disagree with the libertarian bourgeois assertion of unlimited family accumulation put forward by some social theorists.[8] In emphasizing that the family is the seedbed of virtue and the vital institution which socializes and restrains without recourse to the potentially oppressive force of the state, certain scholars have been less than fully attentive to the injustice of the sometimes philanthropic but still self-indulgent family.[9] The family that contributes to injustice and oppression ultimately harms a free commonweal. A certain form of non-Christian pro-family thought is, as John Rawls suggests, equivalent to being against justice for the needy.[10]

In speaking publicly for the family, Christians must be extremely careful not to assert stereotypes about any particular ethnic group. In this culture, African-Amercians are particularly vulnerable to stereotyping:

8. See Robert Nozick, *Anarchy, State, and Utopia* (New York: Basic Books, 1974). See also Friedrich A. Hayek, *The Road to Serfdom* (Chicago: University of Chicago Press, 1944).

9. See *Seedbeds of Virtue: Sources of Competence, Character, and Citizenship in American Society,* ed. Mary Ann Glendon and David Blankenhorn (Lanham, Md.: University Press of America, 1995).

10. John Rawls, *A Theory of Justice* (Cambridge: Harvard University Press, 1971). For example, Rawls refuses to place familial concerns behind his fabled "veil of ignorance."

black men are frequently labeled as absent or uncaring husbands and fathers, and young black women are targeted as representative of the growing problem of unwed teenage mothers. But there is much to be learned from African-American men who are faithful to their wives and children despite overwhelmingly adverse circumstances. Furthermore, out-of-wedlock teen pregnancy is a problem that exists in all races and cultures.

Christians must also avoid criticism of same-sex relations. These relations are complex and deserve the excellent treatment that better-qualified thinkers than I have already afforded them. Procreation as the union of a biological mother and father, in a manner that combines the genetics of two biological creatures with the social experience of raising children who appear in their physical likeness, is not possible in the same-sex context. It is the centrality of creation and subsequent procreation in Judaism and Christianity that makes an emphasis on the blessings of heterosexual marriage and family unavoidable. But this should never result in intolerance.[11] At no point in the Gospels does Jesus indicate intolerance of homosexuality.

On this point, personal history is relevant. As an adolescent, I quickly learned to accept the bisexual orientation of my older brother, a successful popular writer in New York City who died of AIDS in March 1983. Like many families, my family understood that his sexual preferences were what they were. The simple fact is that some men fall in love with other men. It is not my intent to contribute in writing to anything other than understanding in this regard. My working experience has only increased my sense of the need for greater acceptance in other areas of human difference as well. After college, I worked as a research assistant at New York Hospital–Cornell Medical College in the field of pediatric endocrinology and hermaphroditism. I have long questioned the ethics of forcing persons into binary male-female categories of physiology through surgical and endocrinological support.[12] Nothing I write on behalf of permanence in marriage as a basis for optimal child rearing should obscure my respectful attitude toward human differences in sex-

11. Kathy Rudy, "The Social Construction of Sexual Identity and the Ordination of Practicing Homosexuals," *Journal of Religious Ethics* 25, no. 1 (1997): 127-46.

12. This is the topic of an entire issue of *The Journal of Clinical Ethics* (vol. 9, no. 2, Fall 1998).

ual and gender orientation. The Christian voice in the church and in the public square, while affirming the centrality of marriage and family consistent with freedom, equality, and justice, must avoid co-option by intolerant and uninformed forces.

The commonweal is served well by a respectful, civil, and pluralistic discourse that does not diminish the contributions made by specific traditions of understanding and commitment. True democratic discourse celebrates pluralism and refuses to silence the content of the religious voice to assert a draconian secular monism. Edward Shils points out that "The first entry on the agenda of the Enlightenment was . . . to do away with traditionality as such; with its demise, all the particular substantive traditions would likewise go."[13] Traditions have in many ways stood against moral progress, but they can also be critically appreciated for their accomplishments and wisdom in presenting "the ideal of a morally ordered universe in which some things [are] sacred."[14] Furthermore, traditions such as Christianity are always engaged in the process of gaining additional empirical evidence and self-understanding, so that new insight is possible over time. It is to some troubling empirical facts that I now turn.

When the Nucleus Splits

While social-scientific data are often soft enough to be seriously disputed, a remarkably compelling set of facts underscores the general benefits of marriage and family life. Although a great deal of demographic evidence indicates that marital disruption contributes to mortality rates, this is not our epidemiological focus.[15] Beginning in the early 1970s, Judith S. Wallerstein's longitudinal study of families undergoing divorce found that the adverse psychological consequences of marital breakup were considerable for both adults and children.[16]

13. Edward Shils, *Tradition* (Chicago: University of Chicago Press, 1981), p. 7.
14. Shils, *Tradition,* p. 325.
15. Linda J. Waite and L. A. Lillard, "Til Death Do Us Part: Marital Disruption and Mortality," *American Journal of Sociology* 100 (1995): 1131-56.
16. Judith S. Wallerstein and Joan Berlin Kelley, *Surviving the Breakup* (New York: Basic Books, 1980).

12

In particular, Wallerstein's studies challenged the then-current assumption that exposure to degrees of low-level conflict and disharmony in parental relationships is worse for children than the experience of family breakup through divorce. Her work is now universally regarded as scientifically valid. At the time of publication, however, she was ridiculed mercilessly by critics who did not wish to admit the adverse consequences of a divorce curve that became especially steep in the early 1970s and has not leveled off yet; it is estimated that half of the marriages initiated in the 1990s in the United States will end in divorce.[17] Steven L. Nock points out that, just as one would think something was wrong with a company in which half the employees quit or were fired, one would think that something must be wrong with a social environment in which one-third to one-half of all first marriages dissolve. Nock's substantial analysis of an immense amount of data indicates that today, in contrast to the 1950s and even the 1960s, self-interest has come to take precedence over the interests of the family unit.[18] Don S. Browning has brought this troubling reality into the forefront of discussion in the field of religious ethics, coupling his long-standing critique of contemporary psychology's narcissistic images of human fulfillment with his concerns over the damaging impact of family breakup. His project, "The Family, Religion, and Culture," is of great importance.[19]

In their fifteen-year study of divorce, Wallerstein and Sandra Blakeslee found that only 10 percent of children felt better about their lives after parental divorce.[20] After five years, more than a third of these children were suffering from clinical depression; after ten years, unusually high numbers were underachievers; after fifteen years, dispropor-

17. L. L. Bumpass, "What's Happening to the Family? Interaction between Demographic and Institutional Change," *Demography* 27 (1990): 483-98.

18. Steven L. Nock, *The Sociology of the Family* (Englewood Cliffs, N.J.: Prentice Hall, 1987).

19. See Don S. Browning et al., *From Culture Wars to Common Ground: Religion and the American Family Debate* (Louisville, Ky.: Westminster John Knox Press, 1997), chap. 1.

20. Judith S. Wallerstein and S. Blakeslee, *Second Chances: Men, Women, and Children a Decade after Divorce* (New York: Ticknor & Fields, 1989).

tionate numbers were insecure and struggling to establish stable relationships themselves. By the mid-1980s, researchers across the United States were backing away from two decades of optimism regarding the effects of divorce on children.

The harm is not limited to children. Divorced or separated persons, especially men, are disproportionately represented among psychiatric patients.[21] The medical literature abounds with studies indicating that divorce is generally a stressful event associated with physically and psychologically adverse consequences.[22] While remarriages are common, they are complex and difficult for the children involved, who often find them no substitute for the original family.[23] While high-conflict cases of divorce can be justified, a culture of impermanence and unfettered sexual indulgence lead to the following conditions, as summarized by evolutionary psychologist Robert Wright: "A quarter-century of indulging these impulses has helped bring a world featuring, among other things: lots of fatherless children; lots of embittered women; lots of complaints about date rape and sexual harassment; and the frequent sight of lonely men renting X-rated videotapes while lonely women abound."[24] These realities are stark but true.[25]

Even somewhat leftward-leaning sociologists who were once skeptical of studies showing adverse consequences of divorce are now taking a different view. Paul R. Amato and Alan Booth, for example, have studied the assumption that parental unhappiness is worse for children than parental divorce.[26] They analyzed longitudinal child-outcome data from

21. B. L. Bloom, S. W. White, and S. J. Asher, *Divorce and Separation: Context, Causes, and Consequences* (New York: Basic Books, 1979).

22. By far the most thorough compilation of dozens of medical studies is that by David B. Larson, James P. Swyers, and Susan S. Larson entitled *The Costly Consequences of Divorce: Assessing the Clinical, Economic, and Public Health Impact of Marital Disruption in the United States* (Bethesda, Md.: National Institute for Healthcare Research, 1995).

23. Cherlin, *Marriage, Divorce, and Remarriage*.

24. Robert Wright, *The Moral Animal: Why We Are the Way We Are* (London: Little, Brown, & Co., 1995), p. 145.

25. See Stephen G. Post, "Love, Religion, and Sexual Revolution," *Journal of Religion* 72, no. 3 (1992): 403-16.

26. Paul R. Amato and Alan Booth, *A Generation at Risk: Growing Up in an Era of Family Upheaval* (Cambridge: Harvard University Press, 1997).

large national samples and concluded that only 25 to 33 percent of parental divorces ended up being better for the children than if the parents had remained married. Psychological health, self-esteem, socialization, and educational accomplishment are some of the important measured variables. Amato and Booth emphasize that about 70 percent of divorces terminate low-conflict marriages that have some shortcomings but are still reasonably tolerable for spouses and far better for children than divorce. Unprecedented and excessively high individual expectations make many good marriages not "good enough." While low-conflict marriages now routinely become divorces, this was not always the case. Spending a third of one's life in a less than consistently harmonious marriage, the authors conclude, is not too much to ask of parents in order to benefit the children they have brought into the world. This seems reasonable.

Stepfamilies

While the term "blended families" was developed in the 1980s to try to get away from any problems associated with the term "stepfamilies," the truth must be told with due sensitivity. Researchers are now pointing out that stepfamilies present their own set of unique difficulties for children.[27] Martin Daly and Margo Wilson reviewed extensive data and concluded that stepparents generally care "less profoundly for children than natural parents."[28] (These are, of course, general data and should not be used as criteria for individual cases.) They found that fatal child abuse was one hundred times more likely in stepfamilies, and nonfatal child abuse as much as forty times more likely. Robert Wright is not surprised by the finding:

> After all, the whole reason natural selection invented paternal love was to bestow benefits on offspring. Though biologists call these benefits "investment," that doesn't mean they're strictly material, wholly sustainable through monthly checks. Fathers give their children all

27. See *Stepfamilies: Who Benefits? Who Does Not?* ed. Alan Booth and Judy Dunn (Hillside, N.J.: Lawrence Erlbaum, 1994).
28. Martin Daly and Margo Wilson, "Discriminative Parental Solicitude: A Biological Perspective," *Journal of Marriage and the Family* 42 (1980): 277-88.

kinds of tutelage and guidance (more, often, than either father or child realizes) and guard them against all kinds of threats. A mother alone simply can't pick up the slack. A stepfather almost surely won't pick up much, if any of it. In Darwinian terms, a young stepchild is an obstacle to fitness, a drain on resources.[29]

Evolutionary psychologists like Wright suggest that this problem may have roots in the "selfish gene" theory — that is, the theory that greater parental investment in children who carry one's genes is a heavily determined reality.

Regardless of the explanatory paradigm, however, an alarming number of headlines point to difficulty: "A woman's live-in boyfriend murders her child fathered by another man"; "A woman neglects her young stepsister and punishes her so viciously that she dies"; "A stepfather sexually abuses his wife's daughter by a former husband." As these examples drawn from recent news articles demonstrate, the Cinderella story is hardly a fairy tale.[30]

In their monumental study of current data, Sara McLanahan and Gary Sandefur conclude that children in stepfamilies benefit from family incomes that are equivalent to those of the formerly intact families. Nonetheless, they are also two to three times more likely to have behavioral and emotional problems than children in still intact families, twice as likely to have developmental or learning problems, more likely to drop out of high school, more likely to become single teenage mothers, and less able to hold steady jobs as young adults.[31] These authors find that children may be better off with divorce in cases of high-level, persistent conflict between parents. In cases of low-level conflict, emotional distancing, boredom, or a change in one spouse's priorities, however, children would be better off if parents resolved their difficulties and stayed together.[32] Although estimates vary somewhat, divorces resulting

29. Robert Wright, *The Moral Animal,* pp. 103-4.

30. Jane E. Brody, "Genetic Ties May Be a Factor in Violence in Stepfamilies," *New York Times,* 10 February 1998, sec. B, pp. 9, 12.

31. Sara McLanahan and Gary Sandefur, *Growing Up with a Single Parent* (Cambridge: Harvard University Press, 1994), p. 2.

32. McLanahan and Sandefur, *Growing Up with a Single Parent,* pp. 30-31.

from high-level, persistent conflict make up, at most, one-fourth of all cases. It seems possible, then, that many marriages could be saved if parents were better prepared for the realities of marriage, regularly supported in marriage (for example, in conflict resolution), and better educated about the consequences of divorce for their children. In cases of low-level conflict, the children's interests should supersede those of the parents.

There are cases in which the scales balance differently. National surveys indicate that every year 1.5 to 2.1 million women in the United States are physically assaulted by their male partners. Almost three million children in the United States are reported annually to child-protective services as alleged victims of abuse and neglect.[33] Appeals to the moral principle of minimizing harm can therefore justify divorce on a case-by-case basis — but justification is needed. As I have argued over a decade of writing on the concept of *agape,* the essence of Christian love involves mutuality supported by significant degrees of self-sacrifice — but not to the point of requiring radical self-denial and self-immolation.[34] Margaret Farley has provided a casuistical discussion of the making, keeping, and breaking of such commitments.[35]

In England, the report of the Policy Studies Institute, *Britain 2010,* predicts that the normal pattern in Great Britain will be cohabitation, marriage, divorce, and remarriage. Already 2.5 million British children and youths live in stepfamilies. In 1983 England established the National Stepfamily Association to provide advice and support. There is no doubt that those offering pastoral care must marshal great thought and

33. *Family Violence,* ed. Lloyd Ohlin and Michael Tonry (Chicago: University of Chicago Press, 1989).

34. See Stephen G. Post, "Disinterested Benevolence: An American Debate over the Nature of Christian Love," *Journal of Religious Ethics* 14, no. 2 (1986): 356-68; "Communion and True Self-Love," *Journal of Religious Ethics* 16, no. 2 (1988): 345-62; "The Inadequacy of Selflessness: God's Suffering and the Theory of Love," *Journal of the American Academy of Religion* 66, no. 2 (1988): 213-28; and "Christian Love and the Family," Chapter 6 in *A Theory of Agape: On the Meaning of Christian Love* (Lewisburg, Pa.: Bucknell University Press, 1990).

35. Margaret Farley, *Personal Commitments: Making, Keeping, Breaking* (San Francisco: Harper, 1986); see also *Just Love: New Perspectives in Christian Sexual Ethics* (New York: Crossroad, 1995).

energy to help those who have been wounded by family breakdown and now navigate the complexities of remarriage and stepfamilies. In recent decades, the Roman Catholic Church has emphasized the acceptance of civilly remarried persons in the church and the importance of pastoral care and support for them. Its canon law still does not allow the divorced and remarried person to receive sacraments, however, because it wishes to strongly encourage indissolubility.[36]

The "Culture of Divorce"

In her well-received analysis of "the divorce culture," Barbara Dafoe Whitehead points to the psychological ethos of expressive individualism, with its stress on inner experience, as diverting our gaze from the "multiple stakeholders in the unhappy business of marital dissolution: the other spouse, the children, the relatives, and the larger society."[37] Because expressive individualism is too weak to support stable relationships, this ethos really means the death of marriage; it means that children will usually lose the highly personal, daily support of a father, both financially and otherwise. It means that society will inherit the emotional scars. It means that the institution of marriage and family will be weakened for future generations, who have rarely seen fidelity and permanence modeled by their forebears, and modeling behavior is crucially important.

Marriage is a practical social mechanism that is unavoidable if a man and a woman are to be optimally linked over time to their biological children. It enables children to gain support from an identified, responsible father and mother who are living together as a four-handed team committed to furthering their children's short-term and long-term interests. Without marriage there would be no fathers, only inseminators devoid of socially established roles and expectations for sustained investment in

36. For a series of excellent essays on the topic of second marriages within Roman Catholicism, see Kevin T. Kelly, *Divorce and Second Marriage: Facing the Challenge,* 2d ed. (London: Geoffrey Chapman, 1996).

37. Barbara Dafoe Whitehead, *The Divorce Culture: Rethinking Our Commitments to Marriage and Family* (New York: Vintage, 1996), p. 66.

their offspring. Whitehead writes that through marriage, "sexual love is transformed into generative love and passion is transformed into altruism."[38] Unlike friendship, which can be ended for any number of little reasons, marriage is expected to be a lasting union and a source of stability in a sea of instability. Whitehead asks an essential question that we might all want to ask ourselves: "How can children achieve a stable and secure family life, with sustained and high levels of parental nurture and investment, in a system in which the marriage bond is so fragile and vulnerable to disruption?"[39]

Whitehead does a splendid job of tracing a cultural change that was somewhat evident at the start of the twentieth century but began in earnest in the 1960s. "'Til death us do part" has been changed to "So long as each of us feels that our self-interest and passions are being fully realized at every moment." No-fault divorce laws, which emerged ubiquitously in the United States after 1970, establish in legislation and culture the notion that marriage can and even should be terminated without serious cause. Under these cultural and legal terms, Whitehead argues, marriage "loses its status as the institution governing childbearing and childrearing and is demoted to the status of another love connection, subject to the same kind of valuations and measures of satisfaction as living together."[40]

The result of this loss of temporal commitment over past, present, and future is a kind of cultural dementia in which we have begun to lose our lineage memories of what marriage is about. Fewer persons in each generation will remember the warm feelings generated by the presence of parents or will have seen parents successfully navigate conflicts with positive outcomes. Even the less emotionally expressive and directly caring fathers can be remembered for their early-morning commutes to work and their anxiety over paying monthly bills for the sake of their families. There is a hardworking heroism involved in keeping up with expenses. Witness the father who paid the last tuition bill and then sighed, "But I haven't been able to save enough for retirement."

---

38. Whitehead, *The Divorce Culture,* p. 137.
39. Whitehead, *The Divorce Culture,* pp. 139-40.
40. Whitehead, *The Divorce Culture,* p. 143.

As a culture, we seem to have forgotten that family life is the foundation upon which society rests; when marriage, the foundation of the family, is lacking in high ideals, the future will be marked by a lower moral tone and diminished achievement. How does a culture remember that the man-woman-child relationship constitutes something like a holy trinity that has lasting social value? How deep is this forgetfulness? In such a pluralistic world, can people of varying traditions ever assent to this holiness? Can the loss of conjugal and parental fidelity be attributed in part to a half-millennium of Western humanism that has asserted the ultimate value of self-expression? There is the famous Renaissance statement of Pico della Mirandola: "We can become what we will." As John Witte Jr. writes,

> We seem to be living out the grim prophecy that Friedrich Nietzsche offered a century ago: that in the course of the twentieth century, "The family will slowly be ground into a random collection of individuals," haphazardly bound together "in the common pursuit of selfish end" — and in the common rejection of the structures and strictures of family, church, state, and civil society.[41]

Can we resanctify marriage and family in a way that is consistent with pluralism and with the gains of humanism in equality, freedom, and universal rights for women as well as men?

Historian Roderick Phillips, whose study on divorce in the West is considered definitive, introduced the idea that our current and unprecedented cultural shift occurred partly because divorce encourages ever more divorce.[42] He is critical of research on divorce that overlooks "the feedback effect of divorce on itself":

> Although it is true that social and economic conditions can favor the breakdown and dissolution of marriage, it should be clear that divorce itself has become part of the cultural environment in which

41. John Witte Jr., *From Sacrament to Contract: Marriage, Religion, and Law in the Western Tradition* (Louisville, Ky.: Westminster John Knox Press, 1997), p. 215.

42. Roderick Phillips, *Untying the Knot: A Short History of Divorce,* abridged version (Cambridge: Cambridge University Press, 1991). All subsequent references to this volume will be made parenthetically in the text.

marriages exist. To this extent there is a feedback effect, in which the existence of divorce as a viable alternative to marriage, together with the presence of an increasing number of divorces in Western society, contribute in turn to marriage breakdown and divorce. (*UTK*, p. 250)

Phillips shows that ideological considerations are important throughout the history of divorce, and that the ideology of impermanence has now come forcefully into Western culture. He notes that "marriages were generally stable in traditional Western society and that a significant extent of marriage breakdown is peculiar to modern times, notably the past hundred years" (*UTK*, p. 254).

Phillips describes no-fault divorce laws as a "distinct break in the history of divorce," leaving no voice for the common good of society (*UTK*, p. 215). Under these laws, a couple can separate and divorce for any reasons whatsoever, as long as they live apart for the required time. Phillips observes that a Church of England commission endorsed no-fault divorce in 1966 and laid the basis for no-fault legislation in England in 1969. Eventually much of Europe followed suit, including Catholic countries such as Italy, Spain, and Portugal. Meanwhile, New York state went no-fault in 1967, as did the entire United States eventually. It appears that only Ireland has resisted this wave (*UTK*, pp. 216-20). Across Europe, the likelihood of recent marriages ending in divorce lies in the historically unprecedented range of between 30 and 50 percent (*UTK*, p. 215).

Why such high rates? Perhaps we are staking our expectations of marriage too exclusively on one aspect of it — that is, passion. Romance is increasingly viewed as an essential part of marriage. And there are economic and social factors that have changed the face of marriage as well. Widening economic opportunities for women have provided them with more economic liberty. The women's rights movement finally gave them the strength to refuse submissive subordination. Phillips reminds us that cultural attitudes are also central, especially the loss of the scandalous connotations of divorce that reduce "the deterrent of social stigma." With the lessening of such deterrence comes an "emulative factor in the decision to divorce" (*UTK*, p. 241). Let me be clear here. I don't think that reasserting "stigma" is a constructive approach to cur-

21

rent problems; instead, Christians must re-engage in teaching the positive value of lasting marriages and families based as much as possible on empirical data in addition to scriptural and theological sources.

It is remarkable that some branches of Christianity have jettisoned long histories of insight into the natural and theological value of stable marriages and families. Is it not the generally held Christian view that a primary purpose of marriage is the good of children? How can branches of Christianity disregard the interests of the child, who will lose confidence in his or her key social world and struggle with problems resulting from the fracture of a secure union? Weakened father-child bonds, stressed mother-child bonds, decline in high-quality parenting, diminished kinship ties, and the loss of degrees of financial support are well-documented results of divorce — allowing, of course, for some exceptions.

On a final personal note, I write with a sense of family history. In *The Divorce Culture,* Whitehead discusses in great detail the case of Emily Post, the American etiquette writer who, after fourteen years of marriage and two children, divorced my grandfather, Edwin Main Post, in 1906. Edwin was my grandfather by his second marriage, and his relationship with Emily was a matter of some family discussion. Emily's view, carefully documented by Whitehead, was that divorce is always regrettable, especially for children. Whitehead quotes Emily's 1940 edition of the *Etiquette:* "There is no use in pretending that there is any good side from the children's point of view to divorce, excepting in a case where they are protected from a cruel parent or from the influence of a dissolute one. . . . But to the thousands of children who love both parents equally and who can therefore never have more than half a home, the feeling of devastation is quite as great as that caused by enemy bombings. . . ."[43]

Emily, who never remarried, succeeded beyond all expectations as a writer who shaped the ethics and etiquette of America for fifty years. Perhaps she succeeded in part because she always wrote from the heart. She knew that the time she spent with her sons was very important to their well-being, but she also realized that they needed Edwin's fatherly

43. Cited by Whitehead in *The Divorce Culture,* p. 35.

presence and commitment. After my grandfather remarried and moved out to the summer home on Long Island, his two sons by Emily spent their summers with him, the father whom they much loved, and with his second wife (my grandmother) and his other two sons: my father, Henry A. V. Post, and his brother.

Few people appreciate the depth of Emily Post's thought, although it was evident already in her etiquette book; there she declared that it is in the very worst taste to trumpet the news of divorce because "a divorce is a failure, even though both people may agree that it is best, and there is little reason to be proud of a failure."[44] In 1940, thirty-four years after the divorce, she wrote a more philosophical book entitled *Children Are People and Ideal Parents Are Comrades*. In that book she asserted "the children's right to an unbroken home."[45] This is an idea that is certainly worth considering.

Taking into account the emerging field of "men's studies," I wonder if there is anything within the male nature that might suggest a tendency toward permanence consistent with Christianity, even if it is obscured by the culture of modeled divorce. Or does the Christian ideal of permanence impose order that is essentially foreign to the male nature?

Men as Faithful Husbands and Good Fathers?

To a considerable extent, this book belongs in the category of men's studies. It is at least possible to suggest that men are more or less inclined to be pair-bonded husbands and devoted fathers rather than genetically programmed lechers; if the opportunity exists, however, serial monogamy or polygamy may crop up. Does the ideal of permanent marriage require men to rise very far above nature? Evolutionist Matt Ridley writes, "There are characteristically human things we do, like forming lasting bonds between sexual partners, even when polygamous: we are not like the sage grouse whose marriages last for minutes. Nor is mankind polyandrous, like the jacana or lily-trotter, a tropical water

44. Cited by Whitehead in *The Divorce Culture,* p. 36.
45. Cited by Whitehead in *The Divorce Culture,* p. 38.

bird, with big fierce females controlling harems of small, domesticated males."[46]

Monogamy, Justice, and Love

Historically, men have a reasonably strong record of monogamy. Where polygamy has existed, it has been almost entirely the result of the sheer power of despots over men and women. The Incan sun-king Atahualpa kept five thousand women in his harems, and those within his hierarchy followed suit. As Ridley points out, "This left precious few for the average male Indian whose enforced near-celibacy must have driven him to desperate acts, a fact attested to by the severity of the penalties that would follow any cuckolding of his seniors" (*TRQ*, p. 167). In the African kingdom of Dahomey, all women existed for the pleasure of the king, while "ordinary Dahomean men were often celibate and barren"(*TRQ*, p. 168). Evidently men of power and wealth, if given the opportunity, will oppress less powerful men and force women to live imprisoned in harems. The great civilizations of ancient history (Incan, Aztec, Babylonian, Chinese, Indian, and Egyptian) are known not for their civility bur rather for for their despotism and the vast concentration of wealth in one male. In all six civilizations, these emperors recruited young, premenstrual women and "kept them in highly defensible and escape-proof forts, guarded them with eunuchs, pampered them and expected them to breed the emperor's children" (*TRQ*, p. 192). Yet even in this gruesome context, the emperor would have only one queen, suggesting that the concept of monogamy still existed.

Although the norm of monogamy was once heavily distorted by the powerful few, Ridley comments,

> There is one big difference between human beings and chimpanzees and that is the institution we call marriage. In virtually all human cultures, including hunter-gatherer societies, males monopolize their

46. Matt Ridley, *The Red Queen: Sex and the Evolution of Human Nature* (London: Penguin, 1994), p. 170. Subsequent references to this volume will be made parenthetically in the text.

24

mates, and vice versa. Even if he ends up with more than one wife (as a few men do in hunter-gatherer bands), each man enters into a long-term relationship with each woman who bears his children. Unlike a male chimpanzee who mostly loses interest in a female as soon as she is no longer in oestrus, the man remains in close and jealous sexual union with his wife for many years, if not for the rest of his life. Long-term pair bonds are not a cultural construct of our particular society; they are a habit universal to our species.[47]

If we set aside the powerful elite, we find that "even in openly polygamous societies, most men have had only one wife and virtually all women have only one husband" (*TRQ,* p. 171). The historical fact that some human males will use power, wealth, and violence to enslave and monopolize women and oppress other males suggests that monogamy serves not only the moral value of fidelity but also the liberal values of equality, justice, and freedom. It is possible to speak of moral progress that is at the same time largely consistent with essential human nature: "It is our usual monogamy, not our occasional polygamy," says Ridley, "that sets us apart from other animals, including apes" (*TRQ,* p. 204).

Don S. Browning and his collaborators conclude that only monogamy is consistent with the Christian ethical norm of *agape* as equal regard:

> Monogamy offers the possibility of commensurable household structures. Polygyny, polyandry, and single parenthood invariably leave large numbers of adults outside of marital relationships and parenthood. In polygynous societies, wealthy men may hoard young and attractive women. In polyandrous societies, landed brothers may conserve wealth by marrying a single woman, leaving many females out of the marriage system. As single motherhood increases in modern societies, many males are left out of families. Because of its emphasis on individual dignity before God, wherever Christianity spread, the number of monogamous households increased, and the poor and marginalized found mates. Love as equal regard demands equal treatment *between* families just as it does within families.[48]

---

47. Matt Ridley, *The Origins of Virtue* (London: Penguin Books, 1997), p. 92.
48. Browning et al., *From Culture Wars to Common Ground,* p. 297.

The equality inherent in monogamy is consistent with justice, for it should provide everyone who so wishes with a sexual partner in the context of mutual love, with the joys (and disappointments) of parenthood.

With respect to love, Christianity envisions the creation of a lasting personal union based on a foundation of solicitude, and that includes joy, compassion, commitment, and respect: love rejoices in the existence, presence, and growth of the other; love responds supportively to suffering; love is loyal and forgiving to a significant extent; love honors the other's freedom, integrity, and individuality. Marriage exists not just as the foundation for the family but as an end in itself that, even in the absence of children, has immense value as a sphere of love.[49]

Fatherhood

Although some males do abandon paternal duties, I wish to suggest optimistically that the propensity toward fathering remains deep, even if it can be periodically obscured. Robert Wright documents that our evolutionary lineage is different from that of orangutans because it has come to include "male parental investment" (MPI).[50] It is within men's emotional makeup, even when economic or other personal circumstances make it difficult to implement.

MPI is worthwhile from the point of view of continuing the male's genes; thus, Wright explains, a man is genetically inclined "to love his offspring — to worry about them, defend them, provide for them, educate them." The major evolutionary factor appears to be the high vulnerability of human offspring; early on the male realized that "roaming around, seducing and abandoning everything in sight, won't do [his] genes any good if the resulting offspring get eaten." Because the human species developed larger brains, larger heads, and the narrow pelvis and birth canal associated with upright posture, "human babies are born prematurely in comparison with other primates." Thus, they "seriously

49. Karol Wojtyla (Pope John Paul II), *Love and Responsibility,* trans. H. T. Willetts (San Francisco: Ignatius Press, 1981), p. 220.
50. Wright, *The Moral Animal,* p. 57.

compromise a mother's food gathering. For many months, they're mounds of helpless flesh: tiger bait." In this earlier context, fatherly solicitude was thus selectively advantageous, as he would provide for mother and child.[51]

Accordingly, natural selection created not just love for the child in females and males but probably "romantic love," for "the first step toward becoming a solid parental unit is for the man and the woman to develop a strong mutual attraction. The genetic payoff of having two parents devoted to a child's welfare is the reason men and women can fall into swoons over one another, including swoons of great duration."[52] Thus romantic infatuation, while it is relatively fleeting and leaves marriage much in need of *agape,* has a certain value in the process of sexual selection.

The First Wives' Club

According to Wright, the female in a high MPI species "seeks signs of generosity, trustworthiness, and, especially, an enduring commitment to her in particular."[53] Her evolutionary intent is to steer social and material resources toward her children.

Absent a husband's maliciousness, there is no Darwinian pressure on a middle-aged woman approaching menopause to leave her husband. Since a man can still spread his genes, however, new opportunities make sense (in the accounts of the neo-Darwinians). A 1992 study clearly establishes that the single strongest indicator of divorce is a husband's dissatisfaction with a marriage.[54] A man is also more likely to remarry after divorce.[55] Wright argues that a husband's growing intoler-

51. Wright, *The Moral Animal,* pp. 58-59.
52. Wright, *The Moral Animal,* p. 59.
53. Wright, *The Moral Animal,* p. 61.
54. Kim Therese Buehlman, J. M. Gottman, and L. F. Katz, "How a Couple View Their Pasts Predicts Their Future: Predicting Divorce from an Oral History Interview," *Journal of Family Psychology* 5 (1992): 295-318.
55. Joseph Charmie and Samar Nsuly, "Sex Differences in Remarriage and Spouse Selection," *Demography* 18 (1981): 335-48.

ance of a wife he previously loved is not the result of her now being essentially different than she was; rather, it is the result of her being forty-five and without a reproductive future.[56]

I find this sort of argument somewhat plausible. I have known too many middle-aged men who have, to everyone's surprise, taken up with younger women to start second families. Assuming this level of intense MPI for a second time (financial, physical, and emotional) while knowing that one is in late middle age seems to be contrary to rational self-interest. Perhaps it is the underlying power of the mysterious selfish gene that is at work. Most of the time, Wright conjectures, those who choose to start again eventually regret it:

> Many men — and some, but fewer, women — would enjoy the opening stages of those experiments. But in the end they might find that the glimpse of lasting joy the second time around was just another delusion sponsored by their genes, whose primary goal, remember, is to make us prolific, not lastingly happy. . . . The question then becomes whether the fleeting fun of greener pastures outweighs the pain caused by leaving golden-brown ones. This isn't a simple question, much less a question whose answer is easy to impose on one's yearnings. But more often than many people (men in particular) care to admit, the answer is no.[57]

The German philosopher Schopenhauer understood romantic love as "a trick of the species," although now we might say "a trick of the genes."

So what image of male nature would I glean from the above information? Man is essentially inclined to pair-bonding of a reasonably lasting sort and is unusually invested in the well-being of offspring. He has certain wayward tendencies toward promiscuity that are possibly driven by some sort of genetic reproductive imperative. The dismantling of restraint in the culture of divorce simply unleashes tendencies that lurk to some extent below the surface. Lasting unions are by no means alien to man's nature, and fatherhood is of its very essence.

56. Wright, *The Moral Animal,* p. 88.
57. Wright, *The Moral Animal,* p. 132.

Prophetic Families

I have already stated that the Christian family is not to be confused with the insular and over indulgent bourgeois family, or with the family that oppresses women or children. It is imperative that I emphasize this point more fully before proceeding.

Christian commitments to the near and dear should never set aside equally important duties to all of humanity. The family should look outward to serve the needs of others. While parents are usually interested in caring for their own children, their solicitude often does not encompass the children of strangers — especially when those strangers are of different economic, ethnic, religious, or racial backgrounds. The fears of contemporary life (especially the lack of security and economic stability) have produced "solutions" that limit rather than expand our sense of community. Too often, children at extreme risk are only considered when "their" fate impinges on "our" world. This myopic attitude is a violation of the order of love.

The Judeo-Christian notion of a prophetic ethics is a useful starting point, one that combines three distinct, though complementary, social principles (in addition to the theological principle of faithfulness to God). The *first* principle (as elaborated by Amos, Hosea, and Isaiah) is that we give greater protection to the most vulnerable. Here the equality of protection is an equality of proportionality. The *second* principle is that of creation, of fidelity in marriage to ensure for all children the benefit of having both a caring mother and a caring father. (For elaboration, see the following chapter.) This second principle is metaphorically related to the Covenant of Sinai, which is likened to a marriage covenant; its hallmarks are fidelity, fruitfulness, love, and forgiveness. The *third* principle is that within the marriage covenant, women must be treated with equal regard.

The First Principle: Care for All Children

This book is written in the tradition of prophetic ethics, by which I mean the Judeo-Christian notion that active love (solicitude) and jus-

29

tice must proceed first on the principle of care for the most vulnerable (or "the least") among us. The effacement of self-interest must be coupled with a preferential option for the most socially and economically marginal, especially those young enough to have hopes. In response to their God, the prophets of Israel — Amos, Hosea, and Isaiah — wished to establish within social structures both justice *(mishpat)* and righteousness *(sedaqah)*. They threatened the entire community with imminent collapse if renewed justice were not present; they preached with passion a justice first and foremost for those whose fundamental well-being was imperiled because they were outcasts from the society.[58]

This prophetic preferential option for the oppressed constitutes a theory of justice that can be contrasted with the classical utilitarian notion of distribution according to social worth and contribution, the libertarian emphasis on pure survival of the fittest, and liberal theories that seek an abstract balance between liberty and equality. Prophetic ethics is, however, somewhat captured by the natural-law theories that define those "goods" which are absolutely essential for human flourishing and then claim a correlative right to those goods. For example, John Finnis, a natural-law ethicist at Oxford University, lists these goods (not considered an exhaustive list, although one reasonably consistent with cross-cultural images of human fulfillment): life itself, including bodily health and safety; knowledge and education; play, an irreducible aspect of human well-being especially relevant to children; aesthetic experience, whether in the beauty of nature or of human creation; sociability, in its weakest form "a minimum of peace and harmony," but optimally including friendship, neighborliness, and familial care; the opportunity to order one's life according to meaningful hopes; and spirituality and religion, in the sense of pursuing meaning in relation to the Ultimate.[59]

According to prophetic ethics, no human being should be allowed to fall below this minimum threshold of good, and our first duties are to those who do. Thus, the following words are attributed to Jesus of Naz-

58. Walter Harrelson, "Prophetic Ethics," in *The Westminster Dictionary of Christian Ethics,* ed. James F. Childress and John Macquarrie (Philadelphia: Westminster Press, 1986), pp. 508-12.

59. John Finnis, *Natural Law and Natural Rights* (Oxford: Oxford University Press, 1980), pp. 86-90.

areth: "Truly I say to you, as you did it not to one of the least of these, you did it not to me." The first principle of love and justice is this: "The greater the vulnerability of a human being, the greater protection we ought to afford it."[60]

The prophetic ethic is articulated by Jonathan Kozol, who does not shy away from discussion of spirituality in the lives of even the most terribly oppressed children in the worst section of the South Bronx.[61] One boy responds to Kozol's question of what he means by "evil on earth" as follows: "I believe that what the rich have done to the poor people in this city is something that a preacher could call evil. Somebody has power. Pretending that they don't so they don't need to use it to help people — that is my idea of evil" (*AG*, p. 23). Throughout his documentary, Kozol highlights the innocent faith of children who have hope and ideals and thereby enliven the world. The most successful social programs for these South Bronx children are invariably church-sponsored and led by caring pastors, many of them trained in African-American prophetic theology. Kozol concludes his documentary with some pointed questions: "Will the people Reverend Groover called 'the principalities and powers' look into their hearts one day in church or synagogue and feel the grace of God and, as he put it, 'be transformed'? Will they become ashamed of what they've done, or what they have accepted? Will they decide that they do not need to quarantine the outcasts of their ingenuity, and will they then use all their wisdom and their skills to build a new society and a new economy in which no human being will be superfluous? I wish I could believe that, but I don't think it is likely" (*AG*, p. 230).

Kozol quotes Princeton University criminologist John J. DiIulio, who states, "When you look at the gutbucket stuff, the everyday, in-your-face working with troubled kids in these neighborhoods across the country, almost all of it is being done by people who are churched" (*AG*,

---

60. Edmund D. Pellegrino and David C. Thomasma, *Helping and Healing: Religious Commitment in Health Care* (Washington, D.C.: Georgetown University Press, 1997), p. 119.

61. Jonathan Kozol, *Amazing Grace: The Lives of Children and the Conscience of a Nation* (New York: Harper & Row–Perennial Library, 1995). Subsequent references to this volume will be made parenthetically in the text.

p. 42). Churches have always ministered to the poor, run homeless shelters, and provided myriad other programs for those in dire need; as federal commitment to the poor has diminished in recent years, "faith-based" programs have taken over, often with some local tax dollars in support, and have achieved unequaled success (*AG,* p. 45). The question of whether politicians and courts are ready to enter into a new relationship with "faith-based" programs, in which the "faith" element seems to account for a unique level of success (based on social-scientific analysis), remains to be fully answered; it is, however, no longer politically correct to be anti-religion in this context (*AG,* p. 45).

Commitment to children requires a societal belief that all children matter, that childhood is a distinct, formative stage of life in which consistency and security are the building blocks of emotional and spiritual health. This belief must be fostered theologically, philosophically, socially, politically, and economically to enable children's healthy growth in stable families and neighborhoods.

Concern for children seems to be deeply ingrained in human behavior and probably includes elements of altruism.[62] However, many people fail to expand this foundation for self-transcendence, drawing a sharp line between children who are near and dear and children who are strangers. The prophetic voice must expand the circle of moral concern through the spiritual, religious, and ethical insistence on the equal value of all human beings.

Some poor children at extreme risk will eventually surpass those children of economic prosperity who are also much imperiled — by wealth, self-indulgence, substance abuse, sexually transmitted disease, divorce, lack of purpose, and the absence of higher meaning. These children lack the ethos — rather than the material means — for a successful future in which they can take their rightful creative places in society. Despair is rampant among young people — and growing at an alarming rate among those who come from economically comfortable families.

62. Laurence Thomas, *Living Morally: A Psychology of Moral Character* (Philadelphia: Temple University Press, 1989), Chapter Two, "The Biological Basis of Altruism," pp. 35-73.

The Second Principle: Faithful Monogamy

Jesus of Nazareth was clearly within the prophetic tradition of Malachi and consistent with the Dead Sea Scrolls in asserting the ideal of faithful, monogamous marriage by referring to the "principle of creation" evident in Genesis 1–3.

Marriage is the union of female and male that alone allows for a procreation in which children can benefit developmentally from both a mother and a father. In the Gospel of Mark, Jesus draws on ancient Jewish teachings when he asserts, "Therefore, what God has joined together, let no man separate." Regardless of the degree of extension in any family, there remains the core nucleus: wife, husband, and children. Yet the nucleus can be split by various cultural forces (such as infidelity, intentional single parenting, poverty, and patriarchy). This has a costly clinical, economic, and public-health impact.[63] In the United States, even more so than in Europe, we legally sanction divorce for the most trivial of reasons.[64]

In an impartial summary of the trajectory of Christian tradition, historian of religions Geoffrey Parrinder has written, "Every religion has some distinctive characteristics, and Christianity is the only major religion which from the outset has seemed to insist upon monogamy."[65] He points out that Jesus' teachings on marriage, relying on Genesis, provide a "high but difficult morality, and much has been made of these verses in the later Church's rigorous attitudes toward divorce." This rigor is demanding, "but in this instance Jesus seems to have been looking to the purpose of creation, and he took the divine pattern of the creation of man and woman in singleness and unity. In such a context, for a married man or woman to take another partner would be against the unity of their creation."[66] To deter the violation of this unity, Jesus condemned even the

---

63. Larson, Swyers, and Larson, *The Costly Consequences of Divorce: Assessing the Clinical, Economic, and Public Health Impact of Marital Disruption in the United States*.

64. Mary Ann Glendon, *Abortion and Divorce in Western Law* (Cambridge: Harvard University Press, 1987).

65. Geoffrey Parrinder, *Sex in the World's Religions* (New York: Oxford University Press, 1980), p. 202.

66. Parrinder, *Sex in the World's Religions,* p. 208.

wayward imagination, presumably because every violation begins with a thought. Parrinder concludes, "The unity of man and wife in 'one flesh,' commanded by Jesus and referred back to the original action of God at creation, seems to require a single lifelong union."[67]

Some single parents struggle courageously and succeed in raising children of character and accomplishment, while some married couples neglect and abuse their children. While every individual case is unique, there is now strong social-scientific evidence that, *on average,* mother and father together are better able to fulfill child-rearing duties. Across the spectrum of race, gender, and class, children whose parents live apart are twice as likely to drop out of high school, 50 percent more likely to be idle in young adulthood, and twice as likely to become single parents themselves.[68] While a wider circle of relatives can and should be supportive, this is not a substitute for the attentive dedication of two parents. The view that diversity of family types is a sign of progress is contrary to the facts insofar as children are concerned. Against this background, the second aspect of the prophetic tradition that is so powerfully articulated by Malachi and the Jewish Jesus is newly relevant.

The Third Principle: Equal Regard

Browning and his co-authors rightly stress the Christian idea of equal regard. They defend the Christian normative model of "the committed, intact, equal-regard, public-private family."[69] The authors contend that "although Christianity has sometimes supported unjust family practices, its overall direction has been toward a love ethic of equal regard between husband and wife."[70] Respect for women and children, limits on arbitrary male authority, and the denunciation of polygyny (which is unfair to poorer men and turns women into objects) are some of the aspects of Christianity that point toward the authors' normative model, al-

67. Parrinder, *Sex in the World's Religions,* p. 215.
68. Sylvia A. Hewlett, *When the Bough Breaks: The Cost of Neglecting Our Children* (New York: HarperCollins, 1992).
69. Browning et al., *From Culture Wars to Common Ground,* p. 2.
70. Browning et al., *From Culture Wars to Common Ground,* p. 3.

though distortions of the Christian message have sometimes obscured its foundation of equal regard. Thus, the Browning group presents a "new critical familism" that challenges those Christian traditionalists who have misunderstood the Christian moral vision of the family, just as it challenges those who have failed to appreciate the importance of conjugally intact family life. Browning and his collaborators show that neoliberals, neoconservatives, and communitarians all now articulate the adverse consequences of teen pregnancies, out-of-wedlock births, and fatherlessness. While the Protestant affirmations of equal regard and mutuality have been positive, there has been a tendency to see religiously based marriage and commitment as merely one option among others for the organization of sexuality and reproduction.

Browning and his co-authors move from social science and evolutionary psychology to Christian Scripture. In particular, they place the concept of male "headship" over women (Eph. 5:21-23) in historical and cultural context. Against the background of oppressive Greco-Roman patriarchy, the earliest Jesus movement "contained an ethos of genuine egalitarianism between man and woman."[71] The Pauline "love patriarchy" was at least less oppressive than the ancient heroic code of male dominance, for it was a "headship" modeled after the sacrifice of Christ. In an extensive summary of New Testament exegesis and sociology, the authors conclude, "Placed in its proper context, the letter to the Ephesians provocatively but incompletely challenges unilateral authority in families."[72] The fact that Christian wives are counseled to be submissive to their Gentile husbands in 1 Peter 3:1 simply highlights the difference between the patriarchal pagan world and the egalitarian Christian ethos in church and family. The authors make a persuasive argument that better New Testament exegesis points toward equal regard in both church and family. The task of nurturing and sustaining this equality is headed in the right direction but is still a work in progress.

In a discussion of the Christian Right, the authors find Focus on the Family, which is closely associated with evangelical James Dobson,

71. Browning et al., *From Culture Wars to Common Ground,* p. 144.
72. Browning et al., *From Culture Wars to Common Ground,* p. 147.

to be "half-right and half-wrong." While its emphasis on the conjugal family is correct, its stress on male "headship" and "love patriarchy" fails to appreciate the equal-regarding aspects of Christianity, as well as the social-historical context of the pertinent passages from Ephesians and 1 Peter. Promise Keepers is similarly "a step forward and a step backward." The problem of lingering patriarchy is also evident in Catholicism. The authors rightly conclude that "male responsibility and leadership must be a *shared* responsibility and leadership. It must be arrived at through an ethic of communicative discourse, an intersubjective understanding of equal regard. The conservative voices — whether African American, evangelical, or Catholic — have all fallen short of a full understanding of this ethic."[73]

A Qualification: Singleness and Christianity

Any writing on marriage, the family, and Christian ethics is somewhat distorted without a major qualification: according to Christianity, being single is just as much a gift from God (1 Cor. 7:1) as is marriage (1 Cor. 7:7). If Christianity is taken seriously, there should be no regret in not being married; the believer is already a full person without marriage and children. How can there be loneliness when the Christian's first family is the church? The single Christian should appreciate the opportunity that singleness offers to free him or her from anxious concern about spouse and children in order to serve all of humanity. A great deal of pastoral care is needed now to assure Christians that they need not rush into marriage, that they certainly need not remarry, and that they can find all the identity they need in the gift of prayerful solitude, God's love, a believing community, and service to the neediest. It is disturbing that popular Christian bookstores which devote significant space to marriage and family don't devote much shelf space to the gift of singleness; this absence suggests a two-tiered system in which marriage and family rank higher. This is just as diminishing as the reverse ranking that elevates singleness to supremacy. For all that I

73. Browning et al., *From Culture Wars to Common Ground*, p. 245.

write about the importance of lasting unions, I reject the pleasant bourgeois assumption of Samuel Johnson: "The solitary mortal is certainly luxurious, probably superstitious, and possibly mad."

The unreadiness of some Christians to look upon singleness as equally normative with marriage becomes a foreboding specter in our culture of divorce, where so many persons are indoctrinated with the cultural bias against singleness and celibacy. Singleness has been reaffirmed by evangelical theologian Rodney Clapp[74] and, more recently, by theologian Al Hsu.[75] Hsu points out that nearly half of today's adult population is unmarried, and that the community of Christians is roughly similar. Yet being single is explicitly or implicitly viewed as a "problem," and pastors too often try to play matchmaker. Clapp and Hsu, as well as Christian ethicist Stanley Hauerwas, draw renewed attention to the sectarian quality of the Jesus movement, in which singleness was common.[76] Innumerable women converts were happily freed from the stifling family of antiquity, where male authority and childbearing from puberty onward were normative. According to Hsu, singleness is no more a problem than marriage is — although each way of life has its unique difficulties. The New Testament, especially Matthew 19, indicates that "single persons are no less whole people for lack of marriage."[77] In a chapter entitled "The Superiority of Singleness," Clapp argues that single persons are more whole than married ones.[78] While this view is extreme, the message is wonderfully liberating for the single Christian who feels like a second-class believer. Arguably, the fact that the Protestant Reformation precipitated a movement away from singleness exacts a considerable cost in the culture of divorce; it makes it

74. Rodney Clapp, *Families at the Crossroads: Beyond Traditional and Modern Options* (Downers Grove, Ill.: InterVarsity Press, 1993).

75. Al Hsu, *The Single Issue* (Leicester, Eng.: InterVarsity Press, 1997).

76. I am indebted to Stanley Hauerwas for providing me with a copy of his unpublished speech entitled "Why the Christian Family Is Not the American Family." Hauerwas explains that Christianity deeply challenges the family because "Christians do not have to have children to be Christians" (p. 11). Further, "That singleness is the first way of life for Christians does not imply that marriage and the having of children is in any way a less worthy way to be Christian" (p. 12).

77. Hsu, *The Single Issue,* p. 35.

78. Clapp, *Families at the Crossroads,* pp. 89-113.

so "unusual" and "problematic" for Kierkegaard to be Kierkegaard, or, today, for a divorced person to seriously rest content without searching for another mate.

While Christianity must do all it can to keep nuclear families whole, it must also do all it can to make those who are single a genuine part of the larger Christian family.

Religion and the State: A Nonestablishment Partnership?

Given its traditional commitment to the neediest among us, particularly children, Christianity is herein urged to struggle harder against the destructive culture of divorce — both within its own ranks and within the wider society that must be transformed. Empirical data on the adverse consequences of the divorce culture, biblical exegesis, right reason, and the historical thrust of Christian ethics all compel action rather than acculturation. Secular law must again be in accord with the natural dignity of marriage and the family — which, from the believer's viewpoint, is also a sacred dignity. Important issues of birth control, new reproductive technologies, abortion, and same-sex relations should not so dominate discussion as to deflect attention from the institutions of marriage and family. Browning and his collaborators contend that the churches "must help society understand that public policy should not and cannot maintain 'value neutrality' in family matters."[79] The sectarian perspective — that is, that the church should worry only about its own integrity without paying attention to the wider Western culture — may underestimate the extent to which the Christian case for monogamy can be put forward in rational and scientific terms. Browning's group articulates practical, action-guiding principles. Churches must "retrieve their marriage and family traditions, even though they must do so critically"; they must "join with other churches and synagogues to create a new critical marriage and family culture," and "join with other parts of civil society in their local communities to create a critical marriage and family culture."[80] Churches

79. Browning et al., *From Culture Wars to Common Ground,* p. 322.
80. Browning et al., *From Culture Wars to Common Ground,* pp. 307, 309, 310.

must also help society understand that it is unacceptable to maintain value neutrality in public policy on family issues.

Marriage, after all, traditionally fell under the sacred canopy of Western Christianity, which shaped secular law to establish relative permanence. There has, however, been a clear cultural shift to the beliefs of an array of experts on marriage, who very often preach a psychology of self-realization that warns against being highly committed and assumes that the self takes priority over obligations to others when marital tension arises. This focus on the self at the expense of others is contrary to the moral point of view. The Council on Families of the Institute for American Values contends that these experts are also unlikely to discuss data regarding the adverse consequences of divorce for children.[81] Their celebration of impermanence is in stark contrast to the facts.[82] Eminent social scientists write articles pleading for an objective assessment of divorce and family decline.[83]

An example of necessary public comment on marriage and family comes from John Cardinal O'Connor, Archbishop of New York. While controversial for some of his public comments, he is properly concerned about the demotion of marriage in law. When marriage rose to the status of a sacrament, the concern of the Catholic Church was reflected in the immense attention paid to moral and pastoral guidance. The idea that something as important as marriage could be left to the privatized individual remains unacceptable in principle; hence, it is a frequent topic in various papal encyclicals. Yet the church is surrounded by the culture of divorce, in which the terms of marriage are not preset by church or state, tradition or community, facts or social values. Cardinal O'Connor delivered a Sunday homily at St. Patrick's Cathedral on May 24, 1998. He criticized a proposal then under consideration by the New York City Council to make domestic partners the legal equals of married couples. The law

81. Council on Families of the Institute for American Values, *Closed Hearts, Closed Minds: The Textbook Story of Marriage* (New York: Institute for American Values, 1997).

82. See Linda J. Waite, "Does Marriage Matter?" *Demography* 32 (1995): 483-507.

83. Norval D. Glenn, "A Plea for Objective Assessment of the Notion of Family Decline," *Journal of Marriage and the Family* 55 (1993): 542-44.

would cover the nearly nine thousand couples who have registered with the city as domestic partners.

Cardinal O'Connor believes that affording domestic partners such equal status trivializes the importance of committed marriage as a socially essential institution.[84] He points out that the church appreciates the unique contribution that marriage and family make to society, and that it opposes any laws which place the married state and the nonmarried state on equal terms: "This cannot, over either the short term or the long term, fail to influence the young in their attitudes toward marriage and the family, even discouraging marriage in instances when it should be encouraged. It can eventually lead to moral and cultural changes in our society neither anticipated nor traditionally desired from our earliest days as a people."[85]

Cardinal O'Connor cites a letter from John Paul II in which the pope calls upon civil authorities to promote the harmonious growth of the family as essential to the social fabric. He points out that the United States Supreme Court has long refused to elevate unmarried relationships to the level of a constitutional right. John Paul II has stated the Catholic position on marriage as follows: "In a society which accepts sound ethical principles and lives in accordance with them (without hypocrisy and prudery), this institution is necessary to signify maturity of the union between a man and a woman, to testify that their love is a love on which a lasting union and community can be based."[86] As the institution of marriage goes, so goes the institution of the family. When unmarried relationships are elevated, the importance of marriage to spouses, children, and society will eventually reassert itself. In the meantime, however, the costs are high.

The particulars of this New York City scenario are not central here; rather, it is important that religious leaders from whatever faith resist state actions that seem to diminish the uniqueness and the perennial value of legally committed marriage as the seedbed of good

84. Mike Allen, "Cardinal Sees Marriage Harm in Partners Bill," *New York Times,* 25 May 1998, sec. A, pp. 1, 13.

85. Cardinal O'Connor, "Minimizing Marriage" (an essay adapted from the May 24 homily), *The Wall Street Journal,* 29 May 1998, sec. W, p. 9.

86. Wojtyla, *Love and Responsibility,* p. 220.

parenting and of the social future. Marriage is a solemn and public commitment of two people to each other and to the future of children; it is not the same as simply "living together."

It seems that Western societies which have been educated on the importance of marriage to future well-being would want to explore the ways in which our many religious traditions might contribute to solving the problem of the culture of divorce. Training persons in self-government is a necessary precondition for the freedom from government. If religious institutions could better perform the time-honored religious task of preparing couples for marriage and parenthood, society would be well-served.

Given that religions hold such a special place in the experience of so many people, their unique capacity to emphasize the sanctity of marriage and procreation is clearly an important social resource. It would not violate the religious-establishment clause to allow religiously sponsored, publicly funded programs to work in our communities to encourage commitment and responsibility both conjugally and parentally, so long as these programs are open to all who desire them. Indeed, it would be regrettable not to encourage a religious partnership with the commonweal, so long as such public marriage and parenting programs stress commitment and responsibility in marriage and family as basic values. Such a partnership has already worked well in Boston. There, with the help of government funds, Protestant churches have successfully curbed youth violence through an emphasis on nonviolence, respect, and forgiveness.[87] Religions unwilling to develop such public programs should use their own resources to emphasize the sanctity of marriage, procreation, and parenting within their own constituencies.

My urgings here have both a biblical and a cultural basis. After the early Jesus movement, marriage and family became extremely important in Christian thought and life over the centuries. This is a remarkable story that I take up in the next two chapters of this book.

---

87. See Joe Klein, "In God They Trust," *The New Yorker,* 16 June 1997, pp. 40-48.

2

Marriage and Family in the Teachings of Jesus

It is my specific intention in this chapter to address the teachings of Jesus on marriage and family. I do not thereby mean to diminish the place of voluntary singleness in the service of God's kingdom, a possibility that Jesus seems to have endorsed, as passages such as Mark 12:25 and Matthew 19:12 indicate. Mark 12:25 is historically a key text used to support singleness, although it refers to the future resurrection rather than to the current order of creation and human nature. The Sadducees had asked Jesus to comment on the practice of levirate, whereby the brother of the deceased husband marries and impregnates his heretofore childless sister-in-law in order that the husband's name "may not be blotted out of Israel" (Deut. 25:6). Jesus responds, "For when they rise from the dead, they neither marry nor are given in marriage, but are like angels in heaven" (Mark 12:25). As E. P. Sanders interprets this, Jesus was stating that the resurrection would be a new age that would not be "precisely like the present world, but that would none the less be recognizable as world. Even if (in Jesus' view) after the resurrection people will not marry, they will still be recognizable as people."[1] Whatever interpretation is rendered, it is clear that Jesus took this opportunity to cri-

---

1. E. P. Sanders, *The Historical Figure of Jesus* (London: Penguin Books, 1993), p. 187.

tique an overemphasis on the value of biological lineage in the economy of salvation.

Paul cautions against distracting marital obligations in light of the impending eschaton: "Are you bound to a wife? Do not seek to be free. Are you free from a wife? Do not seek a wife" (1 Cor. 7:27); "For the present form of this world is passing away" (1 Cor. 7:31). He wishes that all could be single, as he is, but recognizes his state as "a particular gift from God" that others may not have (1 Cor. 7:7). It should be noted, however, that Paul also insists here that marriage and procreation are no sin, contra those Corinthians who thought that sex in marriage was incompatible with the spiritual life. Yet Paul clearly believed that singleness is superior to marriage under eschatological circumstances.

The passages on singleness can be coupled with the antifamilial elements of the Jesus narrative, including Jesus' harsh conflict with his own family (Mark 3:21, 31-35). The poor and disabled are to be invited to dinner instead of relatives (Luke 14:12-14), and a follower is unfit because he would pause and bid farewell to his household (Luke 9:61-62). Without question, Jesus understood all the spiritual pitfalls of family ties. (See also Luke 11:27-28; Luke 12:49-53; Matt. 10:32-39.)

The singleness passages can also be linked with Jesus' ideal of domination-free relationships, expressed in passages such as this one: "But it is not so among you; but whoever wishes to become great among you must be your servant, and whoever wishes to be first among you must be slave of all" (Mark 10:43-44). This put Jesus at odds with the patriarchal structures of marriage that existed in antiquity and still exist today (Mark 10:2-9; 12:18-27). It is imaginable that his concern with domination and abuse may have further distanced him from the family as hierarchically structured.

Thus the New Testament allows for an ambivalence toward marriage and the family, and it recognizes a place for singleness that contrasts with that of Judaism (and Confucianism). Salvation within Christianity is not dependent on the continuation of a biological lineage. One need not be married and a parent to enter the kingdom of God. How could anything else be concluded when Jesus and Paul were unmarried?

Yet it would be indicative of a serious exegetical bias to ignore the elegant and powerful affirmation of marriage and family that is to be found in the words of Jesus. My discussion focuses upon this affirmation, and at times places antifamilial or afamilial passages in critical perspective. My purpose is to highlight the theme of familial affirmation and to interpret it.

Before I proceed with this discussion, it will be useful to simply quote the principal New Testament text on marriage and divorce:

> Some Pharisees came, and to test him they asked, "Is it lawful for a man to divorce his wife?" He answered them, "What did Moses command you?" They said, "Moses allowed a man to write a certificate of dismissal and to divorce her." But Jesus said to them, "Because of your hardness of heart he wrote this commandment for you. But from the beginning of creation, 'God made them male and female.' 'For this reason a man shall leave his father and mother and be joined to his wife, and the two shall become one flesh.' So they are no longer two, but one flesh. Therefore, what God has joined together, let no one separate."
>
> Then in the house the disciples asked him again about this matter. He said to them, "Whoever divorces his wife and marries another commits adultery against her; and if she divorces her husband and marries another, she commits adultery." (Mark 10:2-12)

The Underlying Principle of Creation

The fact that the Gospels can be read in such a way that they are highly affirming of marriage and family life is passionately articulated by Ernst Troeltsch, the Lutheran historian of Christian social thought. He presented his perspective on the sensibilities of Jesus with respect to the family as follows:

> Starting from the ethical conception of the family, in the pure and chaste sense of later Judaism, Jesus drew upon it for symbols of the highest attributes of God, for the name of the final religious goal, for the original description of the earliest group of his disciples, and for material for most of his parables; indeed, the idea of the family may

be regarded as one of the most fundamental features of his feeling for human life. . . . Hence, his insistence on the indissolubility of the marriage bond, and on the limitation of sex intercourse to married people, even for men.[2]

As Troeltsch pointed out, however, Jesus also reminded his hearers that at times the family may need to be renounced "in response to some imperious spiritual demand."[3] Troeltsch had a Lutheran's distaste for the ascetic turn in the early church, which was "destined to place many hindrances in the way of the nobler result of the Christian ideal of the personalizing, individualizing, and deepening of the family ideal." He blamed this turn for "a grotesque escalation of sexual restraint" and "a low estimate of women."[4]

Troeltsch might have better appreciated the place for asceticism and singleness in most religions. Nevertheless, his ideas on marriage and the family are important. Marriage and family can never be considered prerequisites to a holy life in Christianity, yet they are absolutely essential in the teachings of Jesus; therefore, the "deepening of the family ideal" about which Troeltsch writes is highly significant, even if it ought not to be deepened to the extent that it overwhelms the freedom of God to act in salvation history through the concentrated efforts of those who are single.

This "deepening of the family ideal" of which Troeltsch wrote does derive from the teachings of Jesus, which reflected certain currents within the Judaism of his day. Peter Brown, the eminent historian of early Christianity, points out that the writers of the Dead Sea Scrolls, who were Jewish sectarians living roughly in the same period as Jesus, "took the significant step of presenting the reform of marriage in terms of a return to the single-hearted solidarity of the first couple, Adam and Eve." Brown cites their proscription against any man taking another wife while his first wife is alive; according to their Damascus Docu-

---

2. Ernst Troeltsch, *The Social Teachings of the Christian Churches,* vol. 1, trans. Olive Wyon (1912; reprint, Louisville, Ky.: Westminster/John Knox Press, 1992), p. 61.

3. Troeltsch, *The Social Teachings of the Christian Churches,* p. 61.

4. Troeltsch, *The Social Teachings of the Christian Churches,* p. 131.

ment, this violates "the principle of creation," or the male-female unity. Further, all the radical groups of Jesus' time, such as the one represented by the Scrolls, "believed that the new Israel of the future would be a community of the married, 'fruitful in seed,' an Israel renowned for its disciplined sexuality, from which the abnormalities associated with the present age had been removed."[5]

While Brown acknowledges limited understanding of Jesus' hopes for the imminent "kingdom of heaven," he does conclude that Jesus "seems not to have envisioned the total disappearance of family structures. Rather, like the writers of the Dead Sea Scrolls, he insisted on monogamous marriage as a renewal of the undivided union of Adam and Eve." After the crucifixion, with the growing estrangement between Jesus' supporters and their fellow Jews, "the sense that there would be a natural, undisrupted continuity between the present social structures of Israel and those of the new kingdom" was lost, as was the centrality of marriage to the kingdom.[6] Still, among the writers of the Scrolls, often identified as members of the Qumran sect (through which Jesus may have passed), "marriage and family were the norm."[7]

Few scholars have provided more insight into the importance of Jesus' Jewish origins and identity than Geza Vermes, who writes, "We should note that Jesus, like the Essenes according to the Damascus Document (CD 4.21), saw in Gen. 1.27 ('male and female he created them') and 2.24 ('they become one flesh') the quintessence of marriage established by a divine principle (Matt. 19.4-5; Mark 10.6-8)."[8] Vermes's translation of the Damascus Document as discussed above is as follows: "Whereas the principle of creation is, Male and female created He them (Gen i, 27)."[9] In summing up the meaning of this "principle of creation," Vermes indicates that "remarriage following divorce fundamen-

---

5. Peter Brown, *The Body and Society: Men, Women, and Sexual Renunciation in Early Christianity* (New York: Columbia University Press, 1988), p. 40.

6. Brown, *The Body and Society,* pp. 41, 44.

7. Lawrence H. Schiffman, *Reclaiming the Dead Sea Scrolls: Their True Meaning for Judaism and Christianity* (New York: Doubleday, 1994), p. 130.

8. Geza Vermes, *The Religion of Jesus the Jew* (Minneapolis: Fortress Press, 1993), p. 33.

9. Geza Vermes, *The Dead Sea Scrolls* (London: Penguin Books, 1987), p. 86.

tally conflicts with this quasi-metaphysical unity and, in an ideal world, amounts to adultery, i.e. the destruction of the original bond."[10]

According to exegete John J. Collins, the above-mentioned passage from the Damascus Document is the "first explicit prohibition of polygamy in Jewish tradition." Here is Collins's translation of CD 4:20–5:2:

> They shall be caught in fornication twice by taking two wives in their lifetime, whereas the principle of creation is, male and female he created them. Also those who entered the Ark went in two by two. And concerning the prince it is written, He shall not multiply wives to himself; but David had not read the sealed book of the Law which was in the ark.[11]

Collins argues that the Essene community, from which the Damascus Document emerged among the Dead Sea Scrolls, practiced the high ideal of loyal, monogamous marriage. Even King David's violation of the ideal is not excused but rather is attributed to his ignorance of it.

How close are the moral teachings of Jesus of Nazareth to this Damascus Document? E. P. Sanders writes that marriage was central in the teachings of Jesus, and that "the long form of the tradition about divorce, which includes the appeal to Gen. 1.27 and 2.24 (Matt. 19.3// Mark 10.2-12), or something very like it, represents Jesus' original saying."[12] Sanders goes further:

> Jesus saw himself as God's last messenger before the establishment of the kingdom. He looked for a new order, created by a mighty act of God. In the new order the twelve tribes would be reassembled, there would be a new temple, force of arms would not be needed, divorce would be neither necessary nor permitted, outcasts — even the wicked — would have a place, and Jesus and his disciples — the poor, meek, and lowly — would have a leading role. (*JAJ*, p. 319)

10. Vermes, *The Religion of Jesus the Jew*, p. 33.

11. John J. Collins in *Families in Ancient Israel*, ed. John J. Collins et al. (Louisville, Ky.: Westminster/John Knox Press, 1997), p. 129.

12. E. P. Sanders, *Jesus and Judaism* (Philadelphia: Fortress Press, 1985), p. 257. All subsequent references to this volume will be made parenthetically in the text.

Here Sanders describes a this-worldly fulfillment of God's ideal, a world of worship, justice, peace, and lasting marriage. Sanders sees the prohibition of divorce and remarriage as part of "an overall world view. It can be understood not as an interim ethic nor as an ideal goal which will never be reached, but as a serious decree for a new age and a new order" (*JAJ,* p. 234). He believes that Jesus intended the "restoration" of Judaism (*JAJ,* pp. 106, 116) via the establishment of a kingdom on earth that can be broadly conceived as a world under "the ruling power of God" (*JAJ,* p. 127). This would be "a recognizable social order involving Jesus' disciples and presumably Jesus himself" (*JAJ,* p. 146). These "normal expectations of Jewish restoration theology" cannot be shifted "to the periphery" (*JAJ,* p. 156). Jesus points to "a new order which is analogous to the present one (there is marriage), but not just like it (there is no divorce)" (*JAJ, p. 230).*

According to Sanders's analysis, after the death of Jesus his followers shifted their understanding of the kingdom from "a renewed world situation" to something that existed in "the air" (*JAJ,* p. 230). But Sanders proposes that the disciples originally expected precisely what Jesus himself had hoped for, "a kingdom which did not involve a military revolt, but which was a good deal more concrete than either a collection of nice thoughts about grace and forgiveness, or a *message* about God's love for sinners and his being near" (*JAJ,* p. 232). What Jesus lacked was "a program which could bridge the gap between those who accepted him (some of the poor and outcast of Galilee) and the leaders in Jerusalem" (*JAJ,* p. 235). In his notable review of literature on the historical Jesus, Sanders suggests that Jesus may have died "disappointed,"[13] even as his death brought about atonement.

Yet I do not wish to overstate the case for Sanders's analysis in an area of scholarship that is quite speculative and that does not hold out strong prospects for consensus. I am willing to set aside any hypotheses regarding the nature of the kingdom and the eschatology of Jesus, for my chief interest here is in underscoring the theme of marriage as part of a creation principle.

---

13. Sanders, *The Historical Figure of Jesus,* p. 276.

Monogamy in the Hebrew Bible

A cursory study of the Hebrew Bible suggests three monumental theological claims about marriage and family that lie at the core of the teachings of Jesus. *First,* there are the exuberant and immensely powerful statements of Genesis 1, written by a member of the Priestly (or "P") school, probably in the sixth century B.C.E. Genesis 1 describes a purposeful, ordering God who pronounces that all stages of creation are "good."[14] The relative majesty of this Creator, when compared with the "kindly, jealous, bungling god" of the Yahwist (or "J") writing in the ninth century B.C.E., is well described by biblical exegetes.[15] The author of Genesis 1 proclaims, "So God created humankind in his image, in the image of God he created them; male and female he created them" (v. 27). This God commands the couple, each equally in God's likeness, to "be fruitful and multiply." The divine prototype was thus established at the very outset of the Hebrew Bible.

The dominant theme of Genesis 1 is creative intention. God creates, and what is created procreates, thereby ensuring the continuation of God's created good. The creation of man and woman gives God's handiwork a future.

Second, there is the "J" narrative, first seen in Genesis 2:4, which has an alternative account of creation. Here, woman is made from the rib of the man, a passage regrettably used as a "proof text" for patriarchy (Gen. 2:22). But one passage from J that seems to extrapolate from this same account may easily be understood as profound, even revolutionary, in the autonomy and dignity afforded the married couple: "Therefore a man leaves his father and his mother and clings to his wife, and they become one flesh" (Gen. 2:24); this text suggests intensity and fusion and pleasure. Here is a departure from any social arrangement that would violate the integrity of this "one flesh" union in the name of filial piety or honor.

Consistent with the priority of "one flesh" marriage over the power

14. Karen Armstrong, *In the Beginning: A New Interpretation of Genesis* (New York: Alfred A. Knopf, 1996), p. 9.

15. Stephen Mitchell, *Genesis: A New Translation of the Classical Biblical Stories* (New York: HarperCollins, 1996), p. xliv.

of filial obligations, the Book of J provides the Hebrew Bible with the epochal story of Abraham, the father of Judaism. Here Yahweh sends Abraham and his wife, Sarah, to the land of Canaan, ordering Abraham forcefully, "Go from your country and your kindred and your father's house to the land that I will show you" (Gen. 12:1). God calls a husband and wife to begin a journey of faith, and a mark of that faith seems to be a readiness to depart from the father's house. J provides a passage that lies at the very core of Jewish thought on marriage and family: "I will bless those who bless you, and the one who curses you I will curse; and in you all the families of the earth shall be blessed" (Gen. 12:3). God's blessing, like God's creation, is bestowed on a man and a woman in the union of "one flesh." Paradoxically, at the same time that J is asserting independence from the absolute power of filial duties and describing Abraham and Sarah on a journey of faith that rests on the clear disruption of such duties (they will never see their parents again), he is also describing the creation of a new lineage consistent with God's providential intentions.

Third, there is the prophetic assertion of the absolute spiritual integrity of marriage that is most strikingly delivered in the words of Malachi (sixth century B.C.E.): "And what does the one God desire? Godly offspring. So look to yourselves, and do not let anyone be faithless to the wife of his youth. For I hate divorce, says the Lord, the God of Israel, and covering one's garment with violence, says the Lord of hosts. So take heed to yourselves and do not be faithless" (Mal. 2:15-16). Marriage is, then, a sacred covenant to be honored by those in the community of covenant. In a society gripped by patriarchy, such an absolute is a frightening prospect; but, shed of patriarchy, it promises both a loyal love and children who are socialized and acculturated with the guidance of both a mother and a father.

Malachi (and later, Jesus) presents a sharp contrast to the position of Deuteronomy 24:1-4, which allowed a man to hand his wife a certificate of divorce for even the most trivial of reasons ("she does not please him because he finds something objectionable about her"). The initiative for such divorce rested entirely with the husband. (Centuries later, Talmudic opinion would debate the grounds for divorce.) In rejecting the permissiveness of the Torah in allowing divorce, Malachi seems to anticipate the prophetic position taken by Jesus (Mark 10:2-12). This postexilic prophetic shift away from divorce occurs at roughly the same time that P was writing Genesis 1, suggesting that Israel came to the strong affirmation of the sanctity of monogamous, faithful marriage through time and struggle. The Hebrew oral tradition that was eventually written down by J includes various instances of polygamy and concubinage (notably in the cases of kings Solomon, Saul, David, and Abijah, but there are various others); although God's displeasure with these practices seems evident from the narratives, they cannot be taken as an absolute endorsement of monogamy. After the conquests by Assyria and Babylon, the later Israelite prophets pondered the lessons of Yahweh's punishment and arrived at higher moral standards in wealth and power, in fidelity to God, and in marriage. (See Ezekiel 16; Hosea 1–3; Tobit 6–8; and Malachi 2:16.) However much polygamy and concubinage occurred among the kings, none of the prophets recognized such practices as godly, and monogamous marriage came to prevail as a divine institution established at creation.

The prophet Hosea, whose activity came early in the prophetic period, exemplified the ideal of monogamy and steadfast love of which men are capable when they set aside power: he remained faithful to his wife, Gomer, a prostitute. There could be no better example of love without limit. Hosea was both reversing the practice of permissive divorce by extreme example and providing a human analogy for the steadfast love of God for a wayward Israel that inclined toward Baal worship.[16] The Covenant of Sinai is ever likened to a marriage covenant, in which the God of Abraham, Isaac, and Jacob is always willing to accept a wayward people who sincerely and contritely return to him.

There is, however, a disturbing and negative aspect to the prophet's analogy between God and wayward Israel and the faithful husband and promiscuous wife. In Hosea, Jeremiah, and Ezekiel, according to exegete Renita J. Weems, "naked, battered women's bodies" function as a "poetic device for discussing divine punishment and social anarchy."[17] Weems argues that these negative images of the horribly

16. Edward Schillebeeckx, *Marriage: Human Reality and Saving Mystery*, trans. N. D. Smith (New York: Sheed & Ward, 1965), p. 31.
17. Renita J. Weems, *Battered Love: Marriage, Sex, and Violence in the Hebrew Prophets* (Minneapolis: Fortress Press, 1995), pp. 1-2.

punished unfaithful wife were manipulated by the prophets to win a male audience over to their theological perspective.[18] This suspicion of the prophets is morally valid, although, as Tamar Frankel points out, the "seeds of balance between the sexes" may still be found in the Hebrew Bible as a whole.[19] Feminine images of the deity, for example, may be very important in this endeavor for equality.[20] In asserting the continuing validity of an ideal of marriage and family in the Hebrew Bible, one must equally assert the gap between ideal and sinful reality.[21]

The prophets were rightly critical of the permissiveness of Deuteronomic divorce law, which was still in place in Jesus' time. There was no strict monogamy in Judaism until fairly late in the pre-Christian period.[22] After the return from Babylonian exile, however, polygamy was very unusual and considered contrary to faith in Yahweh.

In summary, marriage and responsible motherhood and fatherhood are, as David M. Feldman writes, "a basic mitzvah in Judaism," according to all codes of Jewish law.[23] One "leaves" mother and father (Gen. 2:24) to create a unity of "one flesh" that places conjugal duties above filial duties. Pleasure and joy in physical intimacy are accepted and encouraged. Mystically speaking, "Divine Presence" rests on the married couple, for they have achieved "completeness" according to the Zohar. Feldman points out that "the example of Abraham and Jacob, and even of Solomon and David, notwithstanding, the biblical ideal is one of monogamy."[24]

---

18. See also Renita J. Weems, *Just a Sister Away: A Womanist Vision of Women's Relationships in the Bible* (San Diego: Luramedia, 1988).

19. Tamar Frankel, *The Voice of Sarah: Feminine Spirituality and Traditional Judaism* (New York: Biblio Press, 1990).

20. Phyllis Trible, *God and the Rhetoric of Sexuality* (Philadelphia: Fortress Press, 1978); see also *Feminist Interpretation of the Bible,* ed. Letty M. Russell (Philadelphia: Westminster Press, 1985).

21. See Judith Plaskow, *Standing Again at Sinai: Judaism from a Feminist Perspective* (San Francisco: Harper, 1990).

22. David R. Mace, *Hebrew Marriage* (London: Epworth, 1953).

23. David M. Feldman, *Marital Relations, Birth Control, and Abortion in Jewish Law* (New York: New York University Press, 1968), p. 28.

24. Feldman, *Marital Relations, Birth Control, and Abortion in Jewish Law,* pp. 35, 37.

According to exegete John Collins, "There is no doubt that both the Priestly theology of Genesis 1 and the Yahwist theology of Genesis 2–3 were conducive to an ideal of monogamy."[25] Further, "Both texts speak of one man and one woman. Neither envisages the dissolution of the union." But the religious ideal of marriage that was prominently displayed at the beginning of Genesis and reasserted by the prophets was always in some dialectic tension with the reality of legally accepted divorce grounded in the purely contractual image of marriage.[26] Especially in the period of second temple Judaism, divorce based on a contractual understanding may have become quite routine. Writes Collins,

> Against this background, we can appreciate the cry of the prophet Malachi, appealing to his contemporaries to be faithful to the wives of their youth and reminding them that what God wants is godly offspring. Jesus of Nazareth, another reformer within the context of second temple Judaism, also took a strict line on divorce.[27]

And it is to the teachings of Jesus that we must now turn. For Jesus was squarely in the reformist and idealist tradition with respect to marriage, and he demonstrated a unique sensitivity to the problems of patriarchal repression and the devaluation of the child.

This essential Jesus, a reformer of marriage and family, is sometimes obscured in the New Testament because of statements condemning the old family loyalties of his converts. Clearly, the powerful social solidarity of the ancient Mediterranean family structure posed a threat to a fledgling religious movement that was socially unaccepted.[28] But the acrimonious conflict between new and old at such an emotionally charged interface should not deflect us from appreciating the fact that the ideal of a renewed and restored family appears absolutely central to the ideology of the "sect of the Nazarene."

25. Collins in *Families in Ancient Israel,* p. 127.
26. Collins in *Families in Ancient Israel,* p. 148.
27. Collins in *Families in Ancient Israel,* p. 149.
28. Stephen G. Post, "Psychiatry and Ethics: The Problematics of Respect for Religious Meanings," *Culture, Medicine, and Psychiatry* 17, no. 3 (1993): 363-83.

Monogamy in the New Testament

Carolyn Osiek and David Balch have written an insightful book entitled *Families in the New Testament World.* They note that according to Roman custom, "divorce was commonly practiced," carried no particular stigma, and could be initiated by a wife as well as a husband. Second and third marriages were common, although the concept of "intimate lifelong marital fidelity continued to be idealized, at least in Roman funerary commemorations."[29] Against this Roman cultural background, Christian teachings presented a sharp contrast. As Osiek and Balch write,

> The unusual Christian prohibition of divorce stands out against its context, but with wide attestation (Matt. 5:31-32; 19:1-12; Mark 10:1-12; Luke 16:18; 1 Cor. 7:10-16). Both of these factors, especially the very early attribution to Jesus in 1 Corinthians, argue for the authenticity of the saying as a teaching of Jesus himself.[30]

As this section will highlight, the teachings of Jesus on the permanent union of marriage are quite forceful.

The Teachings of Jesus

Hebraic roots shape the words of Jesus, which stand within Malachi's prophetic tradition of emphasis on inviolable monogamy. In Mark 10:2-12, cited in full at the outset of this chapter, Jesus quotes Genesis 1:27 ("God made them male and female") and Genesis 2:24 ("the two shall become one flesh"). He uses these passages in his condemnation of divorce. New Testament exegete Richard B. Hays explains the significance of Jesus' pronouncement:

> In sum, Mark 10:2-12, starting from a question about the legal permissibility of divorce, opens out into a symbolic reframing of mar-

29. Carolyn Osiek and David L. Balch, *Families in the New Testament World: Households and House Churches* (Louisville, Ky.: Westminster/John Knox Press, 1997), p. 62.

30. Osiek and Balch, *Families in the New Testament World,* pp. 62-63.

riage as an aspect of Christian discipleship and as a reflection of God's primal purpose in creating humanity male and female. When the question of divorce is seen in this perspective, it becomes clear that divorce is a violation of God's intent; those who are Jesus' disciples will renounce it, just as they renounce many other prerogatives in order to follow Jesus on the way of the cross.[31]

In the New Testament, the appeal to Genesis 2:24 is definitive. (See also Matthew 19:3-12 and Ephesians 5:31.) In Genesis 2:24 Jesus appears to have found an authoritative basis for monogamous marriage. Thus, marriage circumscribes the command to procreate in Genesis 1:28. In Matthew 19:3-12, where the author adapts the earlier Markan account in a pastoral improvisation, the appeal to Genesis 2:24 remains identical, but an allowance is made for divorce in cases of sexual immorality, as it is in Matthew 5:31-32.[32] In Luke 16:18, the demand of the Markan original is again unqualified. As Hays concludes, all these passages strive "to affirm marriage as a permanently binding commitment in which man and woman become one," and to define divorce as a tragic departure from the normative vision.[33]

The firmness of Jesus' statement suggests significance consistent with his concern for the well-being of children, so evident in his blessing of them despite the protest of his adult followers (Mark 10:14-16). It is important and noteworthy that this elevation of the worth of children directly follows Jesus' strong affirmation of steadfast marriage. According to Eduard Lohse, a Lutheran New Testament exegete, Jesus — drawing on the creation story — reliably taught that "God had created humanity as a unity of male and female in order that they might live together in partnership their whole life long (Mark 10:6-7)." Jesus clarified the unity of man and woman according to "the original intent of the creator."[34]

---

31. Richard B. Hays, *The Moral Vision of the New Testament: A Contemporary Introduction to New Testament Ethics* (San Francisco: HarperCollins, 1996), p. 352.

32. Hays, *The Moral Vision of the New Testament,* p. 355.

33. Hays, *The Moral Vision of the New Testament,* p. 361.

34. Eduard Lohse, *Theological Ethics of the New Testament,* trans. M. Boring (Minneapolis: Fortress Press, 1991), pp. 100, 101.

The seriousness with which Jesus treated marriage represents a fulfillment of the Jewish law — which, even when compromised, was nevertheless upheld in principle. For example, polygamy surfaces among rulers and results in the Lord's displeasure with Solomon; murderous adultery appears, but Yahweh punishes King David for his affair with Bathsheba; and, while concubinage occurs in the story of Abraham and Hagar, it is ultimately Abraham's only wife, Sarah, who bears Isaac. God views these untoward acts as reprehensible departures from the ideal of monogamy. It was the Jewish Jesus who claimed to have come to fulfill the law and the prophets, who strongly condemned every man who even "looks at a woman with lust" (Matt. 5:28).

The Crisis Sayings

But if Jesus so strongly sanctioned the principle of creation that gives meaning to marriage and family, what of Jesus' criticisms of familial ties? Such criticisms in no way indicate ambivalence about the meaning of marriage and family. They do indicate, however, that when such relationships prevented converts from following him (e.g., Matt. 10), thereby hindering the expansion of his mission, Jesus was critical.

In this context, Jesus was perfectly consistent with Jewish texts such as Maccabees, in which love for parents, spouses, children, and friends is relativized under *crisis* conditions. Osiek and Balch describe how pursuing the Mosaic way of life might require setting aside "one's own beloved family."[35] Surely such a contingency would never suggest that the family is anything other than central to Jewish ethics and theology. Osiek and Balch indicate that the hard sayings — for example, "Follow me, and let the dead bury their own dead" (Matt. 8:18-22) — are part of a call to proclaim the kingdom of God regardless of familial ties that bind, and that this sort of saying "relativizes family without being anti-family."[36] Such sayings emphatically do *not* suggest a diminishment of the centrality of marriage and family in Jesus' teachings and

35. Osiek and Balch, *Families in the New Testament World,* p. 123.
36. Osiek and Balch, *Families in the New Testament World,* p. 126.

hopes; they do, however, convey Jesus' strong reaction to the absolute patriarchal grip on the family in antiquity. In ancient cultures, family members were virtually shackled by patriarchal control.

The hard sayings, including the warning that the follower "will find enemies under his own roof" (Matt. 10:35-36), do not negate an exceptional reverence for familial ties (Mark 10) and parental love (e.g., Matt. 7:9-11). The sayings occur in an atmosphere of tension between a controversial new religious movement that demanded radical allegiance of its adherents and a society that opposed the movement because it threatened the supremacy of familial allegiance.

Indeed, the tension between the Jesus movement and the family was singularly important. In a compelling social-science commentary on the Synoptic Gospels, Bruce J. Malina and Richard L. Rohrbaugh, drawing on the "hard sayings" against families in Mark, Matthew, and Luke, give this tension the emphasis it deserves:

> In the Mediterranean societies of antiquity, the family of origin is owed paramount loyalty and total attachment. Kinship is the overriding social institution, holding precedence and primacy in the lives of all the persons Jesus dealt with. Persons placing loyalty to some surrogate family above attachment to family of origin, as the disciples of Jesus are asked to do in Matthew, will find that family of origin and the associated social network ("friends") turn against them. Social solidarity within the all-important networks and the honor of the family of origin would require that they do so.[37]

Nothing was more detrimental to the work of Jesus than this pervasive familial resistance; nothing was a harder test of faith for those who were inclined to follow him. Breaking with one's family "could cost one dearly," for it meant enduring loss of status and long-held close relationships, as well as tremendous resentment from loved ones.[38]

The emphasis on early Christianity as "a movement of converts"

---

37. Bruce J. Malina and Richard L. Rohrbaugh, *Social Science Commentary on the Synoptic Gospels* (Minneapolis: Fortress Press, 1992), p. 90.

38. Malina and Rohrbaugh, *Social Science Commentary on the Synoptic Gospels,* p. 101.

who sacrificed familial bonds is further elaborated by Wayne A. Meeks in his study of the origins of Christian morality. The allegiance to kinship group was so powerful that the basic values of the familial sphere were transferred through conversion to the community of faith — that is, following Christ involved "leaving the family of birth and the culture of residence and becoming a sister or brother of those who are God's children."[39] In Paul's first letter to the Thessalonian Christians, "familial affection" ("philadelphia") becomes love for the brothers and sisters in the Christian community (4:9).[40]

The outsiders saw the converted individual as deviating "from ordinary citizen to fanatical member of a group that itself deviates from the norms of the larger society." Meeks adds this rather challenging observation: "Thus middle-class American parents in the 1960s and '70s feared the 'capture' or 'brainwashing' of their children by 'cults.'"[41]

Paul

Paul draws on the same passages from the Hebrew Bible that Jesus does (Gen. 1:27 and 2:24) when he calls the unity of marriage a divine "mystery" (Eph. 5:32). Like Jesus, Paul seems to reject hierarchy in marriage (Gal. 3:28) and confers the highest honor on it by comparing it to the union of church and Christ (2 Cor. 11:2; Eph. 5), although this regrettably seems to reinstate hierarchy. His teachings emphasize the *agape* (serving and loyal love) that should be mutually manifested between husband and wife (1 Cor. 7:3).

A significant break from Judaism is clear in Paul, who provides the Christian with two options: (1) marriage (a mutual and exclusive sexual intimacy that is holy; see 1 Cor. 7:3-4); and (2) singleness (1 Cor. 7:32-35), which Paul himself prefers (1 Cor. 7:7, 38).[42] In this, Paul was surely drawing on the singleness of Jesus. Thus, the hegemony of mar-

---

39. Wayne A. Meeks, *The Origins of Christian Morality: The First Two Decades* (New Haven: Yale University Press, 1993), p. 12.

40. Meeks, *The Origins of Christian Morality,* p. 31.

41. Meeks, *The Origins of Christian Morality,* p. 21.

42. Osiek and Balch, *Families in the New Testament World,* pp. 116-17.

riage and family as the only way of salvation was broken. On the one hand, the fruit of this approach is impressive, for surely those not inclined to marry need to be equally honored and received into the family of God. On the other hand, the endorsement of singleness was misinterpreted by some to mean that marriage and parenthood are really quite insignificant theologically, and that celibacy is superior to marriage even in noneschatological circumstances.

Paul's reason for ambivalence about marriage, something misunderstood by later church ascetics, was that he believed that "the present form of this world" was passing away (1 Cor. 7:29-31); thus, familial responsibilities were not timely. But if Paul's eschatology or philosophy of time and history is set aside, his endorsement of permanence in marriage is clear. His personal singleness, which he did not require of others, was grounded in his belief that the end time was near. For that reason, he encouraged other Christians to forgo marriage if they were able.

Nothing that Paul wrote departs from the idea that marriage between a man and a woman who intend to form a family is filled with divine intentionality and meaning. Yet, as discussed above, Paul endorses singleness and speaks of his own "special gift" (1 Cor. 7:7, 38), allowing a meaningful freedom from marriage and family that does not present itself in Judaism. This endorsement has freed many individuals who are not inclined to marry from the grip of social intolerance.

Christian Love and Parental Heart

Geza Vermes states that although the coming kingdom which Jesus promised remains mysterious in its details, it was nevertheless universal, of this earth, and attainable only with human cooperation.[43] One feature of the kingdom would be the "imitation of divine parental solicitude," since Jesus compared the "essential benevolence of God to the attitude of human parents" (Matt. 7:9-11; Luke 11:11-13).[44] Vermes highlights how often Jesus refers to God as "Father" in the Synoptics (about sixty times),

43. Vermes, *The Religion of Jesus the Jew,* p. 124.
44. Vermes, *The Religion of Jesus the Jew,* pp. 158, 156.

his use of the Aramaic title "Abba" (Father), and parables that draw on the parent-child relationship. According to E. P. Sanders, Jesus looked to a new order in which "divorce would be neither necessary nor permitted, outcasts — even the wicked — would have a place, and Jesus and his disciples — the poor, meek and lowly — would have the leading role."[45]

This notion of the "imitation of divine parental solicitude" is potentially the core of Christian ethics. The parental heart is remarkable in its attentiveness to the details of a child's daily life and needs. It is affectively engaged to the extent that brokenheartedness is a possibility. Jesus' many references to domestic realities suggest holiness in this sphere that Christianity recovered only centuries later. (See Chapter Three of this volume.)

Christian love, or *agape,* was described rather mechanically by Anders Nygren in his classic study, *Agape and Eros.*[46] Love flows downward from God, an overflowing fount, through human agents as conduits or tubes. These metaphors forget an essential factor that gets at the motivation underlying this plenitude of unconditional love — that is, all divine love described in the New Testament exemplifies affective *parental* solicitude. Examples abound. The Parable of the Prodigal Son (Luke 15:11-32) could easily be renamed The Parable of the Loving Father. In Matthew we read, "If you then, who are evil, know how to give good gifts to your children, how much more will your Father in heaven give good things to those who ask him!" (7:11). John declares that "God is love" (1 John 4:8), that he first loved us and gave his Son that we might have eternal life (John 3:16). Paul declares that God sent his Son to die on the cross to save us (Rom. 5:8). And human love for God is entirely *filial* (e.g., Matt. 7:21; Luke 2:49). The Lord's Prayer begins with *Abba,* the Aramaic word for "father." The last words of the crucified Jesus in one Gospel are "Father, into your hands I commend my spirit" (Luke 23:46). The Beatitudes state, "Blessed are the peacemakers, for they will be called children of God" (Matt. 5:9). There is no higher blessedness than to be a child of God.

45. Sanders, *Jesus and Judaism,* p. 319.
46. Anders Nygren, *Agape and Eros,* trans. Philip S. Watson (Chicago: University of Chicago Press, 1982).

To experience divine love as parental is to find the most loyal of loves; to respond to God as Jesus did is to take a filial position; to respond morally to the neighbor is to love as if in a universal family of siblings under God. Love between human beings is brotherly and sisterly love (e.g., Matt. 5:43-45; 1 Thess. 4:9; 1 John 4:7-8, 21).

In *Christian Love,* a book that is not given its due in the history of modern Christian thought on love, and from which I have borrowed many of the above New Testament references, Paul E. Johnson writes, "When we treat all people as members of our own family, love will become universal and cure the social ills of suffering humanity."[47] Johnson claims that "the genius of Christianity is its family design of love."[48]

How, then, does the literal family fare under this Christian ethic of familial love writ large to the inclusive Christian community and to humanity as a whole? The particular family is not at all degraded; instead, its meaning is enhanced and transformed. Arguably, Christianity made a new place for women, overturning repressive domination.[49] Although later Pauline sources reasserted patriarchy, a husband is to relate to his wife through service, not through violence or fear (Eph. 5:23-33). Children were elevated to prototypes of those who will enter the kingdom of heaven (Mark 10:14-15). The Christian tradition would make marriage a holy sacrament, thereby affording it the ultimate sanctity: it would sanction the birth of new life with baptism, requiring parents and godparents to raise children as true children of God.

So the genius of Christian biblical ethics is twofold. First, the power of both vertical (parent-child) and horizontal (husband-wife, brother-sister) familial love is placed at the very center of the entire spiritual universe, and thereby sets the example for universal solicitude. Second, the literal family is enhanced by a sacred canopy that emphasizes love rather than repression and that focuses the family outwardly on God and the universal kingdom of God, not inwardly on itself.

---

47. Paul E. Johnson, *Christian Love* (New York: Abingdon-Cokesbury Press, 1951), p. 35.

48. Johnson, *Christian Love,* p. 97.

49. Lisa Sowle Cahill, *Sex, Gender, and Christian Ethics* (Cambridge: Cambridge University Press, 1996).

Christian ethics is exemplified as a universal family under God, largely but not entirely constituted by many literal families of *agape*.

Conclusion

The teachings of Jesus on marriage and divorce are nothing short of thundering, and they have thundered down through the centuries of Christianity. His elevation of women in his circle of followers, his expressed love for children, his emphasis on love of neighbor that precludes cruelty and violence — all point toward a movement away from the traditional patriarchal family that he doubtless found so distorting of God's original ideal. I consider these teachings of Jesus to have universal value: they can easily be supported by coherent rational arguments for stability and permanence in marriage as a foundation for committed and loving parenthood that is consistent with the dignity of spouses, children, and society.

I realize that interpretations of the core values of Jesus vary in emphasis. Many respected theologians see him as a critic of social and economic injustice, as he doubtless was a friend of the poor; many see him as a healer who harnessed either the power of God or the power of suggestion with remarkable success; many see him as the one who brought forgiveness and love of enemies into a violent world. There is truth in all these prisms. Of at least equal importance, however, is the fact that Jesus brought to his ministry a dramatic new image of marriage and the family. While this image has been somewhat diminished at times in the history of Christianity, it will always remain definitive of the essence of true Christianity. The next two chapters attest to this.

3

The Spiritual Value of the Family

In the previous chapter, I acknowledged a circumscribed New Testament ambivalence about marriage and the family. On certain occasions Jesus asserted the necessity of severing family ties, and Paul regarded marriage as a lesser evil.[1] But much more dominant and impressive is the assertion of monogamy in the teachings of Jesus. The early Christian concern with celibacy and with continence among married couples was shaped by the ambivalent aspect of New Testament teaching, as well as by larger cultural and religious beliefs, which held that the continuity between heaven and earth was disrupted, and that proximity to the sacred could be achieved only through the intermediation of distinctive men whose saintliness was marked by chastity.[2] For a while the natural windows to the sacred were almost closed, among them the kind of naturalism that was emphasized by Jesus in his principle of creation, marriage, and family.

In this chapter I write as an ethicist who, although not a historian, sometimes works with historical materials in shaping an argument. My

1. See J. Goody, *The Development of the Family and Marriage in Europe* (Cambridge: Cambridge University Press, 1983).
2. Peter Brown, *The Making of Late Antiquity* (Cambridge: Harvard University Press, 1978).

task is to interpret and articulate the spiritual and moral validity of the eventual elevation of marriage and family life to a place of holiness.

The New Testament does provide ample hints at the holiness inherent in domestic and family living. By "holiness" I mean, following the Oxford Dictionary, "belonging to, devoted to, or empowered by God." Something is holy if it is set apart as charged with God's own presence and purposes. In the present reality of human sinfulness, however, which includes a tendency toward narcissism and in-group exclusiveness, the holy quality nascent within marriage and the family may become overwhelmed by moral insularity, domination, abuse, or violence. Because the family is considered a separate sphere, often with little public accountability, these adverse realities can easily go unchecked and become "demonic" in a sense — unless the family is shaped and strengthened by participation within the community of the church. Within the sphere of marriage and family, Christians can reach heights of sanctification and moral development as well as depths of evil intent and harm. While holy in essence, marriage and the family are also highly dependent on grace, forgiveness, and participation in the believing community that manifests *agape* and actively seeks to enlarge its boundaries. But the ideal of *agape* — which includes equality, freedom, and justice — must be fully appreciated as providing a strong moral underpinning for family life and therefore as providing a powerful locus that should inform the spiritual and moral tone of the Christian family.

In this chapter I present my interpretation of some factors that eventually allowed for the elevation of the status of the family within Christian tradition, theology, and moral thought. While I draw frequently on the work of historians, I do not intend this chapter to be a historical treatise. It is instead a normative statement on the possibilities for holiness within an institution that can also unleash all that is sinful in human nature.

Marriage in the Early Church: A Time of Ambivalence

The afamilial and sometimes necessarily antifamilial qualities of the early Jesus movement were evident as it struggled to gain the loyalty of converts whose families were anything but accepting of their newfound faith. But this struggle is best understood as one between the insular and controlling forces of family life on the one hand, and the universal and freeing power of the Christian movement on the other. The point is that insularity and domination were at fault, not anything inherent in marriage and family per se.

The early members of the Jesus movement left their homes and were, as Harvard University historian Clarissa W. Atkinson puts it, "adopted into a new family with no stable home in the world." She makes the analogy to contemporary religious movements, which can cause tension between old family and "new" and create severe conflict. The Jesus movement demanded that the insular ties of the past be severed. Atkinson points out that "like other adherents of cults and new religions," the Jesus followers formed a radical new eschatological family that produced an ethic of continence — nicely expressed in Paul's phrase, "remain single as I do" (1 Cor. 7:8) — intended to help them work without obstacle in the short time remaining.[3] Continence was a practical aspect of the freedom from commitments that were obstacles to the fullest devotion both to the Christian community and to all of humanity.

The moral and spiritual struggle against familial insularity and domination was and is necessary for Christians, but this does not imply that sexual asceticism is an end in itself that, under other sociological circumstances, would be extolled. Paul, for example, did not recommend singleness as an end in itself. Indeed, as Will Deming writes, it is no longer possible to see Paul as "one of Christianity's first champions of sexual asceticism." He was "a cautious and measured proponent of the single lifestyle, a form of celibacy characterized by freedom from the responsibilities of marriage and for which the absence of sexual fulfillment was no more than an unintended consequence and an inconvenience, never an end in itself."[4] Paul advocated celibacy because he believed that there was no time remaining for marriage and family.

3. Clarissa W. Atkinson, *The Oldest Vocation: Christian Motherhood in the Middle Ages* (Ithaca, N.Y.: Cornell University Press, 1991), p. 17.

4. Will Deming, *Paul on Marriage and Celibacy: The Hellenistic Background of 1 Corinthians 7* (Cambridge: Cambridge University Press, 1995), p. 4.

But Paul's eschatology was unfulfilled, and the procreative features of the species reasserted themselves. Marriage and family became the way of most Christians.[5] As New Testament scholars Carolyn Osiek and David L. Balch underscore, "We must assume that the vast majority of Christians in these centuries as in every century lived normal married lives."[6]

But this domestic social fact did not issue in a theological appreciation for the holiness of marriage and family. Among those who shaped the thought world of Christian monasticism, ambivalence remained dominant. "In its everyday physical and social meanings," Atkinson emphasizes, "parenthood was excluded from the monastic world."[7] Virginity was holy; motherhood and fatherhood were so only metaphorically.

It is always difficult for a tradition to ensconce one way of life as powerfully normative without relegating alternatives to some diminished status, or even disparaging them. Early Christianity could not assert the superiority of singleness, virginity, and a purely spiritual family and still assert a holiness in marriage and the literal family. Yet in Paul's writings there were hints of a holiness in marriage (see 1 Cor. 7; Eph. 5), and these hints would eventually come to shape theology and sacrament.

The supremacy of celibacy in the early Middle Ages cannot be solely attributed to the flight from familial insularity, although this is always a spiritual and moral subtext. There were clearly other factors involved, including the introduction of spirit-body dualism (which contrasted sharply with the Jewish notion of the whole self) and the ideal of cessation of all desires but the desire for God.

As historian Peter Brown emphasizes, the ideal of cessation of desire proved powerful in early Christian thought. He cites Clement of Alexandria thus: "Our ideal is not to experience desire at all." According to Brown, other Christians set this radical concept in motion with a distinct goal in mind: "By refusing to act upon the youthful stirrings of de-

5. Carol Harrison, "The Silent Majority: The Family in Patristic Thought," in *The Family in Theological Perspective,* ed. Stephen C. Barton (Edinburgh: T. & T. Clark, 1996), p. 91.

6. Carolyn Osiek and David L. Balch, *Families in the New Testament World: Households and House Churches* (Louisville, Ky.: Westminster/John Knox Press, 1997), p. 155.

7. Atkinson, *The Oldest Vocation,* p. 66.

sire, Christians could bring marriage and childbirth to an end. With marriage at an end, the huge fabric of organized society would crumble like a sandcastle, touched by the 'ocean-flood of the Messiah.' "[8] Such extraordinary diminishment of marriage and family was doubtless shaped by a desire to cease desiring. Yet this diminishment was also the means to dissolve converts' divided loyalties between genealogical ties and the spiritual family of believers.

The late historian John Boswell describes early and medieval Christianity as "overwhelmingly ambivalent" about marriage.[9] While critics have rejected his view that "same-sex unions" were blessed ceremonially in the church, Boswell provides helpful documentation of the early theologians' ambivalence about the family because it held such total control over loyalties, conflicted often with religious commitments, and sometimes favored its own kin group at the expense of the poor and outsiders.

While early Christianity diminished marriage and family, this occurred only at a relatively elitist level. Brown argues that the "silent majority" of Christian converts married, raised their children as Christians, and contributed to the welfare of the church through their households.[10] Wayne A. Meeks would concur that "ordinary Christians" in the early church followed the mandates of such well-respected guides as the *Shepherd of Hermas,* in which marriage is held holy, and remarriage after divorce is forbidden.[11] So marriage and family were still considered holy, even if this was less than dominant in the Christian worldview. Brown is right about the "silent majority" who quietly supported marriage and family. But there were some who were not silent in their support.[12]

8. Peter Brown, *The Body and Society: Men, Women, and Sexual Renunciation in Early Christianity* (New York: Columbia University Press, 1988), pp. 31, 32.

9. John Boswell, *Same-Sex Unions in Premodern Europe* (New York: Vintage Books, 1994), p. 111.

10. Brown, *The Body and Society,* p. 61.

11. See Wayne A. Meeks, *The Origins of Christian Morality: The First Two Decades* (New Haven: Yale University Press, 1993), p. 149.

12. *Marriage in the Early Church,* ed. David G. Hunter (Minneapolis: Fortress Press, 1992).

According to the writings of Clement of Alexandria *(Miscellanies),* John Chrysostom ("Homily 20 on Ephesians"), and Jovinian, marriage is as high a form of Christian life as ascetic singleness — and, in some respects, a higher form. Clement indicates that the care of one's family is a human analogue to God's own providential care. In his treatise titled "On Marriage," Clement writes, "Both celibacy and marriage have their own different forms of service and ministry to the Lord; I have in mind the caring for one's wife and children." Clement adds (citing 1 Timothy 3:4) that those who succeed in family responsibilities should be appointed as bishops, for "by their oversight over their own house" they "have learned to be in charge of the whole church."[13] It is remarkable to see in Clement the notion that only through fulfilling duties in the familial sphere does one grow to the point of being able to care for the church as bishop. While surely a minority perspective, this is suggestive enough to indicate a significant pluralism.

Patristic marriage remained, of course, a secular act. But its holiness is evidenced by the nonmandatory priestly prayer and blessing connected with marriage. While the church accepted the state's right to regulate marriage and divorce, Christians generally much appreciated having a priest as a guest at the family wedding feast. Indeed, by the fourth century, the priestly prayer and blessing of marriage came to be known as the "marriage service." This service was not imperative for Christians, however, and it existed alongside the civil and family celebration. (By contrast, the Eastern Church had a mystical and theological conception of marriage that began in the fourth century.[14])

Nevertheless, while marriage was primarily a civil and familial event, its moral grounding and permanence were never in doubt. E. Schillebeeckx makes this statement regarding the early church: "According to Jesus's *logion* on indissolubility, marriage is a consecration of oneself for the whole of one's life to a fellow human being, one's chosen

---

13. Clement of Alexandria, "On Marriage," in *Women and Religion: A Feminist Sourcebook of Christian Thought,* ed. Elizabeth Clark and Herbert Richardson (New York: Harper & Row, 1977), pp. 41-50, p. 48.

14. See E. Schillebeeckx, *Marriage: Human Reality and Saving Mystery,* trans. N. D. Smith (New York: Sheed & Ward, 1965).

partner — and according to Paul's interpretation, doing this just as Christ gave his life for the church."[15]

Clearly, the foundation for a migration of marriage from secular to sacred domain was implicit, and it is to this development that we now turn. A thorough historical discussion of the early Middle Ages can be found in the writings of John Witte Jr.[16] and J. Goody.[17] Pierre Toubert's discussion of "the Carolingian moment" is particularly relevant, for during this time, in the eighth and ninth centuries, a "unifying ideology of the conjugal family" was constructed from the Bible, the church fathers, and the canons of the early councils.[18] The Christian family of "the Carolingian moment" was relatively free of ascetic pressures, and with the next several centuries the natural good of marriage and procreation would be unambiguously asserted by theologians and the church.

The Rise to Consensual Holiness in Marriage

By the second half of the eleventh century, the secular formalities of marriage had been incorporated into the church's form of marriage. At the Lateran Council of 1139, the church excommunicated all those of Albigensian or Catharist persuasion because these heresies condemned marital union. The Catharists saw sex as evil because it continues the natural order. Saint Dominic (c. 1170-1221), a Spanish canon regular, created a small house of preachers to combat the Catharist heresy in southern France. This grew into the influential Dominican Order of the thirteenth century, whose friars preached a message affirming the goodness of marriage, procreation, and nature. Thomas Aquinas (c. 1225-1274), a Dominican, would articulate this appreciation for the natural order more fully than any other theologian.

15. Schillebeeckx, *Marriage,* p. 386.

16. John Witte Jr., *From Sacrament to Contract: Marriage, Religion, and Law in the Western Tradition* (Louisville, Ky.: Westminster/John Knox Press, 1997).

17. Goody, *The Development of the Family and Marriage in Europe.*

18. Pierre Toubert, "The Carolingian Moment," in *A History of the Family,* vol. 1: *Distant Worlds, Ancient Worlds,* ed. A. Burguiere et al. (Cambridge: Harvard University Press, 1996), p. 397.

Marriage was first referred to as a sacrament in 1184 at a local synod in Verona, held in response to the Manichean-like movement of dualism and denial of the goodness of creation, including procreation. In reaction to heresy, marriage became more truly good, and the idea of marriage as a sacrament soon became dominant. That led to other major changes. Christian marriage could be validly established only through the liturgy of the church. Priests assumed functions previously belonging to family guardians and spouses themselves. By the end of the twelfth century, in most parts of Europe it was the priest, not the parent, who asked the bride and groom for their consent to marriage in the wedding ceremony.

As marriage came under the control of the church rather than of the family or clan, free consent came into being. In the twelfth century, Pope Alexander III ratified consensual marriage by issuing the decretal entitled *Veniens ad nos,* which has had as much influence on Western history as any other papal pronouncement. Marriage required the consent of an unmarried man and an unmarried woman, both of whom had to be old enough to give consent and to enter into marriage. Moreover, Alexander argued — in contrast to his teacher, Gratian — that parental consent was neither a necessary nor a sufficient basis for marriage.[19] Historian Jack Goody argues that the church urged this freedom in part to free people from the power of clan and lineage, and in so doing to free them as well to do what they wished with their property — including donating it to the church.[20] This may be true. However, it is also clear that the church came to endorse freedom of consent and the voluntary union of affections as the only meaningful basis for marriage.[21] Sociologist James Q. Wilson contends that this assertion of consent "created an assumption that individuals have a right to accept or reject the conditions of their lives, an assumption that was very different from that which prevailed among cultures committed to clan-controlled

19. See Frances and Joseph Geis, *Marriage and Family in the Middle Ages* (New York: Harper & Row, 1989), pp. 83-98.

20. See Goody, *The Development of the Family and Marriage in Europe.*

21. Goody, *The Development of the Family and Marriage in Europe,* p. 193. See also Georges Duby, *Medieval Marriage: Two Models from Twelfth-Century France* (Baltimore: The Johns Hopkins University Press, 1978), pp. 16-17.

marriage."[22] Wilson suggests that herein lies a key historical turning point in the birth of Western freedom. This is an important truth.

Although the institution of marriage was elevated, its elevation to the level of sacrament was contested through the thirteenth century. There were many prominent theologians who debated whether marriage, which involves sexual intercourse, could ever rightly be viewed as a grace-conferring sacrament. Thomas Aquinas, on the contrary, held marriage to be a sacrament providing assistance toward holiness through grace. This debate was resolved with the conclusion that marriage must bestow grace because it had been declared a sacrament. Protestants would hold marriage to be a state instituted by God but not a sacrament. In response, the sacramental status of marriage was formalized at the Council of Trent in 1563.[23] Thus, marriage became a door to the sacred.[24] The sacramental notion of marriage assumes that a purely natural love is inadequate for the inevitable challenges involved in a marital relationship.

The Family as Holy

The elevation of marriage over the course of twelve centuries was more than an ecclesiastical reaction to heresy; it was also a development grounded in an emerging view of motherhood as holy. Clarissa Atkinson points out that, for a thousand years, physical and spiritual motherhood were understood as distinctly separate; only the latter had heavenly merit. In the later medieval centuries, however, a new appreciation developed for marriage, family, and motherhood; the domestic realm that was once renounced for the cloister became a meaningful spiritual locus. According to Atkinson, "Believers were encouraged to discover and exploit tender family affections, the better to love God." Even "more remarkable," she says, was that "increasing numbers of

22. James Q. Wilson, *The Moral Sense* (New York: Free Press, 1993), p. 204.
23. Wilson, *The Moral Sense,* p. 357.
24. See Joseph Martos, *Doors to the Sacred* (Garden City, N.Y.: Doubleday, 1981), pp. 399-451.

married women were admitted to the company of the saints after the thirteenth century."[25]

Atkinson explains this development in light of a new domestic spirituality. Franciscans and Dominicans of the thirteenth century were mendicant preachers holding forth in marketplaces and other places of domestic import; they were not monastics separated from the world of families. As Atkinson writes, "The friars' accommodation to the spirituality of lay people, including married people, occurred in a context of increasing respect for the estate of marriage." The example of Mary and Joseph became central in piety and dignified marriage; married persons could now aspire to the same loving qualities as the parents of Jesus. The Holy Family became "a kind of earthly trinity." While the sanctity of holy virginity persisted, "new opportunities for sanctity began to be available to married women in the later Middle Ages."[26]

In summary, Atkinson concludes that the piety of the Holy Family shaped a new attitude toward spirituality and the domestic sphere:

> Since the twelfth century preachers and theologians had been reviewing Christian teaching about marriage and family, affirming the goodness of marriage and the importance of parenthood for the church and society. In secular as well as religious art and literature, new attention was paid to families and to the sweetness and attractiveness of children. The Holy Family was presented for example and edification: Christians were encouraged to emulate and even to seek holiness through roles and relationships modeled by Jesus and his mother, foster father, and grandmother.[27]

As the wall between spiritual and physical motherhood began to crumble, mystics who were also mothers, such as Julian of Norwich, went so far as to identify mother love with the divine. The gap between lay and monastic spiritual values narrowed.

Thus the discontinuity between nature and the sacred that was dominant in the period of the early church began to give way to a link-

25. Atkinson, *The Oldest Vocation,* p. 145.
26. Atkinson, *The Oldest Vocation,* pp. 151, 159, 164.
27. Atkinson, *The Oldest Vocation,* pp. 191-92.

ing between the domestic sphere and the divine sphere. There was an increasing pastoral concern with marriage and family, and a theological sense that grace via sacrament could enable persons to endure the trials of conjugal life as occasions demanded. The concept of domestic holiness that Christianity developed was the expression of Jesus' assertion that marriage is, according to divine design, the monogamous union of male and female in lifelong commitment. In a radical and prophetic teaching that must lie forever at the core of Christian teaching, husband and wife "are no longer two, but one flesh" (Matt. 19:6).

This emphasis brings us back to Thomas Aquinas, who strongly affirmed that marriage is properly a sacrament through which nature is assisted by divine grace. Aquinas may be interpreted as the defining theological voice of the recognition of spirituality in the domestic sphere. In clearly affirming the sacred meaning of marriage and family, Aquinas articulated the ontological meaning of Jesus' references to the creation principle, for the natural law is an expression of the eternal law of the Creator.[28] Aquinas's appreciation for the embodiment of human nature and his attention to the givenness of biological structures did much to enhance the theological standing of marriage and family in Western thought.[29]

George Hayward Joyce, S.J., still more eloquently than others, summarized the Thomistic and Catholic doctrine on marriage: "Family life is the foundation on which society and civilization rest. Where the family is lacking in unity, in love, in high ideals, the whole society will soon feel the effects." Marriage exists "primarily for the child."[30] The natural law of procreative responsibility is, like all such moral law, a human participation in the divine blueprint *(logos)*. John Paul II's 1980 encyclical *Familiaris Consortio (On the Family)* could state that the future of society and the Church "passes through the family."[31]

28. Schillebeeckx, *Marriage.*

29. See Stephen J. Pope, *The Evolution of Altruism and the Ordering of Love* (Washington, D.C.: Georgetown University Press, 1994), chap. 2.

30. George Hayward Joyce, S.J., *Christian Marriage: An Historical and Doctrinal Study* (New York: Sheed & Ward, 1933), pp. 23, 19.

31. John Paul II, *Familiaris Consortio (On the Family)* (Washington, D.C.: U.S. Catholic Conference, 1981).

Marriage and Family in Protestantism

While the Protestant tradition rejected the notion of marriage as a sacrament, it nevertheless was fully consistent with the emerging medieval appreciation for the holiness of marriage and family.

Lutheranism

Martin Luther's "The Estate of Marriage," written in 1522, is one of the most influential of all Western statements on marriage and family.[32] Luther rejected the idea of marriage as a sacrament, thereby repudiating Catholicism as unbiblical and manipulative. Yet he strongly urged that the Christian ideal of lasting marital union be firmly ensconced in secular law. He wrote of the mutual honoring of bodies, for the body is "a divine and good creation that is well-pleasing unto God himself." He drew on Genesis 1:27 ("male and female he created them") and 1:28 ("be fruitful and multiply"). These passages from Genesis indicate "that man and woman should and must come together in order to multiply."[33]

In "The Estate of Marriage," Luther described marriage with the language of duty rather than choice. He wrote honestly about the admixture of suffering and good in marriage: "But the greatest good in married life, that which makes all suffering and labor worthwhile, is that God creates offspring and commands that they be brought up to worship and serve him."[34] Luther was thoroughly realistic in recognizing that family life will sometimes lack spontaneous joy, that spiritual and material challenges will usually abound, and that families may not endure in the absence of theological meanings. He believed that lasting joy and an ethic of permanence could be found in knowing that God

---

32. Martin Luther, "The Estate of Marriage," in *Luther's Works,* vol. 45, as found in vol. 2 of *Christian in Society,* ed. W. I. Brandt (Philadelphia: Fortress Press, 1962), pp. 17-48.

33. Luther, "The Estate of Marriage," p. 18.

34. Luther, "The Estate of Marriage," p. 46.

wills this estate. Thus, while he affirmed an ideal form for the family, he never idealized family life by removing its painful realities.

In *The Ethics of Martin Luther,* theologian Paul Althaus provides a thoughtful exploration of Luther's theology of marriage. According to Althaus, Luther saw the family established as a model in Scripture, and he could therefore give thanks and pray for marriage and family. Family love was the work of God, and thus Luther saw family life as pleasing to the creator and as the fit place for spiritual growth, displacing the monastic life entirely. Yet Luther placed family love under the "common order of Christian love," which meant that the Christian family was to serve "every needy person with all kinds of benevolent deeds."[35] Luther gave examples of feeding the hungry, giving drink to the thirsty, forgiving enemies, and praying for all humanity. Thus Luther crafted a theology of the "order of love" in which love for those near and dear is balanced by love for the stranger. Luther's Christian family is set in the narrative context of love for the neighbor, who is everyone and anyone; therefore, the family is not sealed off from wider spheres of *agape.* Such attention to the order of love was consistent with pre-Reformation Catholic thought.

Luther's cultural influence was considerable. Historian Roland Bainton describes how Luther elevated the home as the place where the "gospel precepts can most readily be exemplified." Bainton argues that Luther had a much more significant influence on the sphere of family life than on the spheres of politics and business: "The pious household, where the father was priest as well as magistrate, where family prayers and the recital of the catechism were daily exercises — this picture marked for centuries the Lutheran household." At first, Luther understood marriage in Pauline terms — as a necessary remedy for lust; after his marriage, however, he began increasingly "to portray the home as a school for character."[36]

---

35. Paul Althaus, *The Ethics of Martin Luther,* trans. R. C. Schultz (Philadelphia: Fortress Press, 1972), p. 40.

36. Roland H. Bainton, *The Reformation of the Sixteenth Century* (Boston: Beacon Press, 1952), p. 256. For more discussion of the family and the formation of character, see *Seedbeds of Virtue,* ed. Mary Ann Glendon and David Blankenhorn (Lanham, Md.: Madison Books, 1995).

Although Luther rejected the notion of marriage as a sacrament, Lutheran rites of marriage still deeply encouraged permanence, drawing on Matthew 19:6 ("What God has joined together, let no man put asunder"), Genesis 2:18, and Ephesians 5. Marriage began with a firm marital vow that clarified the intent of permanence and in so doing helped ensure it.[37] Luther considered divorce permissible on the grounds of adultery or desertion, when the spouse had been gone for ten years with no prospect of return. (By the eighteenth century, however, Lutheranism allowed divorce for irreconcilable antipathy, cruelty, and threats of violence.) Luther forbade any thoughts of divorce during stressful periods when a spouse was severely ill and dependent (unless the spouse was an adulterer); he wrote that the caretaking spouse "serve[s] the Lord in the person of the invalid and await[s] God's good pleasure."[38] Luther understood marriage and family as always being imperiled by selfishness and saved by a sense of vocation.

Puritanism

Calvin emphasized marriage and family as a partnership in faith. Like Luther, Calvin did not consider romantic love to be the basis for a successful marriage. He preferred to view marriage and family as a shared labor for the glory of God. Cohabitation between man and woman outside of marriage was to be strictly condemned. God established marriage and sanctified it with a blessing, and "from this it is clear that any other union apart from marriage is accursed in his sight" (2.8.41).[39]

Though they were never champions of romantic love, the Puritans gradually introduced the notions of affection and congeniality as the means to domestic harmony. Puritan parents were willing to allow their children to select marriage partners on the grounds that union in body

37. Kenneth Stevenson, *Mystical Blessings: A Study of Christian Marriage Rites* (New York: Oxford University Press, 1983).

38. Cited in Althaus, *The Ethics of Martin Luther,* p. 94.

39. Calvin, *Institutes of the Christian Religion,* Library of Christian Classics, vols. 20-21, ed. John T. McNeill, trans. Ford Lewis Battles (Philadelphia: Westminster Press, 1960), p. 405.

but not in soul is a misery. Yet the trials of an unhappy wedlock must be endured, for divorce could be permitted only in cases of adultery (Matt. 5:32, 19:9) and desertion. When John Milton eloquently defended divorce on the basis of mere "indisposition," the Puritans resisted this entirely.[40]

Historian Edmund S. Morgan's study on the Puritan family is a classic that is relevant to the current American debate over fatherlessness.[41] He points out that Puritans encouraged warm affections and love between spouses, although they warned against spouses loving one another to the extent that they would descend into idolatry in violation of the "order of being." Parental responsibilities were taken with utmost seriousness and enforced by law. Particularly important was material and financial support: "The laws obliged all parents to perform this duty: no New England father could loaf away his time while the cupboard was bare" (*PF,* p. 65). The neglectful father could be indicted for idleness, although this problem was generally averted with the help of the churches, which insisted on high parental standards of duty.

A principal parental duty was to assist the child in the solemn effort to find his or her "particular calling," since God gives each person gifts that can be discovered with effort, and that serve both the individual and the commonweal: "It was not so much a choice as a discerning of what occupation God called one into" (*PF,* p. 171). The gift would often be discovered by apprenticeship, and Puritan children could change apprenticeships in their search for the fitting use of their energies. Morgan writes, "As far as his children's material welfare was concerned, a Puritan parent could call his duty done when he saw them established in their callings with good husbands and wives" (*PF,* p. 87). Parents, especially fathers, were also responsible for teaching their children to read and to study the principles of Christianity. Literacy was important as a means to help them understand Scripture and thereby bring them "into the covenant" of conversion, and to help them find their vocation.

40. William Haller, *Liberty and Reformation in the Puritan Revolution* (New York: Columbia University Press, 1955), pp. 95, 97.

41. Edmund S. Morgan, *The Puritan Family: Religion and Domestic Relations in Seventeenth-Century New England* (New York: Harper & Row, 1944). All subsequent references to this volume will be made parenthetically in the text.

Three principles informed parental duties: the divine ordinance or sanction of marriage and family, the presence of a vocation in every soul, and the importance of extending the covenant to the next generation. The Puritans understood familial duties to be the keystone of social ethics and political order. Consistent with Aristotle's *Politics,* which was read by Puritan theologians, society was considered an association of families. Morgan describes a familial ideal that required no state:

> This was the first premise of Puritan political and social thought. In the Garden of Eden, which was the world as God had originally planned it, men lived innocently and happily with no need for any social organization apart from that provided by the family. It was only after Adam and Eve had tasted the forbidden fruit that need arose for stronger organizations. (*PF,* p. 173)

As Cotton Mather argued in his classic *Family Religion Urged,* God could have produced millions of people all at once; instead, God produced Adam and Eve, who were to form a family united with God. Because of the Fall, however, the congregation of believers was formed to strengthen worship. The Puritans took God's covenant with Abraham's family as a model. As Morgan explains, "The Puritans, in other words, thought of their church as an organization made up of families rather than individuals" (*PF,* pp. 135-36).

Puritan families conducted regular devotions in the home, including prayer, Scripture reading, and singing. According to Morgan, they believed that if the family failed to inculcate religion and morality, neither the church nor the state could succeed in doing so. The family was prior to and served by the church. Had there been no Fall, there would have been no need for churches. Similarly, the state existed only because the family needed help in enforcing virtue in a degenerate world. Puritan theologian Eleazer Mather wrote that families are "the root whence church and Commonwealth cometh" (*PF,* p. 143). All the Puritan theologians argued that the good ordering of society was possible only if families instructed their members in virtue.

Puritan theologians believed that the intimacy of the marital and familial connection created special moral ties, but they also believed that a Christian should exclude no one from his or her love. The balance of love between those near and dear and those who were distant or strangers was a central concern, as it was in medieval thought and in Luther. Nevertheless, they did not achieve this balance.

Morgan's thesis, which fits well with my concerns regarding the insular bourgeois family, is that the Puritan experiment failed because covenant theology placed so much weight on the redemption of one's children or lineage that the evangelical impulse was paralyzed. "Love thy neighbor" became "Love thy family." In Morgan's final phrase, "When theology became the handmaid of genealogy, Puritanism no longer deserved its name" (*PF,* p. 180). The Puritan failure teaches us that the Christian family cannot be hermetically sealed but must actively turn its attention to the needs of strangers. Clearly, the bourgeois tendencies of the American family have deep historical roots indicating a perennial problem that cannot be easily overcome.

Throughout the Second Great Awakening, various benevolence movements extricated many American Protestant families from insularity. After the Awakening, however, there was a renewed insular tendency. Evidence of this can be seen in Horace Bushnell's classic *Christian Nurture,* published in 1861. It is true that Bushnell contributed much wisdom to the subject of child rearing. He argued against "breaking the will" of a child by physical force or by extreme psychological coercion. And he offered a powerful vision of how a child would respond to a violent and authoritarian father: "If his Christian father is felt only to be a tyrant, he will seem to have a tyrant in God's name to bear; and that will be enough to create a sullen prejudice against all sacred things."[42] Bushnell's positive impact is evident in the history of American child-rearing.[43] Yet Bushnell failed to seriously discuss the conflict between love within the family and love for all of humanity.

The Social Gospel drove hard against Protestant familial insularity by emphasizing issues of distributive justice in the context of the Gilded Age, when wealthy families tried to recreate the golden palaces of aristo-

42. Horace Bushnell, *Christian Nurture* (Cleveland: Pilgrim Press, 1994), p. 298.

43. Phillip Greven, *Spare the Child: The Religious Roots of Punishment and the Psychological Impact of Physical Abuse* (New York: Vintage, 1990).

cratic Europe, as a tour of Newport, Rhode Island, will make painfully clear. But this social criticism does not mean that the Social Gospel was inattentive to the importance of marriage, family, and parenthood. A splendid exploration of the relationship between the beloved and the stranger in the "order of love" is *Dare We Be Christians?* by jouralist-theologian Walter Rauschenbusch. Like all Christian thinkers, Rauschenbusch values love for persons as such, including strangers. But love for the stranger evolves from the experience and lessons of more intimate ties of "solidarity." "The love of fatherhood and motherhood is a divine revelation and a miracle," writes Rauschenbusch. "It is a creative act of God in us." Rauschenbusch continues with this eloquent observation:

> Last year it was not; this year it is, and all things are changed. The dry rock of our selfishness has been struck and the water of sacrificial love pours forth. The thorn-bush is aflame with a beautiful fire that does not consume. The springing up of this new force of love is essential for the very existence of human society. Unless it were promptly forthcoming, children would die like the flies of late summer and the race would perish.[44]

In the family, argues Rauschenbusch, God works through nature to develop our capacities for love and sacrifice that can then be fruitfully extended to the world.

The Christian ethicist must avoid making the broader offering of love seem easy, for ultimately a full Christian love, inclusive of enemies, requires a radical reconfiguration of loyalties that is beyond purely natural propensity. Yet the passage above nicely captures the poetic and theological value accorded parental solicitude.

Anglicanism

Among the most eloquent Anglican statements on the meaning of marriage and family is that of Jeremy Taylor (1613-1667), whose "The Mar-

---

44. Walter Rauschenbusch, *Dare We Be Christians?* (1914; reprint, Cleveland: Pilgrim Press, 1993), pp. 21-22.

riage Ring; or, The Mysteriousness and Duties of Marriage" remains a classic.[45] Taylor wrote of marriage as "hallowed by a blessing" to "increase and multiply." In the early church, "it pleased God in this new creation to inspire into the hearts of his servants a disposition and strong desire to live a single life"; because the dissemination of the gospel required poverty and martyrdom, the single life was advantageous. But after that storm was over, the state of marriage and family "returned to its first blessing." Regrettably, "in this first interval, the public necessity and the private zeal mingled together did sometimes overact their love of single life, even to the disparagement of marriage, and to the scandal of religion." However diminished, marriage came to be considered "the seminary of the church" and a "school and exercise of virtue." It is, wrote Taylor, "the proper scene of piety and patience, of the duty of parents and the charity of relatives; here kindness is spread abroad, and love is united and made firm as a center: marriage is the nursery of heaven."[46]

Taylor had suffered in family life, having buried his first wife and his five sons. He thus had a remarkably realistic and paradoxical assessment of family life as "more merry, and more sad; it is fuller of sorrows, and fuller of joys; it lies under more burdens, but it is supported by all the strengths of love and charity, and those burdens are delightful."[47]

The classic sources of Protestantism are many. They hold in common the ideal of permanent monogamous marriage as following a divine pattern indicated in the first and second chapters of Genesis, the divine origin of human sexuality, the blessing of human propagation, the importance of true companionship between man and woman, and the possibilities of *agape* in overcoming inevitable degrees of insularity.

45. Jeremy Taylor, "The Marriage Ring; or, The Mysteriousness and Duties of Marriage," in *Jeremy Taylor: Selected Works,* ed. T. K. Carroll (Mahwah, N.J.: Paulist Press, 1990), pp. 261-67.
46. Taylor, "The Marriage Ring," pp. 263, 265.
47. Taylor, "The Marriage Ring," p. 256.

Christianity and Divorce

The particular problem of divorce is best treated against the above background in Catholic and Protestant thought.

It is interesting to trace the development of Catholic thought on the matter. It is significant that Christianity from the outset emphasized permanence in marriage (contrary to the permissiveness of Deuteronomy 24:1-2). This belief was based heavily on Mark 10:11-12 and Matthew 5:32, even though the latter allowed divorce based on adultery while the former did not. The church held to the principle of permanence against the permissiveness of secular law, finding support in Charlemagne, who "extended the ecclesiastical doctrine of marital indissolubility to secular courts throughout his empire."[48] Nevertheless, in 826, Pope Eugenius issued a decree based on Matthew 5:32 which stated that divorce was permissible in cases of adultery. By the thirteenth century, however, the position of Mark 10:11-12 had won the day, and absolute indissolubility was established in Canon VII by the Council of Trent. Critics, such as Thomas More and Erasmus, cited church fathers who accepted divorce on the grounds of adultery.

But the canon law held sway, and it categorically forbade divorce. Annulment could be granted on the basis of the impediments of consanguinity and impotence, and separation granted on grounds of adultery, cruelty, heresy, or apostasy. However, divorce, even in the instance of adultery, was forbidden.

The Protestant Reformers were critical of both Catholic thought and practice regarding marriage: they rejected the exultation of virginity and celibacy, pointed to the corrupt practice of granting annulments for money, and eschewed the notion of marriage as a sacrament that thereby confers grace. Still, they understood marriage as a "holy ordinance of God" and were highly reluctant to permit divorce. Luther accepted divorce on grounds of adultery, desertion, or refusal of sexual intercourse, but he did not wish to grant it easily, and he emphasized the importance of forgiveness. Calvin allowed divorce on grounds of adul-

---

48. Roderick Phillips, *Untying the Knot: A Short History of Divorce* (New York: Cambridge University Press, 1991), p. 10.

tery or desertion, but not on grounds of impotence. In actual practice, divorces were exceedingly rare in Protestant countries, and the importance of marriage was indicated by the severity of punishment meted out to violators of its vows. In Calvin's Geneva, for example, fornication (sex between two unmarried persons) was punished by imprisonment and a bread-and-water diet, adultery with an unmarried partner meant banishment, and adultery between two married persons meant death.[49]

John Milton, along with the Strasbourg Reformer Martin Bucer, asserted that mutual consent and emotional incompatibility were also sufficient grounds for divorce. But this was the dissonant view. To the majority of Reformers, as Roderick Phillips explains, "Incompatibility of temperament was not a ground because unhappiness was a result of original sin and must be borne like its other effects."[50] Harmoniousness in marriage was desirable but not necessary or often realistic; the Reformers believed that the institution of marriage and family needed stricter support than the waxing and waning of harmony.

The Role of Women

Historians have long noted that women were accorded higher status in Christian circles than elsewhere in the Greco-Roman world of antiquity, and that women were therefore especially attracted to early Christianity.[51] It can be surmised that women's elevation in status within the Christian community spilled over into the domestic sphere. According to Henry Chadwick, women in the upper classes of society often converted their spouses, and thus came to enjoy "far greater security and equality" in marriage than did their pagan neighbors.[52] Further, as Rodney Stark points out, Christian women "married at a substantially older age and had more choice about whom they married." They thus

49. Phillips, *Untying the Knot,* pp. 15, 16.
50. Phillips, *Untying the Knot,* p. 16.
51. See Robin Lane Fox, *Pagans and Christians* (New York: Alfred A. Knopf, 1987). See also Henry Chadwick, *The Early Church* (New York: Penguin Books, 1967).
52. Chadwick, *The Early Church,* p. 56.

avoided being forced into early, often prepubertal marriages, typically with older men who treated such spouses like the children they often were.[53] And Robert A. Markus makes this comment about Christianity between 330 and 700 C.E.: "If we can trust the figures which suggest that Christians tended to marry at a notably higher age than their pagan contemporaries, Christianity would appear to have reinforced these shifts towards marriage as a more personal and free partnership of equals."[54]

Yet throughout Christian history, the positive impact of faith on relative freedom and equality within marriage practices in the early church has been diminished by those who would assert ancient patriarchal modes of domination under the category of "male headship." The form of Christian marriage supported in this text is one fully consistent with the values of freedom, equality, and justice that are nascent within early Christianity.

The Genesis 1–3 texts have been interpreted by Roman Catholic ethicist Lisa Sowle Cahill as a locus from which to critique patriarchy and subordination in marriage. Cahill concludes that "supremacy and subordination, as distinct from difference and cooperation, are not part of the original creation but of the condition of sin. God's creation of humanity in the divine image, as male and female, and as companions who become 'one flesh,' functions as a standard by which to evaluate and criticize the male and female dialogue and struggle in history." The Genesis texts indicate that the two sexes are equally good and "designed for a harmonious and productive existence."[55] Cahill finds that both Testaments "favor the institutionalization of sexuality in heterosexual, monogamous, permanent, and procreative marriage that furthers the cohesiveness and continuity of family, church, and body politic, and that

---

53. Rodney Stark, *The Rise of Christianity* (San Francisco: Harper, 1996), p. 105. See also Keith Hopkins, "The Age of Roman Girls at Marriage," *Population Studies* 18 (1965): 309-27.

54. Robert A. Markus, "From Rome to the Barbarian Kingdoms (330-700)," in *The Oxford Illustrated History of Christianity,* ed. John McManners (Oxford: Oxford University Press, 1992), p. 69.

55. Lisa Sowle Cahill, *Between the Sexes: Foundations for a Christian Ethics of Sexuality* (Philadelphia: Fortress/Paulist, 1985), pp. 56, 55.

respects and nurtures the affective commitments to which spouses give sexual expression." Such marriage includes pleasurable, reciprocal, affective, unitive sex, but does not condone "sexual trivialization, glorification, manipulation, narcissism, and infidelity," or the sexual hierarchy that underlies these.[56]

Despite the implications of Genesis and the example of Jesus in his openness to women among his audiences and followers, patriarchy was the social reality. Peter Brown argues that in the ancient Mediterranean communities, the average life span was short (less than twenty-five years in the Roman Empire at its height). Young girls were recruited for procreative purposes (the median age at the time of marriage was fourteen) so that the society would not "come to an end for lack of citizens." This was "a world determined to admit no break in the easy flow of civilized life from generation to generation." Except for the few vestal virgins in Rome, "marriage and childbirth were the unquestioned destiny of all other women." Because husbands were invariably older than their wives, they treated them "almost as daughters" and held a position of unchallenged dominance over them justified by appeals to a "natural hierarchy."[57]

Drawing on Brown's work, Cahill argues that the early Christians were struggling against the structure of the Roman family, especially with the unlimited legal power of the husband and father over the wife and children *(patria potestas)*. For this reason, early Christianity downplayed "not only procreation but family ties in any form (Mark 3:31, Luke 19:29 and 8:21)." Its idealization of celibacy was driven by "commitment to communal solidarity and a rejection of the hierarchical and state-controlled functions of the patriarchal family." Parenthood was given little or no attention in early Christianity because in the patriarchal family it perpetuated dominion. In sum, contends Cahill, while heterosexual marriage was assumed to be the proper context for sexual relations, no value was placed on procreation nor any positive significance afforded parenthood. The praise of virginity had "converse effects on attitudes toward marriage and sex." Abstinence meant freedom of

56. Cahill, *Between the Sexes,* pp. 143, 144.
57. Brown, *The Body and Society,* pp. 7, 9, 13.

the soul, but this was achieved through "the denigration of sex, marriage, and parenthood."[58]

Early Christian women must have felt deeply the liberating meaning of a Christ who refused all power except the power of love addressed to free spirits. In *In Memory of Her,* theologian Elisabeth Schüssler Fiorenza thoroughly explores the meaning of freedom in the early Christian missionary movement of the first three or four decades (30 to 70 C.E.), of which Paul was a part. She focuses on the ritual of baptism and the life in the Spirit of those who, through baptism, became members of the Christian community. Whether male or female, slave or free, all those baptized into the freedom of Christ became new creations, shared in ecstatic experiences, and were sent in freedom to proclaim the gospel.[59]

This rite of passage into the Christian community meant that all the coercive hierarchies of the world should be transcended. Women, for instance, served in all the offices in the movement and led house churches; in his letters, Paul acknowledges women who were powerful and respected heads of missionary churches. Junia, Prisca, Phoebe, and Thecla were among them. The strong role that women played early in the movement was changed through a gradual patriarchalization that was firmly in place by the end of the first century C.E. Fiorenza refers to a bitter struggle over women's leadership that led to the active elimination of prominent women from the pages of Christian history.

But this was an unfortunate shift that was not consistent with biblical teaching. On this point, both Fiorenza and New Testament exegete Hans Dieter Betz attach great importance to Galatians 3:26-28.[60] They contend that this passage is pre-Pauline in origin, having functioned as baptismal liturgy in the early missionary movement. They therefore indicate Paul's fundamental proximity to the ethic of freedom associated with new life in the Spirit. The verses read as follows:

58. Lisa Sowle Cahill, *Sex, Gender, and Christian Ethics* (Cambridge: Cambridge University Press, 1996), pp. 151, 152, 172.

59. *In Memory of Her: A Feminist Theological Reconstruction of Christian Origins,* ed. Elisabeth Schüssler Fiorenza (New York: Crossroad, 1984).

60. Hans Dieter Betz, *Galatians* (Philadelphia: Fortress Press, 1979).

For through faith you are all sons of God in union with Christ Jesus. Baptized into union with him, you have all put on Christ as a garment. There is no such thing as Jew and Greek, slave and freeman, male and female; for you are all one person in Christ Jesus.

At baptism, argues Betz, Christians were informed of their new status as children of God. By "putting on Christ," they were transformed into new and free persons. When they began living in the Spirit, worldly distinctions upon which coercion was predicated no longer had meaning. Both Betz and Fiorenza argue persuasively, I think, that the Galatian passages have more than a purely internal significance — that they are meant to inform social and marital relationships. Equality was to be manifest in the relationships between men and women, husbands and wives.

Christianity and Dualism

The ascetic life provided a valuable and necessary alternative to patriarchy and the mandate of reproduction. A problem emerged when, as Max L. Stackhouse argues, "antimaterial" ascetic modes of thought became so pervasive that the "larger ethical vision [the family] was threatened."[61]

There is a powerful — some might suggest dominant — element in early Christianity that was discontinuous with Judaism. While Judaism maintained a great respect and appreciation for the physical union in marriage, early Christianity came to think of sex as something base, according to Morton M. Hunt: "Sex became so sinful and disgusting that even within marriage, as an act allowed by God, it seemed shameful and more ignoble than elimination." While marriage was the only state in which yearnings for physical intimacy could be satisfied, it was viewed by many early theologians as an inferior condition linked with a shameful act that was justifiable only because it was necessary for pro-

---

61. Max L. Stackhouse, *Covenant and Commitment: Faith, Family, and Economic Life* (Louisville, Ky.: Westminster/John Knox Press, 1997), p. 23.

creation. In the early centuries of Christianity, Hunt points out, this tension resulted in the phenomenon of continent marriage.[62]

Thus, a scholar such as Hunt, who writes from outside the circle of Christian faith, concludes with these memorable words regarding the early church and its legacy: "The influence of Christianity upon love and marriage is thus an impossible tangle of opposites — purification and contamination, the rebuilding of the family and the total flight from the family, the glorification of one woman and the condemnation of womankind."[63]

The dualism that I most associate with negative Christian attitudes toward the body and sex can plausibly be derived from Plato and Descartes, but not from Aristotle, Thomas Aquinas, and the Scholastic tradition, for whom the soul is the substantial form of the body rather than a separate substantial entity. Yet even Plato and Descartes (as well as Plotinus) saw physical reality not as evil but simply as the lowest kind of reality on a continuum.

Is substance dualism the cause of the debasement of sex and the body? Or is it the other way around? I do not see a clearly causal relationship between substance dualism and these regrettable realities — for surely history is more complex than that. Yet there is certainly an elective affinity between ideas and social practices.

James B. Nelson, a harsh critic of the sexual alienation of early Christianity, offers this explanation of its development:

> The historical roots of this sexual alienation are not difficult to find. They emerged as two intertwining dualisms. Spiritualistic dualism (spirit over body, mind over matter) emerged with power in late Hellenistic Greece and made a lasting impact upon the Christian church. Championed by Neoplatonists, the dualism viewed the immortal spirit as a temporary prisoner in a mortal, corruptible body. The good life and, indeed, salvation itself required escape from flesh into spirit.[64]

62. Morton M. Hunt, *The Natural History of Love* (New York: Alfred A. Knopf, 1959), p. 127.

63. Hunt, *The Natural History of Love*, p. 126.

64. James B. Nelson, *Between Two Gardens: Reflections on Sexuality and Religious Experience* (New York: Pilgrim Press, 1983), p. 6.

Dualism has resulted in an unduly morbid assessment of the divine good of sexuality, which has led to celibacy and various extreme ascetic tendencies against the care of the body. Nelson encourages a greater appreciation for the incarnation of Christ and the divine gift of sexuality.

Conclusion

The reader who seeks a full history of Christian thought, practice, and legal influence with respect to marriage is urged again to review John Witte's text.[65] It is difficult to imagine a more insightful discussion of Catholic, Lutheran, Calvinist, and Anglican traditions. Witte concludes his book with a strong criticism of Enlightenment contract theory, which deleted the Christian language of permanence and covenant from marriage. In the next chapter, I will critique the ideas of some contemporary Christian ethicists. Too many have simply jettisoned Christian teaching regarding the themes of covenant, fidelity, and a stable base for parenting.

The Christian tradition is complex, somewhat contested, and pluralistic. With appropriate warnings against insularity, however, the tradition holds that those who do marry are bound by God and the common good to intend and to realize a permanence for the sake of an institution upon which the future of children and of society rests.

---

65. Witte Jr., *From Sacrament to Contract*.

4

Toward a Contemporary Theology of the Family

Monogamy plays a significant role in the teachings of Jesus (see Chapter 2). It survived dualistic assaults in the early centuries of the church as well as in later centuries, was ensconced in natural-law theory and the sacramental lexicon, emerged powerfully in the Protestant Reformation as an "order of creation," and became especially central in Puritan theology. Despite somewhat frail beginnings, the idea of lasting marriage as an end in itself and as the precondition for responsible procreation ascended to its high status in Christian tradition. Thus, it is impossible for the Christian who is faithful to the teachings of Jesus to speak of different lifestyles as being equal: it is not good when a woman chooses to forgo marriage and bring a child into the world fatherless; nor is it good for a biological father to act as a mere impregnator who takes no responsibility for the child; nor is the culture of divorce acceptable.

In this chapter I review some of the diverse currents in the contemporary Christian ethics of marriage and family, noting again that, as James M. Gustafson comments, "more attention has been given to homosexuality, abortion, and pre- and extramarital sexual relationships than to marriage and families as communities and institutions."[1] I have

1. James M. Gustafson, *Ethics from a Theocentric Perspective,* 2 vols. (Chicago: University of Chicago Press, 1981-1984), vol. 2: *Ethics and Theology,* p. 165.

organized the material under a series of problematical issues that should, I think, inform future ethical and pastoral discussion. I then conclude by considering the wider theological implications of family theology for our knowledge of God.

The Institution of the Family

Thinking of the family as an institution suggests comparisons with schools, religious bodies, and even hospitals. Social institutions are defined in terms of their places and functions in society. Most schools exist to educate the young so that they may assume their rightful creative role in society's future; churches and synagogues exist to provide a context and community for the expression of human spirituality; hospitals exist to heal or manage illness. Every lasting institution serves society in an irreplaceable way — and the family is no exception. The family exists to teach and to tend loved ones, usually in interaction with various other institutions.

To think of marriage and the family that unfolds from it in institutional terms is useful because it encourages parents to think in terms of their distinctive roles and duties. Alongside other social institutions, the family exists to provide ample parental love and support for children, and to allow husband and wife the opportunity to grow in conjugal love within a context of loyalty and trust. The marriage vow ("in sickness and health, till death do us part") is the beginning of a journey in life that will require remarkable degrees of spirituality, solicitude, respect, self-sacrifice, patience, kindness, forgiveness, and hope. The love that resulted in marriage and then parenthood must be made a thousand times more profound through a journey that will at times be trying. Religious communities, not the state, have generally taken responsibility for preparing the faithful for marriage. It is unfortunate that serious efforts to prepare for marriage have diminished, with the result that too many persons are very poorly prepared for marriage and parenthood. Secular strategies, such as parenting classes in public schools and even a state-sponsored licensing program for would-be parents, have been suggested in response to the current state of necessity.[2] Churches ought to reclaim this social role, partly because the preparation is likely to be more successful when undertaken in a sacred rather than a secular context.[3]

Pastoral Care in the Culture of Divorce

One use of the word "family" is a purely metaphorical one: a family is two or more people who consider themselves tied together by care and love. It is a high tribute to the core reality of the biological family (mother, father, and children) that its special moral tone of consanguinity and mutual support has made this metaphorical use of the term "family" readily understandable to most people through the centuries.

But I am not pursuing metaphors and analogies, although the language of familial relations is central to any discussion of Christian ethics (for example, being equally children of God, we therefore have filial-based duties to brothers and sisters, including all of humanity). Instead, my concern is with the form of those literal families in which procreation occurs. In the Judeo-Christian context, the literal family includes the spiritual and physical union of man and woman joined faithfully in God's sight, which subsequently engenders children who are to be cared for. In the Catholic tradition, this marital union that leads to procreation was afforded a new dignity by virtue of its religious consecration as a sacrament; for Luther and Protestants, this union was afforded dignity by virtue of its being deemed a kind of participation in God's ordering of creation. Classically, pastoral caregivers have devoted a great deal of time and attention to preparing engaged couples for marriage and family through instruction in the meaning of the matrimonial and parental covenants; the importance of married spirituality, in which husband and wife care for one another's souls in prayerfulness; and the significance of caring for children as divine entrustments. More recently, however, pastoral care has often been part of the problem.

Jean Miller Schmidt and Gail E. Murphy-Geiss describe the Meth-

2. Some think that religion has failed so entirely in marriage preparation over recent decades that the state must of dire necessity step into the role.

3. By analogy, it seems clear that the inner-city churches are doing a very successful job of handling a variety of problems ranging from gang activity to welfare dependence. See Joe Klein, "In God They Trust," *The New Yorker,* 16 June 1997, pp. 40-48.

odist movement away from the two-parent family and toward the "changing needs of newer forms." These authors lament the slowness of this movement, and assert, with some degree of truth, that "overall, the Methodist emphasis on grace means that acceptance and compassion must be the norms." They quote a leader from their Board of Global Ministries who calls upon Methodists to accept "the biblical notion of family in which everyone is a brother or sister and the family is the family of God."[4]

This representative mainline Protestant view has three major problems: (1) it ignores the data indicating that, in general, children do better with two parents; (2) it draws solely on the ethic of unconditional acceptance without providing direction consistent with Christian tradition, and is therefore unbalanced; and (3) it too easily ignores the biologically grounded family in favor of the metaphorical one.

Theologian William R. Garrett sees these flaws in the current Presbyterian view. He writes that the accommodation to an "anything goes" approach to the family is now more or less complete:

> By the time the baby boomer generation had begun to reach its childbearing years, Presbyterians had largely forsaken any attempt to transform family patterns in conformity with some normative model, opting instead to develop ministries that related to the spiritual needs of its members regardless of the family forms its members embraced.[5]

While it remains important for pastoral caregivers to begin by unconditionally affirming that God loves people no matter what their circumstances, it is equally important that they emphasize the benefits and meaning of the two-parent family that begins in loyal marriage.[6]

Over the last two decades, many Protestant theologians and pastoral caregivers have embraced familial formlessness, perhaps because

4. Jean Miller Schmidt and Gail E. Murphy-Geiss, "Methodist: 'Tis Grace Will Lead Us Home,'" in *Faith Traditions and the Family,* ed. Phyllis D. Airhart and Margaret Lamberts Bendroth (Louisville, Ky.: Westminster/John Knox Press, 1996), pp. 85-99, p. 98.

5. William R. Garrett, "Presbyterian: Home Life as Vocation in the Reformed Tradition," in *Faith Traditions and the Family,* pp. 114-25, p. 123.

6. Joanna Bowen Gillepsie, "Episcopal: Family as the Nursery of Church and Society," in *Faith Traditions and the Family,* pp. 143-56.

they do not wish to cause any discomfort. In their study of theology of the family and pastoral care, for example, John Patton and Brian H. Childs state, "There is no ideal form for the Christian family toward which we should strive. There is, however, a normative function: care." While there is much value in their definition of care as a combination of appreciation, respect, compassion, and solicitude, they refuse to "argue for or against any particular form of the family or for who ought to be living together and for how long."[7] For Patton and Childs, who are both liberal Protestants, any form is acceptable, for however long, if redemptive "care" is present. No formative order, *nomos,* or empirical data shapes their thinking. If, however, the generalized benefits of having two parents joined in loyal marriage are taken into account, an ethics of care may in fact require a more directive pastoral approach than Patton and Childs allow.

Other liberal Protestant thinkers also mistakenly link care with such relational chaos. In 1978, the highly influential James B. Nelson published his book entitled *Embodiment.*[8] Nelson's assertions of the goodness of the body and of sex must be lauded as a contribution to marital fullness: he affirms the goodness of creation, the body, and *eros;* he is properly critical of male images of sexuality that result in the abuse of women instead of affective intimacy. His Freudian framework can be questioned on empirical grounds, as can some of his derivative assertions about the absence of sexual expression inviting "self-destruction." Nevertheless, his analysis of the relationship of sex to human well-being is helpful, particularly since some of Christianity, in contrast to Judaism, has been unduly suspicious of sexual intimacy (although the sexual sphere is as prone to exploitation as any other area of human activity).[9]

Yet, apropos of the principle of creation, Nelson departs from the moral signposts of Christian ethics when he indicates that, in some cases, marital fidelity is fully consistent with nonexclusive sexual inti-

7. John Patton and Brian H. Childs, *Christian Marriage and Family: Caring for Our Generations* (Nashville: Abingdon Press, 1988), p. 12.

8. James B. Nelson, *Embodiment: An Approach to Sexuality and Christian Theology* (Minneapolis: Augsburg, 1979).

9. See Stephen G. Post, "Love, Religion, and Sexual Revolution," *Journal of Religion* 72, no. 2 (Winter 1992): 403-16.

macies. This "open marriage" departure from the sexual exclusivity associated with Christian monogamy represents a serious criticism of the tradition. Nelson argues for personal relativism: he asserts that the form of marriage ought to be "congruent with the authentic needs of persons" and, further, that we ought never to "absolutize" a particular institutional form.[10]

But Christian tradition teaches an exclusive monogamy, as indicated by the New Testament, even if it allows for divorce in compelling cases. Christian thinkers have attached great importance to fidelity in marriage: biblical warrants require it; marriage is considered a one-flesh union for the duration of partners' lives (an increasingly lengthy commitment in our aging society); the pattern of Christ's own faithfulness is considered an ideal for marriage. On the matter of fidelity, a position such as Nelson's will stir response from thoughtful conservative Christian ethicists. Gilbert Meilaender, for example, summarizes Nelson's position to mean "I promise . . . unless and until new possibilities for growth and self-realization lead me to a new partner."[11]

Like Nelson, Protestant ethicist Christine E. Gudorf does not affirm monogamous marriage and the two-parent family. In her discussion of marriage, Gudorf cites Jessie Bernard's well-known assertion (made in 1971) that married women are "more phobic, passive, and depressed" than single women. This claim is questionable. No doubt some women have been and are oppressed by marital patriarchy through control of property and the potentially stifling role of full-time mother. But Bernard's analysis reflects a form of anti-family feminism that was eventually moderated through the later writings of Betty Friedan and others. Gudorf does indicate that the best solution to the problem of marriage and family is to abolish patriarchal inequalities rather than the husband-wife form itself. However, she supports alternatives to the two-parent family: "Families need not be based on marriage. Families can be collections of persons who are committed to the physical, moral, spiritual, social, and intellectual development of other

---

10. Post, "Love, Religion, and Sexual Revolution," p. 149.

11. Gilbert A. Meilaender, *The Limits of Love* (University Park: Pennsylvania State University Press, 1987), p. 126.

members of the collective unit in an ongoing way." And she goes on to claim that "marriage can take many shapes and forms." She also leaves dangling, in a troubling way, this query: "Is there a purpose and content to marriage once it is no longer about the ownership and control of woman and children, once both entering and remaining within marriage are voluntary?"[12] Clearly there is a reason for marriage: providing children with the love of both a mother and a father.

In today's culture of divorce and alternative relationships, pastoral caregivers must reassert (without shaming) the form of the family — that is, mothers and fathers in loyal marital partnerships, working and caring together. Of course, separation by death and justifiable divorce will occur — but these splittings of the nucleus assume that a whole nucleus was once in place, and this is the responsibility of Christian pastoral caregivers. The principle that it is good for a child to have both a committed father and mother is difficult to improve upon.

The question now is whether the empirical data can begin to turn pastoral care around. It would be helpful, for example, if all students in pastoral-care programs could be required to read social-scientific studies such as that of Paul R. Amato and Alan Booth, who conclude that about 70 percent of divorces occur due to "low conflict" between spouses and should be avoided in order to benefit children.[13] Such divorces are unnecessary and break important familial bonds.

Resisting the Acculturation of Christianity

Contemporary theologians and pastoral caregivers should be teaching that marriage and family, over the long term, require a more mature form of love *(agape)* than a burst of romanticism. Secondly, they should be teaching that marriage is a covenant rather than a contract.

---

12. Christine E. Gudorf, *Body, Sex, and Pleasure: Reconstructing Christian Sexual Ethics* (Cleveland: Pilgrim Press, 1994), pp. 74, 79, 80.

13. Paul R. Amato and Alan Booth, *A Generation at Risk: Growing Up in an Era of Family Upheaval* (Cambridge: Harvard University Press, 1997).

Passion Contained by Agape

Though it was published in 1940, I consider Denis de Rougemont's *Love in the Western World* to be prophetic and cogent in its analysis of the problem of a divorce culture. A lay Catholic, de Rougemont much appreciated the institutional aspects of marriage and family. He contrasts two "rival moral systems," one that made marriage into a sacrament and another that essentially viewed it as a mistake. The rival of marriage is the religion of passion — and, in effect, adultery. De Rougemont explains that the church viewed adultery as both a sin and a crime:

> In the eyes of the Church, adultery was at one and the same time a sacrilege, a crime against the natural order, and a crime against the social order. For the sacrament conjoined in one and the same act two faithful souls, two bodies capable of begetting, and two juridical persons. It was therefore a sacrament that made holy the fundamental needs of both the species and the community.[14]

Today the religion (or "ultimate concern") of passion and adultery so permeates modern culture as to make such lasting unions appear ridiculous. Adultery swoops down to destroy what would otherwise have lasted. The pain is very real and often leads to emotional and familial disaster. Oddly, however, our culture tends to think of passionate violations of marriage (and, therefore, of family and society) as interesting. The potency of such passion does wear off as reality asserts itself over time and the inflamed mind regains reason; but by then the damage has been done. While the passion had dominion, it was more real than the world and obligations to spouse and children — even to self. As a culture, we esteem passion more than social stability.

De Rougemont reminds us that marriage requires a conversion to the love of neighbor, even the love of enemies, because there will be moments when a spouse will feel like an enemy. No loyal husband or wife can honestly say that at some point he or she did not ask, quietly and alone, "Why did I marry this person?" Perhaps the marriage began in

14. Denis de Rougemont, *Love in the Western World,* trans. M. Belgion (New York: Harper & Row, 1940), p. 275.

the heat of passion, but no attention was given to aims in life and common interests that might make for an enduring and interesting sexual friendship.

Christianity requires creative fidelity "for better, for worse." Although it cannot possibly anticipate future contingencies, it does not need to — since the marriage vow is categorical rather than hypothetical. As de Rougemont notes, "Fidelity is extremely unconventional. It contradicts the general belief in the revelatory value of spontaneity and manifold experiences. It denies that in order to remain lovable a beloved must display the greatest possible number of qualities."[15] The idea of marriage has to do with containing passion through the power of committed love for spouse and children.

To the extent that our culture has lost sight of this form of love in its fervor to exalt momentary feeling, it means the end of order; the end of order brings with it the eventual loss of freedoms. Our world of presidential philandering, of talk-show promiscuity, jealousy, and rage, is the public expression of a disorder that dominates over love and God's design. This design does not require self-immolation or the tolerance of domestic violence and cruelty; it does require considerable self-sacrifice and much forgiveness.[16]

Covenant, Not Contract

Another way of approaching the above concerns is with the more Protestant language of covenant. The notion of a marriage contract ensures that a marriage will last only as long as it serves the love of the self, including the self's infatuations. The language of covenant versus contract has started to capture public attention and to stir debate about the role of law in shaping moral behavior.

Little moral or spiritual dignity remains when marriage is re-

15. De Rougemont, *Love in the Western World,* p. 307.

16. Questions of Christian love and self-denial were the focus of my earlier book, *A Theory of Agape* (Bucknell, Pa.: Bucknell University Press, 1988). This work was based on my doctoral dissertation, entitled "Love and Eudaemonism" (Ph.D. diss., University of Chicago Divinity School, 1983).

garded as a mere civil contract that can be dissolved without justification. Catholicism would contend that the very idea of marriage as anything other than a sacrament over which the church alone is ultimately empowered automatically diminishes its dignity. Protestantism would contend that, even if marriage is rightfully controlled by the state, it is nevertheless a divinely ordered state that is obligated to uphold in law and policy the design of God. Marriage and the family should not be governed by the dictates of contractual self-interest, which should be confined to marketplace consumerism.

Legal historian John Witte Jr. makes the finest current statement about the problems of secularization and the diminishment of marriage through the language of contract. He underscores the fact that marriage law was shaped by models of Catholic sacrament, Lutheran social estate, Calvinist covenant, and Anglican commonwealth, all of which have in common the notion of relative permanence. With the Enlightenment, however, this deeper ethic was set aside:

> The essence of marriage, Enlightenment thinkers argued, was not its sacramental symbolism, nor its covenantal associations, nor its social service to the community and commonwealth. The essence of marriage was the voluntary bargain struck between two parties who wanted to come together into an intimate association. The terms of their marital bargain were not preset by God or nature, church or state, tradition or community. . . . Couples should now be able to make their own marital beds, and lie in them or leave them as they saw fit.[17]

This change was too radical to transform much nineteenth-century law. And at the turn of the twentieth century, leading legal authorities in England and the United States still referred to marriage as "the highest state of existence," "a public institution of universal concern," "a state of existence ordained by the Creator," and so forth. The U.S. Supreme Court spoke of marriage as "more than a contract," "a sacred obligation," and a "foundation" of civilization.[18] Nevertheless, Enlighten-

17. John Witte Jr., *From Sacrament to Contract: Marriage, Religion, and Law in the Western Tradition* (Louisville, Ky.: Westminster/John Knox Press, 1997), p. 10.
18. Witte, *From Sacrament to Contract,* p. 11.

ment ideas gradually began changing the concept of marriage. The transformation began "slowly at the turn of the century, gained momentum with the New Deal, and broke into full stride during the 1960s and thereafter." According to Witte, the Enlightenment call for a *"privatization* of marriage and the family has come to greater institutional expression."[19] Recent history supports this statement. By the late 1970s, all states in the U.S. had passed unrestricted divorce laws. At the end of the twentieth century, the legal language of marriage has become completely secularized. In addition, marriage law has accommodated itself to the full realization of the individualist model, with no recognition of institutional or social responsibility.[20]

Nevertheless, there are some signs that the pendulum is swinging back. On August 15, 1997, Louisiana changed its domestic relations law. A couple can now choose between a contract marriage, with unrestricted access to no-fault divorce, and covenant marriage. The latter includes premarital counseling about lifelong commitment, obligation to seek marital counseling if needed, and restrictive grounds for divorce or separation (adultery, physical or sexual cruelty to the other spouse or the child, imprisonment for a felony, and lengthy separation). There are no clear data regarding the number of couples who choose covenant marriage, largely because marriage records are not centralized there. Still, the choice of covenant marriage is a promising sign.

The idea of covenant marriage law has not yet caught on with lawmakers across the U.S., although about twenty states have considered it in the context of ongoing policy reform. Objections come from lawyers concerned with the complexity of restoring fault in divorce proceedings, from libertarians and liberals concerned with government intrusion, and from those concerned with the risk of increased domestic violence.[21] The fate of covenant law still remains to be determined, and other roads to reform will also be tried. These include required or voluntary premarital counseling, marriage and parenting education in the schools, and waiting periods before allowing divorce.

19. Witte, *From Sacrament to Contract,* p. 194.
20. Witte, *From Sacrament to Contract,* p. 209.
21. These facts are taken from various newspapers and television media in the summer of 1998.

In this context, pastoral caregivers should emphasize the fact that Christian tradition does not accept the contract privatization of marriage, that marriage is of concern to church and society, and that marriage should be neither entered into nor terminated lightly. Any discussion of covenant models leads back to the deeper discussion of the nature of love.

The idea of legislating morality, once the Christian center of Western culture, has lost its hold. Nevertheless, one role of the law is to instruct. The call for a new ethics and spirituality of marriage and the family must come from within our religious communities, and the law should resonate reasonably well with this ethics. Jesus' words on divorce are radical, yet Christians are bound to take these words seriously and to implement them to the greatest possible extent. Unless theologians, pastoral caregivers, and church leadership take on the problem of the divorce culture from a Christian perspective, the integrity of Christianity will be eroded.

Fatherhood Lost?

There is nothing in the experience of men quite like becoming a father. Fatherhood is a new way of being in the world. Many fathers still fail; but many succeed in becoming responsible and caring and, in some cases, morally and spiritually resurrected. It is worth recalling that Christianity teaches that humanity was saved by the birth of a child.

Ideally, fatherhood occurs within the context of marriage. Marriage harnesses the energy of males to help in rearing children and engages their lifelong commitment and investment. Polygamy, polyandry, and adultery are not altogether incompatible with this process, but they are detrimental to stable reciprocal attachment. Who has ever met a wife or a husband who is pleased to have only a share in a spouse's loyalty and affection? The usual outcomes are jealousy, discord, and rage, rather than the family love and dignity that a spouse rightfully deserves. Anything other than loyalty and exclusive intimacy is fundamentally degrading to the partner.

The reproductive process involves males and females in ways that are distinctly different. This distinction has been the perennial model for much cosmological, philosophical, and theological speculation. There is the *animus* and *anima* of Jungian analysis. The image of male and female joined together in a creative, integrative, species-continuing wholeness is expressed in the Tantric Buddhist Jewel and Lotus, the Hindu Lingam (Shiva) and Yoni (Shakti), the Chinese Yang and Yin, and in Genesis 1:27 as well as Jewish mysticism.[22] The male-female partnership that produces children is highly respected, if not revered, in many traditions. As David Bakan has written from the Jewish context, the man-woman-child "holy trinity" is an "ultimate paradigm of wholeness, wholesomeness, and holiness."[23]

Catholic philosopher Gabriel Marcel wrote his highly regarded essay entitled "The Creative Vow as Essence of Fatherhood" in 1943.[24] Marcel contrasts the man imbued with the spirit of fatherhood with "the man who gives free rein to his progenitive instinct."[25] As Marcel views it, fatherhood is a "hazardous conquest" that is "achieved step by step," consistent with "an unfathomable order, divine in its principle."[26] In his earlier essay, "The Mystery of the Family," Marcel had sketched a metaphysic conferring on the family a "sacred character" as a reflection of divine nature. Without such theological consecration, the family "decomposes and dies."[27] My earlier study of theology and the family is an effort to further this line of analysis.[28]

Whatever one's conclusions about the need for a sacred canopy over the family, one would have to admit that the state of the family and of fatherhood is undermined today. Everywhere we look, fatherhood is diminished. My own memories of a hardworking father who was capa-

22. David Bakan, *The Duality of Human Existence: An Essay on Psychology and Religion* (Chicago: Rand McNally, 1966), pp. 107-8.

23. David Bakan, *Slaughter of the Innocents: A Study of the Battered Child Phenomenon* (Boston: Beacon Press, 1971), p. ix.

24. Gabriel Marcel, *Homo Viator: Introduction to a Metaphysic of Hope,* trans. Emma Craufurd (1951; reprint, Gloucester, Mass.: Peter Smith, 1978), pp. 98-124.

25. Marcel, *Homo Viator,* p. 107.

26. Marcel, *Homo Viator,* p. 121.

27. Marcel, *Homo Viator,* p. 96.

28. Stephen G. Post, *Spheres of Love: Toward a New Ethics of the Family* (Dallas: Southern Methodist University Press, 1994).

ble of giving reassuring hugs and who sacrificed so much for our family's economic comfort and education are mostly (but of course, not entirely) positive. Yet the current impression is that fathers are unimportant and incidental. Movie stars are portrayed on the covers of magazines with the newly arrived baby and a caption such as "And Baby Makes Two." The message is clear: If an unmarried movie star such as Jodie Foster can have a baby without a father in the vicinity, then it must be perfectly fine.

But everything is not fine — either for society or for Christianity. In the year 2000, 40 percent of American children will be born out of wedlock, and about one-fourth of these out-of-wedlock babies will be born to women who deliberately chose single parenthood. The consequences? Nearly 30 percent of children will live in single-parent homes, mostly headed by mothers; nearly half of these will grow up poor, untended for long periods of the day (and therefore less socialized and less disciplined), and wondering whatever happened to dad. They will be more likely than their peers to be put on detention in school, more likely to run away from home, more likely to suffer from depression and commit suicide. These are the dark statistics.

It doesn't take a social scientist to appreciate the many losses that divorce creates for children. Practically speaking, it is more difficult for a father to stay financially and emotionally involved with his children when they do not reside together, and when he spends a part of his income on maintaining a separate residence. In the many difficult moments of rearing a child, from handling diaper changes and wild temper tantrums to simply running out to the store for more milk, there will be two hands rather than four. A boy will lack a fully responsible male role model, and a girl will lack the example of a committed and solicitous male who will hopefully shape her expectations in her future choice of a mate. The mother who cannot share responsibilities with a father is likely to experience greater physical and emotional stress.

Sociologist David Blankenhorn's summary of the social cost of "the flight of males from their children's lives" raises issues of universal concern. "Over the past three decades," he observes, "many religious leaders — especially in the mainline Protestant denominations — have largely abandoned marriage as a vital area of religious attention, essentially

106

handing the entire matter over to opinion leaders and divorce lawyers in the secular society."[29] Blankenhorn writes that fatherhood is "less the inelastic result of sexual embodiment than the fragile creation of cultural norms."[30] The rate of fatherlessness is higher than ever — since 1994, 40 percent of the nation's children have not lived with their fathers. Driven by divorce and out-of-wedlock childbearing, we have "split the nucleus of the nuclear family." It is true that some single women do a fine job of rearing their children. Nevertheless, on average, fatherless children will be less able to take their rightful creative places in society.

Youth violence, especially among males, is due in some measure to the absence of a father-mentor, which can result in undisciplined lives and deep resentment. "Prisons cannot replace fathers," Blankenhorn says bluntly. To salvage the future from violence, "we must fashion a new cultural story of fatherhood," "change from a divorce culture to a marriage culture," and affirm that "being a real man means being a good father."[31]

Procreation guided by the principle of creation ensures that men become fathers not just in body (inseminators) but in the spirit and action of steadfast covenant love. Christian churches have a responsibility to encourage caring fatherhood. As feminists have pointed out, however, there can be no solution to the problem of fatherlessness until men and women achieve harmony based on equality and intimacy. Paul Ramsey once wrote, "A reflection of God's love, binding himself to the world and the world to himself, is found in the claim He placed upon men and women in their creation when he bound the nurturing of marital love and procreation together in the nature of human sexuality."[32] The too-often deep harms of familial patriarchy afflict women, children, and, eventually, the very structures of society.[33] But Christianity remains a

---

29. David Blankenhorn, *Fatherless America: Confronting Our Most Urgent Social Problem* (New York: Basic Books, 1995), p. 223.

30. Blankenhorn, *Fatherless America,* p. 65.

31. Blankenhorn, *Fatherless America,* p. 223.

32. Paul Ramsey, *Fabricated Man: The Ethics of Genetic Control* (New Haven: Yale University Press, 1970), p. 38.

33. Susan Moller Okin, *Justice, Gender, and the Family* (New York: Basic Books, 1989).

powerful source of wisdom in response to the new problematical issue of fatherlessness.[34]

My own parental experience tells me that the relationship that my daughter and son have with their mother is qualitatively different from their relationship with me. This doesn't mean that one is better or worse — just different in texture. The wisdom of God in giving each child both a mother and a father is incalculable. The full implementation of this wisdom seems to point toward models of co-parenting, in which both mother and father are deeply bonded with their children.

Patriarchy and Divorce

Formlessness is one response to a tradition of marriage and family that is plagued by patriarchy. But the plague of patriarchy doesn't mean that the form of the two-parent family can be rejected in principle; without it, children will suffer, and an essential element of New Testament Christianity will be lost. The fact of patriarchy, explicit in all the classical Protestant statements and the source of much oppression historically, continues to undermine the future of the Christian family. But this headship patriarchy is giving way to the hard-won influence of feminism and gender equality in both the family and in society. In their essay in *Religion, Feminism, and the Family,* Anne Carr and Douglass J. Schuurman assert that the harmful structures of patriarchy are part of "a sinful, fallen world which God wills to redeem."[35] Redemption is possible, argues Mary Stewart Van Leeuwen in *Gender and Grace,* and Christianity does have the resources to mediate between strong family relations and feminist concerns for equality.[36]

---

34. Lisa Sowle Cahill, *Sex, Gender, and Christian Ethics* (Cambridge: Cambridge University Press, 1996).

35. Anne Carr and Douglas J. Schuurman, "Religion and Feminism: A Reformist Christian Analysis," in *Religion, Feminism, and the Family,* ed. Anne Carr and Mary Stewart Van Leeuwen (Louisville: Westminster/John Knox Press, 1996), pp. 11-32, p. 28.

36. See Mary Stewart Van Leeuwen, *Gender and Grace: Love, Work, and Parenting in a Changing World* (Downers Grove, Ill.: Intervarsity Press, 1990).

The literature on feminism, faith, and family is well discussed in the above-mentioned sources. Without question, the problem of women fleeing from marriage is to a considerable degree the problem of men creating the circumstances that prompt flight. It is also the result of a general societal movement over the last four decades toward a broader individualism, in which self-fulfillment has became more important than responsibility to others, and taboos against easy divorce and having children outside marriage have faded quickly.[37]

The question of whether men and women can live equally and well together is resolved in each marriage as a matter of practical commitment. When marriages do fail, children are more prone to fail. But children aren't the only ones who suffer. Divorce also has costly consequences for many men and women.

The research on the negative effects of divorce is quite striking. For example (as mentioned in Chapter 1), when Judith S. Wallerstein and Joan Berlin Kelley undertook a longitudinal study in the 1970s of sixty families undergoing divorce, they expected that most normal, healthy people would work out their problems within a year of divorce. Contrary to this original assumption, many people were still struggling to cope with their familial breakup long after divorce. Follow-up interviews conducted five, ten, and fifteen years after the divorce indicated that consequences can persist especially for children, but also for adults.[38]

Indeed, marital disruption is "the single most powerful predictor of stress-related physical as well as emotional illness," according to the National Institute of Mental Health.[39] Mortality rates, including suicide, are much higher for divorced men; suicide rates for divorced women are considerably higher than rates for never-married, married,

37. Daniel Yankelovich, "Trends in American Cultural Values," *Criterion* 35, no. 3 (1996): 2-9.

38. Judith S. Wallerstein and Joan B. Kelley, *Surviving the Breakup* (New York: Basic Books, 1980).

39. B. M. Rosen, H. F. Goldsmith, and R. W. Rednick, *Demographic and Social Indicators from the U.S. Census of Population and Housing: Uses for Mental Health Planning in Small Areas* (Rockville, Md.: National Institutes of Mental Health, 1977), p. 24.

and widowed women.[40] Mortality from accidents and the incidence of acute and chronic illnesses in general are higher among divorced women.[41] In a study designed to assess the correlation between education level and levels of heavy drinking, it was discovered that men and women who were separated or divorced were 4.5 times more likely to become dependent on alcohol than the comparison group of married persons.[42] In addition to the adverse health and life consequences for many children of divorce, the physical and emotional impact of divorce *on spouses* is considerable. A powerful objective summary of the data has been published by the National Institute for Healthcare Research.[43]

Certainly there are numerous cases of justified divorce in which a man or a woman may be healthfully liberated from a very repressive context. However, easy divorce is no panacea (literally, "healing remedy"), although too many spouses suffer under the illusion that it is just that.

The nuclear form of marriage, which uniquely ensures children a mother and a father, should be seriously undertaken, even though every rule admits of some necessary exceptions. No woman, for example, should have to endure domestic violence, an aspect of patriarchy that seems never to go away.[44] Nevertheless, divorce, especially in the context of long-term health consequences for both children and adults, ought not to be casual.

40. D. A. Smith and G. R. Jarjoura, "Marital Status and Risk of Suicide," *American Journal of Public Health* 78 (1988): 78-80.

41. L. M. Verbrugge, "Marital Status and Health," *Journal of Marriage and the Family* 41 (1979): 267-85.

42. R. M. Crum, J. E. Helzer, and J. C. Anthony, Level of Education and Alcohol Abuse and Dependence in Adulthood: A Further Inquiry," *American Journal of Public Health* 83 (1993): 830-37.

43. David B. Larson, James P. Swyers, and Susan S. Larson, *The Costly Consequences of Divorce: Assessing the Clinical, Economic, and Public Health Impact of Marital Disruption in the United States* (Rockville, Md.: National Institute for Healthcare Research, 1995).

44. See *Family Violence,* ed. Lloyd Ohlin and Michael Tonry (Chicago: University of Chicago Press, 1989).

Men and Women in Rapprochement

Many feminists as well as male theologians now wish to discuss how marriage and family life can be enhanced by equality and intimacy. Evangelical theologians are among them.

In contrast to some of the liberal Protestant views outlined above, Paul K. Jewett's *Man as Male and Female* stands out as a gem. A faculty member at Fuller Theological Seminary, Jewett wrote as a thoughtful and informed evangelical scholar. In this book, Jewett states that while the classical notion of *imago Dei* refers to Man's "unique powers of self-transcendence," it can also be asserted that "Man's creation in the divine image is so related to his creation as male and female that the latter may be looked upon as an exposition of the former."[45] Thus, the relationship of wife and husband hints at certain features of God. Jewett reaches this conclusion:

> Since God created Man male and female, both must acknowledge the call of God to live creatively in a relationship of mutual trust and confidence, learning through experiment in relationship what God has ordained that they should learn in no other way. This calls for integrity on the part of the man to renounce the prerogatives, privileges, and powers which tradition has given him in the name of male headship. And it calls for courage on the part of the woman to share the burdens and responsibilities of life with the man, that in love and humility they may together fulfill their common destiny as Man.[46]

Jewett's key insight, informed by Genesis 1:27, is that the image of God includes maleness and femaleness, and that the human completion of this image includes both marriage and Pauline equality (Gal. 3:26-28). The love of parents for children reflects within human nature a central aspect of God's love for each human person. There could hardly be a stronger sacred canopy for marriage and family.

Among the most influential statements of an evangelical familial

45. Paul K. Jewett, *Man as Male and Female: A Study in Sexual Relationship from a Theological Point of View* (Grand Rapids: William B. Eerdmans, 1975), p. 13.
46. Jewett, *Man as Male and Female*, p. 149.

ethics is the book by Gary R. Collins entitled *Family Shock: Keeping Families Strong in the Midst of Earthshaking Change*. Collins summarizes the end-of-the-century cultural forces that he believes threaten the stability of marriage and family, and he calls upon the churches to give direction. He embraces a form of "Christian feminism" endorsed by moderates:

> These moderates reject the caricature that a woman's place is solely in the home, waiting on her husband and forced to squelch her gifts, abilities, interests, and calling so she can stick around the house and do her husband's bidding. But these women — their numbers include many Christians — value motherhood, support strong family ties, applaud both those who work in the marketplace and those who work at home, believe in the sanctity of marriage, and are committed to sexual purity and faithfulness.[47]

Christian feminists, argues Collins, are prepared to acknowledge that radical feminism has helped to "improve the lot of women" and "bring healthy balance to many marriages." This influence — probably not as pervasive as Collins suggests — opens the possibility for Christian (or good) feminism, described thus: "In its more balanced, biblically sensitive forms, feminism brings honor to the Creator and strengthens families."[48]

While some evangelicals — most notably Jewett — have attempted to employ a constructive theology to strengthen a form of nonpatriarchal marriage and family consistent with fidelity, some liberal Protestant thinkers have departed from the ideal of the principle of creation altogether. Jewett is truer to Christianity.

Perhaps the most compelling statement from a more liberal Protestant thinker is that of James M. Gustafson. Rejecting the model of family that draws on male hierarchy, Gustafson attempts to delineate a different model. According to him, "The divine empowering and ordering of life takes place in and through 'nature': through human biologi-

---

47. Gary R. Collins, *Family Shock: Keeping Families Strong in the Midst of Earthshaking Change* (Wheaton, Ill.: Tyndale House Publishers, 1995), p. 302.
48. Collins, *Family Shock,* p. 303.

cal relationships first of all." Given the normal balance between male and female, monogamy remains normative. Further, Gustafson affords marriage and family a theological dignity and a central role in "the order of human love."[49]

Gustafson emphasizes stewardship, mutual commitment, and "vocation" in marriage. One of the rewards of marriage and family is the love and gratitude that can be shared among family members. But there are also problems and difficulties to be faced: "There is pain and suffering in our stewardship: the anxiety and sufferings of others become our own; our intentions for the well-being of others are sometimes misunderstood, and sometimes are misguided."[50]

The potential burden of stewardship can tempt individuals to put themselves first. Ultimately, the "human fault" of egocentrism can destroy marriage and family. Drawing on Marcel's writings, Gustafson views "fidelity" and loyalty as imperative for good stewardship in this and any context. Fidelity allows the family to become a school for piety and morality. In the family, individuals develop the senses of "dependence, gratitude, obligation, remorse and repentance, possibility, and direction that ground piety and ultimately theology, and morality and ultimately ethical thought."[51]

A socially responsive Christianity must construct a new ethics of marriage and family that, informed by equality between men and women, thinks deeply about what spouses owe each other, their children, and outsiders near and far. In such a Christianity, family becomes a central concern of the church — but never so as to exclude or burden those who are called to singleness, or to tolerate patriarchal abuses. Practically, the church cannot succeed unless families support its beliefs and values; by the same token, families need the support of the fellowship of believers lest they become insular and exclusionary. Christianity points to love in the family and the church as looking outward in the spirit of the Good Samaritan.

While human contingencies and social injustices result in neces-

---

49. Gustafson, *Ethics and Theology,* pp. 158, 164.
50. Gustafson, *Ethics and Theology,* p. 166.
51. Gustafson, *Ethics and Theology,* p. 173.

sary but always regrettable splits in the family nucleus, the Christian ideal remains: the family in its full ideal form is the culmination of marriage between man and woman as marked by the birth of children in covenant love or by the adopting of children. Bringing children into the world and rearing them with love and discipline are the main functions of the family, the essential fruit of marriage, the seal of a couple's union, and the opportunity for profound moral growth through motherhood and fatherhood.

The ideal form of the family articulated above is more than an impressive image that, while easily acknowledged, need not be implemented. Scriptural teachings on the permanence of marriage and on the sanctity of motherhood and fatherhood need to be taken much more seriously as guides for actions and behavior.

Love is manifested in solicitude for the welfare of self and the other, and usually in a delight in the presence of the other. Love is the abrogation of the self-centered tendency. Many partial descriptions of *agape* can be combined to suggest that, building on a foundation of solicitude, love includes joy, compassion, commitment, and respect; love rejoices in the existence, presence, and growth of the other; love responds supportively to suffering, although it is present in the absence of suffering; love is loyal and patient; love honors the other's freedom, integrity, and individuality. Ultimately this love is sustained by the conviction that a caring, parental God exists at the center of the universe, as revealed in the love of Jesus toward even the least among us. This is the same Jesus who taught that faithful marriage is consistent with the principle of creation. He must have loved children, since he wanted to see each child enjoy the attentive presence of both a mother and a father.

Conclusions for a New Family Theology

The love of a child for his parents can only be a response to the love of those parents for that child; it is the first love that a child can experience, and it is therefore important for the child's development that parents create the conditions under which it can be elicited. As psychiatrist Willard Gaylin writes, human beings are unique because of the prolonged period each of us has from the "moment of birth to the moment of self-sufficiency or independence." Emphasizing biological and evolutionary realities, he continues, "If there is no pouch, then the loving responses of the maternal organism must be its substitute. Otherwise, no species so designed could survive."[52] Helplessness, survival, and care are thus linked. The caring capacity is complex, and some parents are abusive, but remarkably, given the demands of rearing children, abuse is more or less unusual. As Gaylin observes, "These occasional abnormalities cannot refute the inclination to caring clearly resident in the biological nature of the species."[53] He notes that the highest form of sacrifice in Judaism is Abraham's sacrifice of his son Isaac; in Christianity it is God's sacrifice of his only Son. The natural inclination of parents to care for their children and, by extension, the childlike and the helpless, significantly supports the foundation of the moral life.

Daniel Mark Epstein, in his study of "the natural history of the heart," makes this astute observation: "We are born from total darkness into a blinding light in which we cannot distinguish ourselves from mother or anything else in nature. Yet even before we recognize ourselves or our surroundings, love has been working on us for some time." Epstein reflects as far back as he can on his childhood, and he concludes what most fortunate people would agree to: "The first experience of love is being loved, by our parents." Early mother-love in particular elicits the initial return of love from the child, Epstein suggests. "As I got older," he concludes, "I became more conscious of my feelings, but the basic emotion of filial love did not change after childhood."[54]

Without the experience of parental love, the child feels resentful and angry, which makes it much more difficult for him to love others; a likely result of such absence of parental love is that the child will inflict harm, emotional or physical, on himself and others. For this powerful reason among others, potential parents must be prepared to care for the children they will bring into the world, lest a generation of children be lost to themselves and society.

52. Willard Gaylin, *Caring* (New York: Alfred A. Knopf, 1976), p. 27.
53. Gaylin, *Caring*, p. 39.
54. Daniel Mark Epstein, *Love's Compass: A Natural History of the Heart* (Reading, Mass.: Addison-Wesley, 1990), pp. 16, 41.

Following the lead of Judaism, Christianity has emphasized the importance of the child, one of its many contributions to Western familial culture. In Mark 10:13-16, Jesus indignantly rebukes his disciples for preventing children from approaching him and tells them to let the children come to him: "And he put his arms around them, laid his hands upon them, and blessed them." These verses follow immediately after the verses that prohibit divorce (Mark 10:10-12), suggesting that in this prohibition, Jesus had in mind the welfare of children as much as the sanctity of conjugal love. Christianity makes a new place for children in the family, sanctioning each new life by a christening in which parents vow to provide love. The protection and nurturing of children becomes the primary value of the family. When this value is consistently practiced, children grow into love.

But even the most affective and directly loving parent is uncertain of filial response. There is no better narrative for reflecting on this point than the Parable of the Prodigal Son, which reads in part as follows: "So he set out for his father's house. But while he was still a long way off, his father saw him, and his heart went out to him. He ran to meet him, flung his arms around him, and kissed him" (Luke 15:20-21). And there is no better interpretation of the prodigal for our purposes than that of Henri J. M. Nouwen. When the prodigal returns, the father emanates forgiveness, manifesting a love that is too great for force or constraint, which gives the son freedom to reject or return that love. The son had run away to a distant country, and the father had been powerless to prevent that. But he had remained hopeful and loving. Nouwen sees in this father and his relation with his son all the essentials of a constructive theology:

> Here is the God I want to believe in, a Father who, from the beginning of creation, has stretched out his arms in merciful blessing, never forcing himself on anyone, but always waiting; never letting his arms drop down in despair, but always hoping that his children will return so that he can speak words of love to them and let his tired arms rest on their shoulders. His only desire is to bless.[55]

55. Henri J. M. Nouwen, *The Return of the Prodigal Son: A Meditation on Fathers, Brothers, and Sons* (New York: Doubleday, 1992), p. 90.

This is a grieving, forgiving, and generous God.

In his interpretation, Nouwen considers the meanings in Rembrandt's painting entitled *The Return of the Prodigal Son*. Especially significant are Nouwen's insights into the hands of the father in Rembrandt's great depiction. Several art critics have commented that the father's left hand is masculine and probably the artist's own, while his right hand is distinctively feminine. So the father as Rembrandt captures him is not only the great patriarch but the mother as well. Observing the actions of both hands in the painting, Nouwen adds, "He holds, and she caresses. He confirms, and she consoles. He is, indeed, God, in whom both manhood and womanhood, fatherhood and motherhood, are fully present." There is unconditional love from a God who is "Father as well as Mother."[56] The return of the prodigal son was cause for celebration after the father's long suffering. In these images, as I mentioned, Nouwen finds the analogical beginnings of a very simple yet profound theology — that is, God is to humanity as parent is to child. It is in the love that mothers and fathers have for their children, rooted in evolutionary psychology and essential human nature, that the universe reveals a moral beginning point.

56. Nouwen, *The Return of the Prodigal Son,* pp. 94, 102.

5

Adoption, Love, and Justice

Adoption is, in may ways, the most lasting and beneficent solution for children whose birth parents doubt that they will ever be able to raise their children safely and responsibly. Christian ethics supports the bonding in covenant love of adoptive families brought together by sometimes painful circumstances. While the Christian tradition is firmly supportive of the idea that birth parents should rear their children, it also supports adoption as a way of assuring the spiritual dynamic of care for children in the stable married presence of a mother and a father.

Catholic theologian Lisa Sowle Cahill points out that in addition to allowing infertile couples to "nurture a child without requiring a reproductive alliance of one member of the couple with a third party," adoption can help meet the needs of "parentless children worldwide." She describes her own adoption of three children from Thailand in the context of social justice: "Parties to adoption can recognize that the sundering of the biological and social relationships of birth parents to children often arises from social injustices, and that the causes behind the availability of children for adoption should be addressed in their own right." Even in such cases, adoption succeeds in "the matching of adults' needs and children's needs in an equation in which a double negative can become a positive accomplishment."[1] The very complex issues of adoption justice, of relin-

1. Lisa Sowle Cahill, *Sex, Gender, and Christian Ethics* (Cambridge: Cambridge University Press, 1996), p. 247.

quishment of a child in the context of a forced option, and of adoption as a partial solution to the problem of children at risk are important to any full discussion of Christian ethics and the family.

In this chapter I will attempt to interpret the Christian tradition with respect to the moral value of adoption; to examine child relinquishment as a reasonably free *agapic* act, even if it is inevitably and to some degree a forced option accompanied by at least a degree of compunction; and to counter the view of adoption as an inferior form of parenting and as unhealthy for children. I will also attend briefly to the various policy and legal aspects of current adoption practices, and to adoption as an important counterpoint to the "family preservationist" ideology, in which blood kinship is valued to the extent that a child is sometimes left too long with an abusive birth parent. Before I turn to these issues, however, I wish to define the problem of blood kinship (which is in different ways pertinent to all three issues) under the rubric of genealogical essentialism.

An Argument against Genealogical Essentialism

The genealogical family combines the bearing and the rearing of a child in a manner that the principle of creation strongly recommends. In his response to an earlier version of my discussion of adoption, Catholic natural-law theorist William Werpehowski points out that a married couple's wish to have their "own" child captures something fundamental. Drawing on the work of medical ethicist Leon Kass, Werpehowski finds important meaning in the biblical language of "flesh of my flesh" and "sprung from my loins." There is no question that the sciences of evolutionary biology and evolutionary psychology, grounded in the biological investment of parents in continuing their genotype into future generations, support the fundamental nature of the drive to raise a child of one's own making. A mother and a father see themselves in the child of their conjugal union; correlatively, the child benefits from identifying with the narratives of a biological lineage, from which he or she develops a sense of having roots. Werpehowski contends that some social workers, whom I have criticized for trying too hard to "preserve" some devastated families, may have at heart a child's need to be raised by his or her genetic parents.[2]

Ideally, a man and a woman join together in permanent marriage before a child is conceived and then raise the child in covenant love. As I have argued previously, there is something in this process that, analogically considered, hints at the creative mystery of a Mother-Father God.[3] At its best, this relationship can provide a child with love, nurture, and stability. But adoption into a two-parent family can also provide these things, even if neither parent has a biological-genetic investment in the child. The successful practice of adoption is proof that parents can transcend the "selfish gene" of the evolutionary psychologists, and that children can prosper without the narrative of a biological lineage (which can easily be idolatrous).

It is out of the legitimate sense of the importance of connecting bearing and rearing that the adoptive parent-child relationship has been described in law with the terms "as-if-begotten" and "as-if-genealogical."[4] But it seems to me that in some ways there can be "overconnection": the adopted child is granted a new birth certificate; the adopting parents are usually matched with a child who has basic physiological features similar to theirs, so that the child will seem to take on the characteristics of the birth parents and not "miss" a sense of biological ancestry. However understandable, this mimicry goes too far. As soon as the child is informed of the adoption, which is now universally recommended in order to avoid parental complicity in a cascade of lies as the child inquires about his or her lineage, such mimicry is set aside.[5] The majority of adoptive parents inform the child early, generally around age five, although some wait longer.[6]

2. William Werpehowski, "The Vocation of Parenthood: A Response to Stephen Post," *Journal of Religious Ethics* 25, no. 1 (Spring 1997): 177-82.

3. Stephen G. Post, *Spheres of Love: Toward a New Ethics of the Family* (Dallas: Southern Methodist University Press, 1994).

4. Judith S. Modell, *Kinship with Strangers: Adoption and Interpretations of Kinship in American Culture* (Berkeley and Los Angeles: University of California Press, 1994), p. 2.

5. Mary Watkins and Susan Fisher, *Talking with Young Children about Adoption* (New Haven: Yale University Press, 1993).

6. Marshall D. Schecter and Doris Bertocci, "The Meaning of the Search," in

This mimicry also has the unfortunate result of implying that the genealogical family is the "real" one, fueling the opposition of the Adoptees' Liberty Movement Association (ALMA) to closed adoptions. (Prior to the 1930s, U.S. adoptions were all open.) The Association states with considerable hyperbole that "the denial of an adult human being's right to the truth of his origin creates a scar which is embedded in the soul forever."[7] ALMA has created consent forms for parents and children who mutually wish to unite, as has Adoptees-in-Search.[8] There is nothing wrong with this process of consent, although it must be strongly stated that many relinquishing parents as well as adopted children do not wish to unite, and would be horrified at the idea of someone appearing at the door decades after the adoption. The Adoption Rights Movement, by so insisting on the essentiality of blood lineage, has contributed to the unfortunate perception of the adoptive family as inferior to the biological one.

Something akin to what I term "genealogical essentialism" has been popularized by Betty Jean Lifton. In her influential autobiographical book entitled *Twice Born*, she argues for the importance of contact between the birth parents and the birth children on the grounds that knowing blood kin is essential for establishing stable personalities and identities.[9] As an adoptee, Lifton contends that every adoptee is "beached like a whale" on the shores of a "deficient narrative," for he or she will never know the story of his or her biological lineage. But a number of her claims are wrongheaded. For example, her innumerable negative images of adopted persons — she claims that they have tendencies toward violence and sexual indulgence, and are plagued by a sense of meaninglessness and inadequacy — have no basis in fact. Moreover, Lifton suggests that birth mothers are continually in search of their relinquished children, just like the Greek goddess Demeter,

---

The Psychology of Adoption, ed. David M. Brodzinsky and Marshall D. Schecter (New York: Oxford University Press, 1990), pp. 62-90.

7. Schecter and Bertocci, "The Meaning of the Search," p. 8.

8. Katrina Wegar, *Adoption, Identity, and Kinship* (New Haven: Yale University Press, 1997).

9. Betty Jean Lifton, *Twice Born: Memoirs of an Adopted Daughter* (New York: Penguin, 1977).

who never gave up trying to find her lost daughter Persephone. This is a flawed analogy, however, because Demeter had raised Persephone since birth and had never relinquished her.[10] And Lifton overlooks the fact that many birth mothers don't want to find their children. Overall, Lifton tends to use her own personal experience too freely to make simplistic generalizations about all adopted persons. While I will acknowledge that the search for biological lineage is important for some adopted persons, the practice is far from widespread; moreover, it is untrue that an estimated five million adopted people in the United States all suffer from Lifton's proposed psychological condition of "adoption syndrome."

The gradual geneticizing of our culture through scientific development lends support to the anti-adoptionism of Lifton's camp. The gene has been described as "a cultural icon, a symbol, almost a magical force," and as the secular equivalent of the soul: "Fundamental to identity, DNA seems to explain individual differences, moral order, and human fate."[11] Sociologist Marque-Luisa Mirangoff has defined genetic welfare as a distinctive worldview that insists on degrees of genetic perfection, somewhat to the detriment of the social welfare, which stresses the importance of environment and social intervention. It makes people begin to see the world differently. "The emergence of Genetic Welfare," writes Mirangoff, "unlike the 'passionate movements' of the past, is a quiet revolution insinuating itself into everyday life in incremental fashion."[12] Such insinuation has a range of negative implications.

While Christian ethics is deeply appreciative of the birth ties between parent and child as a matter of natural law, it neither suggests pretending that the blood connection exists in cases of adoption nor supposes that the adopted individual will necessarily need to search for his/her genealogical or supposedly "true" familial self-identity. Chris-

10. Betty Jean Lifton, *Lost and Found: The Adoption Experience* (New York: Harper & Row, 1988).

11. D. Nelkin and M. S. Lindee, *The DNA Mystique: The Gene as a Cultural Icon* (New York: W. H. Freeman Press, 1995), p. 2.

12. Marque-Luisa Mirangoff, *The Social Costs of Genetic Welfare* (New Brunswick, N.J.: Rutgers University Press, 1991), p. 24.

tianity challenges the assumption that the only real kinship is based on birth, biology, and blood.

Werpehowski, the father of two adopted children himself, both understands and laments the narrowness of a culture in which the adoptive father is not considered the child's "real" dad.[13] This sort of bias against adoption is unacceptable, even if it is a reflection of profoundly significant human procreative propensities.

Under the freedom of God, the ties of nature are important but not absolute. Families can be built as well as they can be begotten; every principle in action admits of some exception.

Christian Tradition and Adoption

The Christian moral tradition has made a significant place for adoption. Describing the contours of the Christian tradition on adoption is difficult, however, because of the paucity of writings on the subject and the pluralism within the tradition. Adoption has been discussed in modern Christian ethics mainly in the narrow context of providing an alternative to abortion.[14] While this context is an important one, it is not the context that shapes my concerns in this book.

The idea of adoption was contributed to Christian tradition by Saint Paul. Five of Paul's texts mention adoption as a means of obtaining permanent enjoyment of an improved status as legal heir and having old debts canceled. The Pauline appropriation of a theology of adoption is beyond the scope of this discussion; what is relevant to note here is that it is clearly a part of his vision of Christian membership and salvation.[15]

Historians have pointed to periods of Christian ambivalence regarding the social practice of adoption, even as the theological concept

13. Werpehowski, "The Vocation of Parenthood," p. 177.

14. James T. Burtchaell, *Rachael Weeping: The Case against Abortion* (San Francisco: Harper, 1984).

15. James M. Scott, *Adoption as Sons of God: An Exegetical Investigation into the Background of Huiothesia in the Pauline Corpus* (Tübingen, Germany: J. C. B. Mohr, 1992).

played a central role in liturgical ceremonies and theology. Kristin Gager, for example, argues that Christian leaders in France during the early medieval period opposed the practice of adoption because it allowed the continuation of pagan family cults.[16] At that time, the church attempted to restrict the power of clans and lineages by limiting the opportunity for nonbiological heirs through a ban on adoption. This meant that more land would pass to the church by default.[17] Under different circumstances and in different periods, however, the church has been accepting of adoption. (Roman Catholicism, for example, is today among the strongest institutional supporters of adoption, partly due to its pro-life position.)

In England there was also some marked resistance to adoption at times. In post-Reformation England, for example, needy children were placed under poor-law guardians and apprenticed; nineteenth-century English practice stressed institutionalization, emigration, and foster placement. The English were very reluctant to allow adoption because they so overemphasized the centrality of blood lineage. Indeed, adoption wasn't legally sanctioned in England until 1926.[18] Thus, I do not wish to argue that the strength of a theology of adoption translated consistently into social practices across the scope of Christian history.

A tension between Protestant and Catholic attitudes in nineteenth-century America demonstrates variations within Christianity at that time. Protestants promoted the removal of needy and neglected children from the city streets of New York to family farms in the West. Reverend Charles Loring Brace organized the Children's Aid Society in 1853, and by 1890, 84,000 children at risk had ridden the "orphan trains" from eastern cities to western states like Ohio and Michigan, even against the protests of biological parents.[19] (This was far from an

---

16. Kristin Elizabeth Gager, *Blood Ties and Fictive Ties: Adoption and Family Life in Early Modern France* (Princeton: Princeton University Press, 1996).

17. Jack Goody, *The Development of the Family and Marriage in Europe* (Cambridge: Cambridge University Press, 1983), pp. 68-73, 93-96.

18. Harry Hendrick, *Child Welfare: England, 1872-1989* (New York: Routledge, 1994).

19. See Jean Bethke Elshtain, "The Chosen Family," review article in *The New Republic,* 14 and 21 September 1998, p. 47.

ideal solution: The children who rode West were all expected to work, and not all of them were adopted by their foster families; some just drifted.) The Catholic Church, by contrast, was unwilling to so casually break up biological families, so it developed numerous children's institutions to provide temporary church-sponsored relinquishment for Catholic parents.[20] This suggests that Catholic natural-law ethics and affirmation of the biological structures of human moral experience may have informed a hesitancy with regard to relinquishment and adoption that Protestant reformers did not have. Catholics were also concerned that Protestants were interested in taking children away from Catholic parents in order to evangelize them. Thus, political undercurrents shaped the tension between preserving the biological family and disrupting it.

American adoption statutes emerged in the mid-nineteenth century on the wave of Protestant reform movements attempting to replace almshouses as a means of providing for the welfare of dependent children.[21] Broadly considered, these statutes fit within the ethos of "disinterested beneficence" that shaped the antebellum Protestant reform movements which followed the Second Great Awakening. In contrast to Roman law, which emphasized adoption as a means of establishing family heirs, American law sought to "establish an institution to ameliorate the condition of the neglected and dependent child. Inheritance rights were only incidentally considered."[22] Thus, in its historical origins, American adoption emerged from *agapic* roots rather than proprietary ones. According to Leo Huard, a historian of law, the motives for legalized adoption "lay in the increasing concern for the welfare of neglected and dependent children, which became apparent at many points in this country beginning about 1849. Statutes, therefore, took an immediate and radical departure from a basic concept of Roman law in that the primary concern of our laws was the welfare of the child rather

20. Elizabeth McKeown, "Adopting Sources: A Response to Stephen Post," *Journal of Religious Ethics* 25, no. 1 (Spring 1997): 169-75.

21. Stephen B. Presser, "The Historical Background of the American Law of Adoption," *Journal of Family Law* 11, no. 2 (1972): 443-516.

22. Fred L. Kuhlmann, "Interstate Succession by and from the Adopted Child," *Washington University Law Quarterly* 28 (1943): 223.

than concern for the continuity of the adopter's family."[23] This, argues Huard, represents moral progress.[24]

Premodern Tradition

Was the Protestant support of adoption consistent with an earlier strain of Christianity? Because the historical record is contested and fragmentary, the question is hard to answer. The late historian John Boswell endeavored to reconstruct a history of adoption theology and practice in early Christianity. While Boswell's work has received some criticism, his investigation in *The Kindness of Strangers* is still interesting in its basic arguments.[25] Boswell maintains that the biblical injunction to care for widows and orphans (James 1:27) "probably included abandoned children" (*KS,* p. 153). In both Pauline and early church writings, salvation of the Gentiles is characterized as "adoption" by God through Christ; in these writings, the term is the same as that used for "adoption of abandoned children" (*KS,* p. 154). Paul's Letter to the Galatians "contrasts the position of natural heir, which is no better than that of a slave, with the superior position of the adopted son" (*KS,* p. 154). To some extent, the paradigm of adoption was intended to undercut the Jewish emphasis on biological lineage; Christianity "discounted the importance of lineage and descent, which had been prominent in Jewish religious identity" (*KS,* p. 155). Boswell points out that even though two Gospels begin with lengthy lineages leading up to Jesus, he is cared for by Joseph, his nonbiological father.

Yet Christianity accepted the theology of adoption in a context much larger than Jewish polemics; Christians believed that God had "given up a child to them," a child sacrificed by his "natal" father (*KS,* p. 155). Converts all believed that they were adopted into the faith, and they sometimes left hostile biological families in the process. They were

23. Leo Albert Huard, "The Law of Adoption: Ancient and Modern," *Vanderbilt Law Review* 9 (1956): 749.

24. Huard, "The Law of Adoption," p. 172.

25. John Boswell, *The Kindness of Strangers* (New York: Random House, 1988). All subsequent references to this volume will be made parenthetically in the text.

"provided with a 'birth' through baptism — a kind of rescue of abandoned children" (KS, p. 156). The convert had "spiritual parents" who took special care in nurturing his or her faith; much like adoptive parents, these parents "took up" the "child" in the faith.

Boswell writes that all this conveyed "the complementary notions that parental love is a great good, but not inherently incompatible with relinquishing a child." This meant, among other things, that early Christians understood literal adoption as a necessary and central response to poverty and other adverse social conditions (KS, p. 155). When viewed against the background of the theological concept of salvation by adoption (for example, Romans 8:15, Galatians 4:5, and Ephesians 1:5), adoption in social life seemed significant. This applied not only to the kindness of taking in a child, which was solemnized in ritual, but to relinquishing one. Boswell describes the association made in the medieval period between relinquishing a child for oblation (service to the church) and divine *agapic* sacrifice. He notes as well that Christians drew on Old Testament accounts of the accomplishment of God's purposes through acts of relinquishment — for example, the relinquishment and providential rescue of Moses.

By the close of the thirteenth century, Boswell notes, the heretofore Christian emphasis on "the kindness of strangers" and its diminution of biological lineage began to fall into eclipse. In part this can be seen in the increasing number of foundling homes (KS, p. 394). Adoption was still common, but "the increasing social significance of lineage and birth" created a greater reluctance "to acknowledge that a family relationship was not biological." Families still raised abandoned children, "but they almost invariably pretended the child was a biological heir" (KS, p. 431). In its natural-law formation, Christianity still emphasized that child bearers should in most all cases also be child rearers.

Given the medically unmitigated frailties of human experience in the medieval period and beyond, however, "the kindness of strangers" remained a social imperative. In the late eighteenth century, for example, in French cities such as Lyons, Toulouse, and Paris, one child in every three or four was known to have been relinquished to the care of others. Throughout Europe at that time, 15 to 30 percent of the children registered at birth were relinquished (KS, p. 15). In addition, many households in Europe and the American colonies adopted children who were apprenticed as young as seven or eight. Boswell comments that such statistics are significant "both as indication of what a reasonably prosperous society might experience or tolerate in the absence of effective means of contraception, and as counterpoise to the incredulity the subject provokes when viewed from the peculiar vantage of the twentieth century" (*KS*, p. 19).

Although Boswell's work remains controversial, he does provide an interesting summary of the history of the perception of adoption. Early Christianity endorsed adoption theologically as a metaphor for salvation; although more historical study is needed, it was also endorsed in practice as a necessary response to human contingencies. In ancient Rome, relinquishment occurred under a mythological canopy: a statue of a she-wolf suckling the foundlings Romulus and Remus stood over the forum in Rome from the third century B.C., "conveying to Romans who passed under it, for many subsequent centuries, the potentially happy prospects for abandoned children" (*KS*, p. 271). The benefits of relinquishment were thus creatively ensconced in cultural symbol and ethos. With the development from Roman antiquity to Christianized Europe in the fourth and fifth centuries, a new sacred canopy captured the happy prospects of the relinquished infant and the acceptability of the birth mother's gift, which at that time took on deeper religious meaning. Christians believed that "they had been 'substituted' — not unlike an abandoned child — for the posterity of Abraham" (*KS*, p. 155). Given the centrality of this theology to the post-Constantinian formation of Western culture, "Christian literature was filled with positive and idealized images of adoption and of transference from natal families to happier and more loving adopted kin groups" (*KS*, p. 178).

At this juncture it must again be acknowledged that Christianity considers adoption to be an important exception to its teachings and practices that have bound together begetting and rearing children, whether grounded in natural law or covenant love. My point is that it would be unfair to conclude from the central affirmation of the God-given connection between begetting and rearing that Christianity is suspicious of adoption and reluctant to embrace it when needed. Of course, Christianity does not see adoption as existing alongside the requirement that biological parents rear their offspring, as though birth parents might select one option or the other under ordinary circumstances. But when the birth parents simply cannot raise the child (the moral-philosophical dictum of "ought implies can" indicates that we are excused from duties that would ordinarily hold if we lack the wherewithal to fulfill them), the child's best interests, coupled with an appreciation for the circumstances of the birth parents, require recourse to adoption. While adoption is, then, a secondary option, Christianity nevertheless solemnizes it and ensconces it theologically as the right response to the child in need.

Next I turn to an area that needs more examination: the tension between the responsibility to rear and, in some circumstances, the responsibility (or at least the permission) to relinquish.

Adoption and Procreation

Philosopher Alan Donagan rightly insists on the moral centrality of a principle he identifies with the Hebrew-Christian tradition: "It is impermissible for human beings voluntarily to become parents of a child, and yet refuse to rear it to a stage of development at which it can independently take part in social life."[26] This traditional view, argues Donagan, derives from the precept of parental responsibility. A child deserves a stable marital union and nurture by his or her natural parents. However, he continues, "For a child whose natural parents cannot assume this authority, for any reason from death to temperamental unfitness, other arrangements must be made, for example, adoption; but they are considered to be intrinsically inferior."[27] While it is significant that Donagan's summary of the tradition includes ample reference to the parent-child relationship, and while he is correct about the appropriate dominance of the expectation that "natural parents" will raise their children responsibly, I disagree with his assertion that adoption is "consid-

26. Alan Donagan, *The Theory of Morality* (Chicago: University of Chicago Press, 1977), p. 101.
27. Donagan, *The Theory of Morality,* p. 102.

ered to be intrinsically inferior." I will allow that adoption is a secondary rather than a primary aim that emerges in dire necessity. This does not, however, suggest the label "inferior."

Still, Donagan does capture an essential parental and covenantal precept of Judaism and Christianity. Among theologians, this precept has been forcefully stated by Paul Ramsey, whom I have quoted earlier (in Chapter 4). In his characteristic appeal to *agape* and creation ordinance, he summarizes Judeo-Christian thought as follows:

> We procreate new beings like ourselves in the midst of our love for one another, and in this there is a trace of the original mystery by which God created the world because of His love. God created nothing apart from His love; and without divine love was not anything made that was made. Neither should there be among men and women (whose man-womanhood — and not their minds or wills only — is in the image of God) any love set out of the context of responsibility for procreation, any begetting apart from the sphere of love.[28]

Ramsey writes that God binds together "nurturing marital love and procreation," an "original mystery" of God's covenant with creation *in imagine Dei* (in the image of God). To bring a child into the world but not to rear it is "a refusal of the image of God's creation in our own."[29] Without quarreling over Ramsey's presentation of Christian expectations concerning covenantal bonds, I am asking when the mysterious connection between procreation and parental love might be reluctantly set aside in the best interests of the child consistent with *agape*.

Among Roman Catholic thinkers, few have been more articulate in affirming the importance and mystery of parental love than Gabriel Marcel. Marcel adds an important point about adoption: "Reflection shows us none the less clearly, that adoption must always be exceptional, that a society in which it became very frequent would be in danger of devitalization, for it can only be a graft of the tree of life, some-

28. Paul Ramsey, *Fabricated Man: The Ethics of Genetic Control* (New Haven: Yale University Press, 1970), p. 38.
29. Ramsey, *Fabricated Man*, p. 39.

times marvelous and sometimes, alas, abortive."[30] I find myself in partial agreement with Marcel. Consistent with the principle of creation, he designates adoption as "exceptional." And I think that he is rightly suggesting the social vitality in child rearing by birth parents. (I do not side with Plato's utopian notion of state child-rearing.) Nevertheless, I think the word "devitalization" is unfair to those many adoptive parents without whom society would suffer. Like Donagan, Marcel does not include sufficient positive evidence of the full contribution of adoption to social life. (On a biographical note, Marcel and his wife adopted two children after they discovered that Madame Marcel was sterile.)

Karl Barth rightly emphasizes that while the idea that birth parents should rear their child is central to Christian thought, it should not be absolutized. In addition to certain practical circumstances ("ought implies can") that make this ideal impossible to fulfill, "under divine command parenthood will necessarily involve readiness for exceptional circumstances" when it may be disturbed by God's "extraordinary claims and constraints" through providential necessity. Barth holds that parents must realize "it is not their relationship to their children which is divine but the will of God in which this relationship is rooted."[31] The first commandment precludes idolatry: God may require that one reluctantly set aside a parental relationship at great sacrifice when it is clear that the best interests of the child, whom God also loves, are at stake.[32]

The Christian tradition provides an impressive cultural and spiritual umbrella for the principle of rearing the children one brings into the world. The fact that Christianity creates a sacred canopy for rearing one's birth children is important, since the stability of cultural life and the well-being of the vast majority of children are both secured by this moral imperative. Nevertheless, Christianity also provides a sacred can-

30. Gabriel Marcel, "The Creative Vow as Essence of Fatherhood," in *Homo Viator: Introduction to a Metaphysic of Hope,* trans. Emma Craufurd (1951; reprint, Gloucester, Mass.: Peter Smith, 1978), p. 124.

31. Karl Barth, *The Doctrine of Creation, Part 4,* Vol. 3 of *Church Dogmatics* (Edinburgh: T. & T. Clark, 1961), p. 285.

32. Barth, *The Doctrine of Creation,* p. 245.

opy for the adoptive family, and this is equally important. By this means, the Christian community legitimizes families that are created purely by *agape* rather than begotten biologically. (Christianity has diminished the importance of lineage and descent that is prominent, but not absolute, in Jewish identity.[33]) The Christian community also constructs a system of meaning for those parents who cannot provide for the children they bear and must therefore relinquish them. But if the act of relinquishing a child is to be meaningful, it must be performed freely.

Theological Meaning and Freedom

Under the Christian canopy of cultural approval for relinquishment, so far as it can be discerned from limited sources, relinquishment can be an expression of *agape*. There is no reason to assume, for example, that a woman today who relinquishes her child cannot feel a certain benefi-cence in her action.

Barbara Katz Rothman, who has done extensive empirical re-search with birth mothers who have relinquished their children, points out that for every child adopted, there is a child relinquished. But how a woman arrives at the decision to relinquish makes a crucial difference. Rothman cites two poems, one written by a woman pressured into relin-quishment:

> In the night we feel
> Sorrow, the twisting, churning
>   Of nothingness.

The other poem was written by a woman content with her actions:

> I loved you and still do
> But I can't let that love into my life.
> I gave you life so your mother could love you.
> I signed papers that said I was "Abandoning" you.

33. Elie Spitz, "Through Her I Too Shall Bear a Child: Birth Surrogates in Jewish Law," *Journal of Religious Ethics* 24, no. 1 (1996): 65-97.

But with love,
With the knowledge that a family waited for you,
Waited with joyous outstretched arms.
I've seen the joy of families with special babies
Like you.
It is matchless.
I've no regrets.[34]

Rothman concludes, "The birth mother without regrets may express and come to terms with her grief. The loss is there, but she can live with it, take joy in the satisfaction she created, the life she created and gave away." It is, Rothman argues, not the choice of relinquishment that leads to regrets but the yielding to pressure to relinquish. Birth mothers who relinquish with a "deep sense of the rightness of what they are doing" can feel good about themselves and their generosity.[35]

However, assessments of the importance of relinquishment for society can be taken too far. Philosopher Raymond M. Herbenick, for example, holds that any woman who makes a voluntary decision to abort is guilty of abandonment *in utero,* thereby justifying state custody of the infant for its own good and for "legitimate redistributive interests on behalf of minorities denied the equal opportunity of parenthood" because of infertility.[36] Herbenick concludes that "a parent in an elective abortion and abandonment" decision should be required as a matter of justice to carry the fetus to term in order to provide others with a scarce resource.

While I certainly see the social value of relinquishment, I am also concerned that a birth mother's sense of rightness about relinquishment be encouraged and strengthened. How can this be done? Maybe through the kind of coalition that Jewish ethicist Richard N. Levy would like to see develop: "Somehow a coalition should be able to de-

34. Cited by Barbara Katz Rothman in *Recreating Motherhood: Ideology and Technology in a Patriarchal Society* (New York: W. W. Norton, 1989), p. 126.

35. Rothman, *Recreating Motherhood,* p. 129.

36. Raymond M. Herbenick, "Remarks on Abortion, Abandonment, and Adoption Opportunities," in *Having Children: Philosophical and Legal Reflections on Parenthood,* ed. Onora O'Neill and William Ruddick (New York: Oxford University Press, 1979), p. 55.

velop of those who want but cannot bear and those who bear but do not want [or cannot raise]."[37] If a birth mother can appreciate the joy that relinquishing a child brings to a couple who would otherwise be without children, she may feel the generosity of her deed more fully.

This is not to say that relinquishment is a spontaneously joyful and altruistic act. It is what William James termed a "forced option," meaning that the choice is thrust upon the individual by circumstances in which no choice will be an easy one. It is therefore useful that some ethicists like Paul Lauritzen have voiced concern about the problem of coercion. He considers the term "unwanted children" to be misleading in cases "where a woman is relinquishing a child not because she is unwilling to care for her child, but because she is unable to do so."[38] He cites several studies of American natal mothers who relinquished their children due to "external factors," including family opposition, pressure from physicians or social workers, and financial limitations. Thus, the suspicion of relinquishment: according to Lauritzen, it is unlikely to be a matter of "choice," and it violates an emotional bond with the child that he sees as developing during gestation.

Lauritzen's general point is not without value. But let us look carefully at the studies he cites to support the view that relinquishment is generally coercive. He relies heavily on the often-quoted 1982 article by Edward K. Rynearson, a psychiatrist, who discusses the problem of "repressed maternity" in three pages, suggesting that women who experience this problem may also have dreams about losing a baby and excessive fears of infertility.[39] Rynearson himself admits that his "preliminary" study has no statistical support. His sample is a clinical population of twenty patients under psychiatric care for various reasons, all of whom happen to have relinquished infants in adolescence. He states that further study is needed of a nonclinical population of devel-

37. Richard N. Levy, "Abortion and Its Alternatives," *Sh'ma: A Journal of Jewish Responsibility* 8, no. 144 (1977): 214.

38. Paul Lauritzen, *Pursuing Parenthood: Ethical Issues in Assisted Reproduction* (Bloomington: Indiana University Press, 1993), p. 126.

39. Edward K. Rynearson, "Relinquishment and Its Maternal Complications: A Preliminary Study," *American Journal of Psychiatry* 139 (1982): 338-40.

opmentally mature women who chose to relinquish to see if they exhibit similar fantasies and behaviors.

There are a number of studies besides those Lauritzen cites that offer a range of opinions on the subject of relinquishment. An article by Eva Y. Deykin and colleagues is ambitiously entitled "The Postadoption Experience of Surrendering Parents." It is cited frequently for its claims that 69 percent of women who relinquish do so because of external factors, and that 65 percent initiate searches for the child later in life. Deykin's study sample is taken from members of Concerned United Birthparents (CUB), a support group for birthparents founded in the late 1970s. As the article acknowledges, "Participation in a support organization such as CUB may be more likely for those who experience continuing conflicts over the surrender of a child or who have a particular interest in searching."[40] The authors also acknowledge that involvement in such a group can deeply color recollection of and attitudes toward prior events.

A more cautious analysis of relinquishing natal mothers is "Solomon's Mothers" by Leverett Millen and Samuel Roll. Still, this study of twenty-two relinquishing mothers in psychotherapy is, like Deykin's, highly selective. The authors point out that a woman who signs away her legal claim to her child "is often perceived as the most unnatural of women, a rejecting mother."[41] Thus they strongly suggest that any woman considering relinquishment must be counseled regarding all alternatives (single parenthood, foster care, abortion, relinquishment). Among the women in their study, they do detect anguish, even years later. Their recommended first step toward the resolution of grief is to de-stigmatize the loss, although they admit that "removing the stigma from a woman's decision to relinquish her child will be slow."[42] They also recommend grief counseling and support for the mourning process. That process should eventually include some form of public rite to bring

40. Eva Y. Deykin, Lee Campbell, and Patricia Patti, "The Postadoption Experience of Surrendering Parents," *American Journal of Orthopsychiatry* 54, no. 2 (1984): 278.

41. Leverett Millen and Samuel Roll, "Solomon's Mothers: A Special Case of Pathological Bereavement," *American Journal of Orthopsychiatry,* 55 (1985): 411.

42. Millen and Roll, "Solomon's Mothers," p. 417.

it to social and psychological closure. (According to Boswell, many relinquishments in medieval times were supported by ritual — for example, the reading of providential stories of adoption.) The authors further contend that if the stigma is lifted and the grief process dealt with rather than suppressed, the relinquishing mother can be satisfied with thoughts of her child in a happy adoptive home.

In *The Adoption Life Cycle,* Elinor B. Rosenberg concludes that the crucial factor in successful relinquishment is that the birth mother take the time to consider all possible options and make the decision on the basis of her own thoughts and feelings: "We have become aware of the lifelong anguish felt by those who allowed themselves to make a decision based on other's judgments rather than their own."[43]

Carol Schaeffer can attest to the wisdom of this. Like many other young women in the 1960s, she felt forced to relinquish. Now, in a book called *The Other Mother,* she writes bitterly about the experience.[44] Schaeffer was in college when she became pregnant. Her boyfriend's family opposed marriage, and so she relinquished her child. This was not her true desire, and she prayed daily for her lost son. When her son reached legal age, she was finally able to search for him — and she found him. The reunion was gratifying for both mother and son, and the adoptive parents were highly receptive to it. Schaeffer's criticism is not of relinquishment per se but of being pressured into it by others.

The suspicion about relinquishment points out the need for authentic choice. It should be recognized, however, that none of the three available options for the potential relinquishing mother is entirely happy and free of regret. She may choose abortion, itself an action that under some circumstances she may later regret; she may decide to raise the child, despite inadequate education and income; or she may decide to relinquish the child. Given the choices available to women, critics of relinquishment may expect too much if they expect that choice to produce perfect happiness. All the choices are regrettable to a certain ex-

43. Elinor B. Rosenberg, *The Adoption Life Cycle: The Children and Their Families Through the Years* (New York: Free Press, 1992), p. 108.

44. Carol Schaeffer, *The Other Mother: A Woman's Love for the Child She Gave Up for Adoption* (New York: Soho Press, 1991).

tent, depending on the situation and temperament of the individual and on the cultural context in which she makes her decision.

One of the elements that can make relinquishment difficult is the bond that a woman feels with the child she has carried. But not all critics admit to the power of this bond. In fact, in an unusual line of argument, philosopher Sara Ruddick understates the affective bonds that normally develop between mother and infant. Ruddick claims that she does "not believe that any one relationship between birthgiving and mothering is mandated by morality or nature."[45] She argues that *all* children should be considered as adopted because birthgivers who become mothers make a decision to adopt, and if they do not wish to become mothers, they relinquish. Ruddick concludes that "all mothers in-the-world are adoptive."[46] Moreover, she claims that "the work of a birthgiver is not compromised if she carefully transfers to others the responsibility for the infant she has birthed."[47]

In some ways Ruddick's perspective is a welcome contribution to the debate and enables mothers who are not "birthgivers" to feel just as qualified to be mothers as biological mothers are. While Ruddick may underestimate the connections between birthgiving and mothering, she provides a necessary response to the argument that relinquishment is entirely "unnatural"; if Boswell is accurate, she has some of history and Christian thought on her side. Nevertheless, I would question Ruddick on the grounds of experiential credibility in making the mothering role of the "birthgiver" so entirely a matter of choice alone, as though nothing in her nature inclines her toward this role. Christian teachings would surely reject such a separation of birthing and rearing.

Another obvious criticism of Ruddick's position is that relinquishment emerges as an option only when some kind of pressure makes it difficult for the birth mother or parents to sustain a transition from gestation to parenting. Under ordinary circumstances, the birth mother is naturally inclined to parent; this inclination is supported and enhanced by powerful social expectation. Birth mothers do not relinquish sponta-

45. Sara Ruddick, *Maternal Thinking: Toward a Politics of Peace* (New York: Ballantine Books, 1989), p. 211.

46. Ruddick, *Maternal Thinking,* p. 218.

47. Ruddick, *Maternal Thinking,* p. 51.

neously. Thus, relinquishment is rarely, if ever, "free" in the sense of representing only and perfectly the will of the mother. A birth mother usually chooses relinquishment because she knows it is the best or only option *in her circumstances.* She may not regret the decision in the sense of wanting to change it, but she may regret that her situation was not otherwise. And even if she continues to believe that she made the right decision, she may later desire to see the child.

What more can be said about freedom? First, it is a mistake to overstate the oppressive aspects of relinquishment, which is a potentially liberating option when the natal mother is unable to provide for her child. She may well be an adolescent or college student who is without a profession and a stable income. She is not oppressed so much as she is simply starting out in life — getting an education, learning to make a living, and so forth. This is a dominant pattern in our era that applies increasingly to women as well as to men. Few doubt that children who bear children would be better off free of maternal duties, and that their children might fare better as well.

By virtue of divine command or natural law, the Christian ethicist must acknowledge that all relinquishments are bound to be difficult decisions that go against the grain of nature or conscience (contra Ruddick); these decisions can, however, be made with purpose and with considerable internal freedom. Few of the tough and tragic decisions made by individuals are unconstrained by circumstances, including economic ones; we do not consider these decisions to be automatically devoid of responsibility and freedom. By investing the act of relinquishment with spiritual and moral value, Christian ethics can allow a birth mother to be free from negative cultural stereotypes that painfully interfere with her choice or convince her that she has none.

The Adopted Family as Inferior?

Thus far, I have attended almost exclusively to the experience of the relinquishing mother. At this point I want to say some things about the relationship between Christian ethics and adopting parents.

A Christianity that is aware that the social practice of adoption is grounded in a theological concept of adoption should appreciate adoption as a valid option. After all, a child of God is restored by adoption and thereby raised into divine grace. (See John 1:12 and 1 John 3:1-6.) Paul describes Christians as new creatures who receive the assurance of adoption (Rom. 8:15-16). The theologians of the early church viewed adoption as the immediate effect of baptism; through it we become children of God and heirs of the kingdom. Adoption is an act of God's grace whereby we gain the privileges of being children of God; literal adoption is also an act of God's grace whereby we gain the presence of caring mothers and fathers.

Sadly, in this culture, adopting parents are oppressed by the assumption that a family built through adoption is inferior to a biological one. William Werpehowski, whom I cited earlier, describes this oppression from firsthand experience:

> Anne [his wife] and I are raising two adopted children. . . . Intentionally and unintentionally, our culture deals cruelly with all the parties to adoption: "He's not your real dad!" "I'll bet you love the little guy just as much as if he were your own." "How could you give this precious darling creature away?"[48]

This assumption of inferiority is unfair, even though the connection between bearing and rearing a child has validity. Given his experiences, Werpehowski suggests that whenever a tradition views one practice as powerfully normative, it is difficult to avoid some degree of disparagement and disapproval of other practices. One of the theological responses that Werpehowski gives to this problem is that we must realize that "the Christian vocation of parenting is always also an act of relinquishment."[49] Drawing on Karl Barth's idea that parents' authority and dignity come from their being abiding witnesses to God in the presence of their children, Werpehowski theologically annexes Ruddick's notion that all mothers are in some sense adoptive, as are fathers. It is this sort of insight that he believes can help lift away any assumed inferiority of the adoptive family. These are wonderful ideas, even though I remain

48. Werpehowski, "The Vocation of Parenthood," p. 177.
49. Werpehowski, "The Vocation of Parenthood," p. 181.

convinced that it is rather unrealistic to imagine birth parents perceiving themselves as adoptive.

Drawing on personal experience, Elizabeth Bartholet of Harvard Law School has provided a pedagogy for stigmatized adoptive families in *Family Bonds*. She wishes to explode the bias that defines personhood and parenthood in terms of procreation, demotes adoption to a last resort vastly inferior to biologic parenting, and creates an obsession with the medical "techno-fix" of reproductive technologies. Bartholet tells of her ten years of struggle with infertility, during which none of the dozens of doctors and nurses with whom she spoke ever suggested that she consider adopting; some even discouraged it as a terrible idea. She wants more regulation of this area of medicine to ensure that those who consider or pursue in vitro fertilization have meaningful information regarding risks and failure rates, and that counselors are committed to undoing the adoption stigma. She asserts that few doctors "see it as their job to help patients work through the advantages and disadvantages of treatment as compared with parenting through adoption."[50]

Bartholet is convinced that infertile women are oppressed by the overwhelming cultural stigma against adoption, which drives them to seek technological fixes in the first place. She is at her best when she calls for a major cultural shift toward a positive view of adoption. She believes that closed adoption sends the message that the family built through adoption is somehow flawed and inferior and must be founded on the lie of a false birth certificate: "If the parent-child relationship in the adoptive family were as powerful and legitimate as other parenting relationships, there would be no need to seal the adoptive family off from threats that birth parents might appear on the scene to usurp the parenting role."[51] Adoptive parents are the "real" parents; moreover, in today's society, so many children shift into new family formations that the adoptee need not be protected from a sense of "difference," as might have been the case when traditional nuclear families were dominant.

And what of the fate of children who are adopted? In 1992 the Na-

---

50. Elizabeth Bartholet, *Family Bonds: Adoption and the Politics of Parenting* (Boston: Houghton Mifflin, 1993), p. 31.
51. Bartholet, *Family Bonds,* p. 51.

tional Institute of Mental Health funded the Search Institute, a Christian-based institution in Minneapolis, which recently completed the largest study of adopted families ever done in the United States. The report, entitled *Growing Up Adopted: A Portrait of Adolescents and Their Families,* has been widely praised. This study looked at 715 families who adopted infants between 1974 and 1980. Conducted in 1992 and 1993, the study included adopted children between twelve and eighteen years old. The families were randomly selected from the records of public and private adoption agencies. The report includes a number of positive findings: (1) the self-esteem of adopted children compares favorably with that of a national sample of 12- to 18-year-olds; (2) adoption is accepted by the majority of adopted children with relative ease, with only 27 percent indicating that adoption "is a big part of how I think about myself"; (3) being adopted typically does not complicate adolescence (this finding contrasts with that of previous studies whch took their samples from clinical contexts and from adoptions in which the children were beyond infancy at the time of adoption); (4) adopted children are as deeply attached to their adoptive parents as are their non-adopted siblings; (5) adoptive families have considerably lower rates of divorce and separation than do biological families, creating a relatively stable context for adopted children; (6) adopted children have a slightly higher degree of psychological health than that indicated by the national norms for all adolescents; and (7) transracially adopted children (mostly of Korean birth mothers in this study) do as well as their counterparts in same-race families, although the fact of being adopted will never recede into the background in these situations.[52] In *Family Matters,* E. Wayne Carp emphasizes another positive finding: 95 percent of adopted children are never referred to professionals for therapeutic assistance, exploding the myth that mental instability and ill health follow when children don't know their genealogical roots.[53] In short, the four percent of Americans who are adopted are prospering quite well.

52. Peter L. Benson, Anu R. Sharma, and Eugene C. Roehlkepartain, *Growing Up Adopted: A Portrait of Adolescents and Their Families* (Minneapolis: The Search Institute, 1994).
53. E. Wayne Carp, *Family Matters: Secrecy and Disclosure in the History of Adoption* (Cambridge: Harvard University Press, 1998).

Adoption and Its Alternatives

There is a widely shared sense in the United States that the child protective service system, which includes public and private aspects, needs reconfiguration to respond to the urgent plight of many of our country's children. There is no simple solution, and children's protective services cannot solve this monumental social problem alone. As a general principle, the task of government, consistent with the Catholic social-ethical principle of subsidiarity, is to create the conditions under which the family can solve its own problems. But this can be extremely difficult for certain families, and the question inevitably arises: At what price are families sometimes preserved?

Family Preservation: At What Cost?

Some critics complain that child protective services cling to the illusion of reuniting children with severely troubled families; as a result, children are left to languish in foster care or other less-than-ideal situations when they could be freed for adoption.

By most estimates, about a half million American children are growing up in a context of radical impermanence, rotating between a single mother, relatives' homes, foster homes, and group homes. The feeling of being unwanted is painful to these children, who "age out" of the system by the time they're eighteen. (Those with mental disorders or physical disabilities are allowed to stay in foster care until they reach twenty-one.) Sixteen thousand teenagers age out of the service system every year, and although some show great resilience, their prospects are often dim. Most leave high school without a diploma, have no job experience, and have nothing to fall back on. Forty-five percent end up on welfare or in prison; 25 percent become homeless. African-Americans constitute 15 percent of the population in the United States, and 47 percent of the children in foster care. Too many children stay too long in foster care, partly because foster parents receive a monthly stipend and regular visits from a social worker; adoptive parents, on the other hand, must fend entirely for themselves. If the current system worked properly, these children would spend eighteen months at most in foster care; at that point they would either be returned to their rehabilitated birth parents or be placed with adoptive parents. But only two-thirds of children in foster care ever return "home," and half return to foster care more abused than before.[54]

And then there are those whose lives are lost in this struggle to do what seems best for all. Six-year-old Elisa Izquierdo, who was killed by her mother, graced the cover of *Time* magazine several years ago (11 December 1995). Five-year-old Marisol is a plaintiff in a class-action suit against New York City's Child Welfare Administration because her drug-abusing birth mother locked her in a closet for months and forced her to eat cardboard; this punishment was the result of Marisol's expressed wish to be adopted by her ready and willing foster mother of three years. These tragedies, along with many less publicized and even undocumented cases of abuse and neglect, illustrate the need for a rethinking of children's services.

Do we sometimes pay too much attention to the interests of the birth parents and not enough to the best interests of children? Should caseworkers perceive themselves as "family advocates" or as child advocates? Is family preservationism driven by legitimate values, or is it attractive because foster care is more expensive? Even when the birth family might be marginally preservable, should society act on the preferences of children who genuinely wish to be removed from their birth parents?

Answering these questions is difficult. And assessing the risk of every child is a multifaceted challenge — more of an art than a science. Ultimately, the Juvenile Court must review and approve every removal to foster care, as well as every reunification decision. Because of U.S. legislation passed in 1980, more decisions have been made in favor of reunification in the last few decades.

Since 1980, child protection services have been required by federal law PL 96-272 (The Adoptions and Assistance Act) to make "reasonable efforts" to keep children with their birth parents whenever it is "safe" to do so — a contrast with earlier policies that encouraged swift removal to foster care and to adoptive parents. Child-welfare workers thus aim to

---

54. See Jennifer Toth, *Orphans of the Living: Stories of America's Children in Foster Care* (New York: Simon & Schuster, 1996).

avoid taking children from their parents and to implement preventive measures against child abuse and neglect.

Family preservationists assert that more must be done to enable birth parents to provide the child with a reasonably good quality of life. Preservationists appeal to the best interests of the child and assume (some would suggest too simply) that these interests can be fully met only by the birth parents. But their dominant line of argument draws on anti-discrimination and the civil rights of the parents.

However one assesses preservationist thinking, it is important to note that family preservation can succeed only if appropriate services are provided — and federal resources to deal with the biological parents in crisis (substance-abuse counseling and treatment, mental health services, day care, parenting classes, housing support, etc.) have dwindled. Frequent support visits by professionally trained caseworkers over an extended — even indefinite — period of time are also lacking. If family preservation is to be taken seriously, more funds must be budgeted for these services.

Social workers and the courts struggle to determine the point at which a child should be removed permanently from his or her biological parents in order to facilitate adoption — which, in contrast to foster care, provides a lasting and stable home. When parents cannot be rehabilitated, or when parents' problems are too complex to be resolved in the short term, children bounce between the biological family and foster care, drifting from foster home to foster home. In such cases, the family preservation–foster care dyad does not serve the best interests of the children. While the overzealous removal of children from their birth homes should be avoided, the best interests of children are not always consistent with the interests of birth parents. Children who cannot be protected within their birth families must be removed from them. That leaves several options, including residential care and adoption.

Residential Care in Group Homes

If residential care for children at extreme risk exists in well-supported and developed forms, it should not be viewed as a last resort after all else has failed. It can be introduced into a child's life on a short-term basis at various points, according to need; used in this manner, it can enhance family preservation, foster care, and adoption services. This approach to residential care is both creative and consistent with history.

A century ago in the United States, "orphanages" were the first resort for children in need. By 1933, there were 1,613 orphanages, many begun by religious groups. Altogether they served 140,000 children;[55] most facilities housed fewer than eighty children. "Orphanage" was clearly a misnomer: in most cases, the resident children had at least one living parent who had to work and usually paid a small sum of money to the residence. Parents usually retained custody of their children and would visit monthly and exchange letters with them. Every parent could advocate for the child and remove him or her to a different institution at will. The orphanage wielded similar power: a child who was not "compliant, respectful, and well-behaved" could be dismissed and returned to the parent. Temporary placements were common, according to historian E. P. Smith. "Although some children stayed for 10 years or more," he explains, "others went home when widowed parents remarried, when deserting fathers returned, or when single parents could either take them or place them with extended family or friends." In the 1920s, 32 percent of children in orphanages spent less than one year there.[56]

A policy change toward foster care was implemented in the early 1930s, based on the shift to the view that family care is better than institutionalization. However, residential care remains highly beneficial for young people who require structure, nurture, and discipline. The youth homes in Israel, among others, prove this point.

Adoption

The time-honored tradition of adoption deserves serious reconsideration as a significant option — although at this point in time it faces

55. E. P. Smith, "Bring Back the Orphanages? What Policy Makers Today Can Learn from the Past," *Child Welfare* 74 (1995): 115-42.
56. Smith, "Bring Back the Orphanages?" pp. 127-28.

some serious challenges. According to R. P. Barth, adoption research has "lost vigor and rigor in recent years" and is limited by the "relatively narrow thinking of practitioners."[57] Currently there are few areas of family and child policy that are more confused and restricted. And, as adoption reaches across social and racial lines, the process is more complex, and sometimes hotly contested. Perhaps the most controversial area today is that of transracial adoption.

Opposition to transracial adoption has been spurred by preservationist organizations such as the National Association of Black Social Workers (NABSW) and the National Indian Child Welfare Association (NICWA). The adoption of African-American children by Euro-American parents was increasing steadily until 1972, when NABSW took the position that only same-race placement is acceptable.[58] Since then, children's services agencies across the United States have emphasized same-race placement. NABSW and NICWA have asserted that transracial adoption is a form of racial and cultural genocide — that is, a form of blatant discrimination and assimilation to the dominant culture hidden under the thin veneer of "the best interests of the child," particularly when the possibilities for same-race placement have not been developed or fully exhausted. This position is understandable. Certainly one way to destroy a cultural group quickly is to take away its children.

Any minority group, especially if it feels oppressed by a dominant assimilating culture, is inclined to view the loss of its children through transracial adoption as an assault on its distinctive identity. The psychological impact of transracial adoption — indeed, of adoption generally — on the birth parents who do not want to relinquish thir infants is a further consideration, much intensified by the relatively high incidence of relinquishment in the oppressed group vis-à-vis the dominant population.

A few decades ago, Indian children were at a particular disad-

57. R. P. Barth, "Adoption Research: Building Blocks for the Next Decade," *Child Welfare* 73 (1994): 637.

58. Penny R. Johnson, Joan F. Shireman, and Kenneth W. Watson, "Transracial Adoption and the Development of Black Identity at Age Eight," *Child Welfare* 66 (1987): 45-55.

vantage. In the early 1970s, 20 to 30 percent of Indian children were being placed in non-Indian families.[59] At this point, U.S. legislators stepped in. In addition to passing PL 96-272 (referred to earlier), they passed the 1978 Indian Child Welfare Act to discourage the devastation of Indian families. This act requires that foster care or adoption in the extended family be the first option, after which efforts should be made to place the child within the child's tribe or, if need be, with parents in another tribe. Transracial foster care or adoption can be undertaken only if these efforts are unsuccessful, and cultural ties with the child's Indian heritage must be maintained. Similarly, programs across the country try to recruit same-race adoptive parents in the African-American communities.

Preservationists contend that the sense of connection with cultural heritage is essential to a child's psychological, social, and mental stability. This "root-seeking" tendency should not be trivialized; indeed, many do not believe that it can be satisfied without the child being raised in a household that participates fully in the relevant cultural heritage.

The many reasons to preserve same-race adoption need to be respected. And yet it should be remembered that transracial adoption, if undertaken in the right manner and spirit, can be a positive experience. It can be, among other things, a very powerful way to assert the underlying unity of all humanity. Reinhold Niebuhr once wrote that "the chief source of man's inhumanity to man seems to be the tribal limits of his sense of obligation to other men."[60] This inhumanity generally involves a politically powerful racial group that oppresses a less powerful one. Niebuhr pointed out that neither a common language nor a common Protestant faith with the white majority could overcome "the hazards of an obvious 'color' mark of race."[61] America, he concluded, has experienced immense difficulty "in acknowledging the common humanity with a racial minority."

59. See W. Byler, "Removing Indian Children: The Destruction of American Indian Families," *Civil Rights Digest* 9, no. 4 (1977): 18-27.

60. Reinhold Niebuhr, *Man's Nature and His Communities* (New York: Charles Scribner's Sons, 1965), p. 84.

61. Niebuhr, *Man's Nature and His Communities,* p. 90.

Legislation has also underscored the value of transracial adoption. On April 24, 1995, the U.S. Department of Health and Human Services announced new federal rules pressuring states to reverse long-standing, racially based practices that have prevented the placement of minority children in permanent homes. The new rules implement the 1994 Multi-Ethnic Placement Act, which prohibits states and adoption agencies (public or private) receiving federal support from denying or delaying placement of a child based solely on race, color, or national origin. The rules do require states and agencies to actively recruit potential foster and adoptive parents who share the ethnic and racial background of the children needing homes. However, the Act does not allow race to be a "controlling factor," and it states that recruitment efforts must be balanced with the child's pressing need for a stable family; the earlier the adoption, the better the long-term outcomes. Thus the Multi-Ethnic Placement Act serves the inclusive ethic of love for all humanity.

Conclusion

Even in the best of biological families, youth lose their way. When this happens in adoptive families, there is a tendency to blame adoption. This is further evidence to support William Werpehowski's claim that a powerful dominant practice tends to cast alternatives in a disparaging light. This light is so disparaging, in fact, that some who have been adopted, such as Betty Jean Lifton (cited earlier), tend to attribute a gloomy malaise to all those who have been relinquished. Adolescent schoolchildren typically remark, "Well, that girl is strange, but she was adopted."

Given this state of affairs, Christianity needs to create a pedagogy for all oppressed adopted persons, who deserve liberation from the social stereotypes that they may even internalize and self-impose. Women who relinquish their children also deserve respect, for they make a difficult choice based on a self-assessment of their own capacities to rear a child; for the most part, they have the best interests of the child in mind. Parents who adopt do the world a profound service; by providing the love of a mother and a father, they do much to ensure that an otherwise disadvantaged child will be able to take his or her rightful creative place in society. Jean Bethke Elshtain's warning is worth pondering: "Combine the new prestige of blood [96 percent of unmarried teenage mothers now keep the children they have borne] with the collapse of any stigma surrounding out-of-wedlock birth, and you have what might be called a crisis of care."[62] But there is a solution, she argues:

> We rightly favor biological families to do this work, in part because most of the time this is precisely what biological families do, what they are there for. When biological parenting does not work, however, there is a noble alternative, a human grace that has stood the test of time. It is based on something more powerful than blood. It is based on love.[63]

Ultimately, it is the love of a mother and a father that, hinting at the image of God, holds out hope for the child in need.

62. Elshtain, "The Chosen Family," p. 48.
63. Elshtain, "The Chosen Family," p. 54.

6

The Challenge of Intensive Family Caregiving

Any parent who has cared for a child with retardation, major physical handicaps, or serious developmental deficiencies knows the challenge of care under difficult conditions.[1] Any spouse who must shoulder the financial and emotional responsibilities of the family when the husband or wife is suddenly and severely disabled would gladly return to easier times. Any adult child or elderly spouse who has cared for an elderly person with progressive dementia knows what it means to speak of a 36-hour day.[2] And many women in this culture know what it feels like to be sandwiched between responsibilities to their families and to their aging parents; regrettably, women still do most of the direct caretaking.[3]

In this chapter I want to focus on the sort of monumental challenges I've just described because they're becoming so much more commonplace and protracted in our technological age. Seriously ill

---

1. Stanley Hauerwas, *Suffering Presence: Theological Reflections on Medicine, the Mentally Handicapped, and the Church* (Notre Dame: University of Notre Dame Press, 1986).

2. Nancy L. Mace and Peter V. Rabins, *The 36-Hour Day* (Baltimore, Md.: The Johns Hopkins University Press, 1991).

3. Elaine M. Brody, *Women in the Middle: Their Parent Care Years* (New York: Springer, 1990).

persons who in an earlier century would have died sooner now have much longer life spans. In some instances these challenges pit families against a health-care system that often insists on the heroic rescue from death but offers little or no long-term support for the caregiving family.[4] To what extent can families be expected to shoulder the burden of care?

Solicitude is often sufficient to motivate caring. Nevertheless, it is likely that at some points the more arid sense of duty must be invoked when the spontaneity of solicitude wanes, even if it then waxes again. The affective basis of solicitude may become less central in caregiving than the deontological perception that, because "I am parent, spouse, or adult child of this person," certain obligations exist, regardless of a loss of joy and spontaneity. When caregivers can act with joy, spontaneity, and love under trying circumstances, we tend to see a certain saintliness in them that is apparent not only in their speech but also in their attentiveness to the small gratifications that become so large in the lives of disadvantaged loved ones.

Very often this sort of caring has a spiritual basis — that is, the perception of a divine solicitude at the heart of the universe that sustains care and from which inspiration can be drawn. Christians have traditionally spoken of the *imitatio Christi*. This phrase may first bring to mind the great saints of history, but there are also everyday saints who do their best to image Christ in the domestic sphere despite immense hardship. These caregivers may experience periods of despair that can be described as dark nights of the soul, but they are sustained by a sense of tremendous optimism and joy that grows out of their faith.

In what follows I will focus on caregiving in the sphere of dementia of the Alzheimer's type, an issue to which I have devoted much of my professional life for the past nine years.[5] During that time I have met numerous family caregivers, some of whom have taken care of loved ones requiring constant attention around the clock. Were I to avoid the

4. Hilde Lindemann Nelson and James Lindemann Nelson, *The Patients in the Family* (New York: Routledge, 1995).

5. Stephen G. Post, "The Fear of Forgetfulness: A Grassroots Approach to an Ethics of Alzheimer's Disease," *The Journal of Clinical Ethics* 9, no. 1 (1998): 71-80.

topic of such intensive family caregiving, this book would rightly be criticized as being inattentive to current realities.

The Family in an Aging Society

Ours is an aging society in which the fastest-growing segment of the population is the "old-old" (a gerontological term for those eighty-five years of age and older). Demographers speak of the historically unprecedented transition from a classic demographic triangle, with the old-old at the apex and the relatively younger and young filling out the base, to a demographic rectangle with roughly proportionate numbers of relatively young and old. No other society in the history of the world has had to navigate this transition. Discussion now abounds on the issue of justice between the generations, and some ethicists call for age-based rationing of life-extending medical technologies.[6]

Marriage vows and promises to family were not quite so demanding when many women died in childbirth and when most serious infections and diseases cut life short. But modern sanitation, public health programs, and amazing advances in medicine and technology now rescue many from the grip of death; thus, the average life span is much longer now than our ancestors could ever have imagined. As a result of this transition, the demands of parental, conjugal, and filial morality are much greater than they were in previous centuries.

The biblical command to "honor thy father and mother" is considerably more complex in an aging society. A hundred years ago, most parents died in their fifties. Now many parents will live, on average, into their late seventies, with women outliving men by several years. Alzheimer disease (AD) affects about three percent of those aged sixty-five, and rises steeply to affect an estimated 50 percent of those over eighty-five. By 2030, it is estimated that the numbers of affected persons will quadruple. AD is, of course, epidemic in industrialized countries. As a

6. Daniel Callahan, *Setting Limits: Medical Goals in an Aging Society* (New York: Simon & Schuster, 1987); for a rejoinder, see *Too Old for Healthcare? Controversies in Medicine, Law, Economics, and Ethics,* ed. Robert H. Binstock and Stephen G. Post (Baltimore, Md.: The Johns Hopkins University Press, 1991).

result, conjugal and filial caregivers are confronted with astounding new duties; in earlier times, few people lived long enough to experience the devastation of progressive and irreversible dementias of the aged.[7] And we will continue to live longer and longer lives — with potentially dire results. Researchers predict a time when the average individual will live to be one hundred years old; unless the morbidity of dementia and other chronic illnesses of old age can be prevented, delayed, or cured, the medical-scientific dream of longer life will have to be considered the success that failed and overwhelmed.[8]

The moral and institutional role of the family, given public support as needed, is to create a framework of values and a sphere of care in which vulnerable family members can be loved and supported. Family caregivers can challenge existing social stigmas against vulnerable loved ones and create a hospitable milieu for them. They can also learn what radically dependent persons need, and then struggle for the necessary public entitlements and financial support that constitute justice for them. Through voluntary associations, such as the Alzheimer's Association, they can become public-policy advocates for the constituency they know best. Philosophical theories of justice have little, if any, impact on the actual allocation of social goods. However, the appropriate advocacy of a voluntary association built on experience and sacrifice can create change for the most oppressed and disabled. It is, as Reinhold Niebuhr appreciated, love that does justice.[9]

Family caregivers demonstrate a loyalty based on close ties and gratitude without which, according to classical sociologist Georg Simmel, "society simply could not exist."[10] Radically dependent persons require nonjudgmental solicitude and respect from family caregivers, something that professional caregivers may approximate but will rarely

7. Stephen G. Post, *The Moral Challenge of Alzheimer Disease* (Baltimore, Md.: The Johns Hopkins University Press, 1995).

8. Patricia B. Coughlan, *Facing Alzheimer's: Family Caregivers Speak* (New York: Ballantine Books, 1993).

9. Reinhold Niebuhr, *The Nature and Destiny of Man* (New York: Charles Scribner's Sons, 1941).

10. Georg Simmel, *The Sociology of Georg Simmel,* ed. K. H. Wolff (New York: Free Press, 1950), p. 379.

equal. Indeed, those who are ill expect their family to be their "haven in a heartless world" — although they may forget how difficult this might be without caregiver respite provided by wider communities (e.g., neighborhoods, churches, and synagogues) that offer strong support.

The Challenge of the Most Deeply Forgetful

I use the expression "the deeply forgetful" as a term of compassion meant to convey that we are all increasingly forgetful as we age, some of us more precipitously than others. Yet I admit that in some ways the term "the deeply forgetful" trivializes the dementing diseases such as AD that constitute human development in reverse. These diseases take every benchmark of infant and child development, from swallowing to communication by speech, and reverse them in a process that amounts to the tragic peeling away of capacities and even of the sufferer's life story. Temporal glue between past, present, and future time is lost, and eventually the sufferer lives life more or less in the pure present. AD can afflict anyone in old age. Yet, because it appears that several genetic risk factors exist, the assault of AD does tend to increase within susceptible families.[11]

Most people with AD live at home until they enter the advanced stage of disease. Given the sharply rising numbers of AD sufferers, the modern nuclear family — parents and children living as an isolated unit, perhaps with grandparents in the home or nearby — faces a caregiving crisis. The nuclear family is the last remnant of the extended family, and public policies for its support when it is facing a caregiving crisis are far from ideal. This heightens the challenge to the family, since AD is a multifaceted disease that can ravage both the afflicted one and the caregivers.

AD, after all, is not just a disease of cognition; it also affects behavior and function. Behavioral difficulties make family caregiving unusually

11. *Genetics and Alzheimer Disease: Clinical and Ethical Perspectives,* ed. Stephen G. Post and Peter J. Whitehouse (Baltimore: Md.: The Johns Hopkins University Press, 1998).

difficult. Memory loss, disorientation, apraxia, aphasia, agnosia, increased impulsivity, sleep disturbance, and diminished problem-solving skills are all well-known manifestations. When the affected individual becomes aware of his or her diminished intellectual and cognitive functioning, he or she may direct anger at others, as well as experience nonspecific anxiety, suspiciousness, and sadness. The individual may also experience an astonishing range of other feelings and behaviors: frustration, panic, hopelessness, self-blame, worthlessness, and embarrassment; frightening and persistent agitation, frequent or constant wandering, incontinence, hallucinations, and delusions. In the early stages of the disease, the individual often becomes depressed as he or she grieves over lost capacities. If there is any "kind point" in the progression of dementia, it may be in the later stages, when the person forgets that he or she forgets.

Fortunately, there are a number of things that caregivers can do to ease the distress of the person with AD. They might, for example, be able to correct an environmental or interpersonal cause of a behavioral problem. They can often reassure the affected person with a touch of the hand. They can promote a sense of security by preserving familiar home routines, seeking out the causes of symptoms and carefully limiting further exposure to them, and not hurrying the person. Other positive actions include responding to forgetfulness with gentle reminders and humor rather than anger, listening attentively even when conversation strays, and making use of the person's remaining capacities through activity-focused care. All of these endeavors are works of love that uphold the dignity of the person with dementia.

Tom Kitwood, who led the Bradford Dementia Group at the University of Bradford until his untimely death in 1998, was respected internationally for his pioneering work in describing how the person with AD can be respected in these many ways.[12] One of Kitwood's key arguments was that respect for the person with AD involves much more than the preoccupation with choice, advanced directives, and proxy decision-making. Respect for the person is much broader than the autonomy model suggests, although respect for choice is very important. Respect

12. Tom Kitwood, *Dementia Reconsidered: The Person Comes First* (Buckingham: Open University Press, 1997).

entails communicating as much as possible with the person, being attentively present and assisting with small needs as well as large, allowing hope to be maintained in its emotional and relational aspects, encouraging self-expression through the arts, and exposing the person to the pleasures of natural settings. Respect for the person is based on human dignity, a dignity that is both still inherently present to degrees but also the creation of others in the context of a caring community.

That caring community usually begins with the family. Caregiving within the family is a precious moral resource — so precious that it should not be exhausted. The interests of the person with dementia and of his or her caregivers are practically and ethically interwoven and interdependent. This is one of the many reasons why the churches have an awesome responsibility in our aging society to provide a community of care for persons afflicted with AD and for their family caregivers. Christian families need the wider context of the church to care for the elderly person with dementia just as much as to care for the growing adolescent. Christian support is important at all stages, including the advanced stage of the disease.

At this point, the afflicted person often does not recognize others and can no longer communicate; thus, he or she has become the neighbor, who is anyone in need. The personal connections based on a life story of relationship within the family are now resigned to other people's memory. Caregivers sometimes remark that their loved one is "no longer there," "gone," "absent." Thus, love for the near and dear is finally reconciled with love for all humanity. Care is given now to the neediest, who has lost much of his or her self-identity. This demanding care is anything but self-interested, and it continues in the absence of reciprocity. Kierkegaard's definition of true Christian love as love that cannot be reciprocated is here fulfilled in a particularly painful way, for the neighbor who is a stranger was once a beloved spouse, parent, or friend.

Caregiving and Society

Providing care for those with dementia can be very demanding and draining. Yet for a number of people, this kind of caregiving is a highly rewarding task. In my work, I am often amazed to see how often filial and conjugal love rise to the occasion. The patience, humor, and devotion of caregivers is a tribute to the human spirit. One wonders whether this is ineffable divine grace in action.

Some caregivers who have sacrificed themselves radically out of love for a family member with cognitive deficits claim to have discovered themselves. Paradoxically, by losing themselves in service to a loved one, they find themselves. In *Families against Society,* for example, Rosalyn Darling describes how caring for her retarded child transformed her. Initially she was full of self-pity and a sense of overwhelming tragedy. But over time she accepted this situation and recognized that she was able to care for her child successfully. And eventually she became angry that society was not providing adequate services in support of the kind of care she was providing — a reaction that led her to political advocacy.[13] Other caregivers may thrive from the outset because they find caring to be the most meaningful of human activities, especially if they are part of a religious community with a tradition of nonjudgmental and nonappraisive solicitude at its core.[14] While this ethic of meaningful self-denial that is also true self-discovery may not be for everyone, its perennial power must be respected and those who live by it admired. Clearly, the notion that "love beareth all things" can result in the oppression and harm of family caregivers (usually women) and is therefore properly suspect; nonetheless, our pedagogy of the oppressed must not go so far as to ignore the remarkable depths of genuine idealism and the possibilities for fulfillment that caregiving affords when it is taken up with a sense of vocation.

Caregiving, like the experience of dementia itself, is interpreted through some heuristic prism that colors it, thereby adding or detracting from its meaningfulness. The evaluation of caregiving is a matter of worldview and the identity of a specific community, and can vary dramatically between communities.[15] Even with heuristic support, however, caregivers can reach the point of exhaustion. It is the responsibility

13. Rosalyn Darling, *Families against Society* (Beverly Hills, Calif.: Sage, 1979).
14. See Hauerwas, *Suffering Presence.*
15. See Hauerwas, *Suffering Presence.*

of communities of care, whether religious or secular, to provide them with assistance. Where communities of care do not exist or are insufficient, government assistance is necessary. The classical political and philosophical principle of subsidiarity indicates that family, religious groups, and community should be encouraged to mobilize moral commitment and resources as much as possible; one of the things that people with dementia contribute to society is a reminder that we are ultimately interdependent.

Caregiver counseling and respite, financial assistance, adult daycare, support groups, and visiting-nurse support — all should be available as needed to prevent excessive strain on caregivers. Respite services provide supervised activities appropriate for people with dementia, allowing caregivers time to run errands, keep appointments, shop, or just take some quiet time for themselves. People with dementia and their caregivers are often better served by respite services than by the tertiary-care hospitals, with their still inadequately tempered bias toward prolongation of morbidity.

Currently, public policy focuses too much on the needs of those individuals whose families have relinquished care because of a lack of social and financial support. As I see it, it is poor public policy to allow caregivers to become so desperate that they surrender their parent, spouse, or child to an institution. In fact, society ought not to allow families to reach the point of surrender in the first place.

Given the frequent absence of support for caregivers, however, we must be tolerant of those who are unable to handle the stress of stewardship and must relinquish direct care. Philosophers have argued that "ought implies can," that no person is morally obligated to attempt anything that he or she could not have succeeded in doing, however strong the motivation. It is a maxim of moral philosophy and common sense that no one is bound to do the (practically) impossible. It is tragic that family members who want to provide care cannot do so because of the old myth that the family, like the individual, must be self-reliant.

In summary, families are deeply strained by caregiving demands that are the result of our aging society and the unnecessary protraction of morbidity in advanced-stage dementia. There have always been people who lived into old age and became dependent on family caregivers, but never before have there been so many. Now that the extended family has all but vanished in the United States and is quickly disappearing in many other parts of the industrialized world, the network of caregivers that prevented too much of the task from falling on any one person's shoulders is largely gone. Thus, when a caregiver in the nuclear family becomes ill or exhausted, the consequences are grave. In a culture of divorce, this problem is much exacerbated. Those couples who stay together provide a paradigm of love and care.

Spousal Care

In an aging society, human beings are forced to realize their dependence on others as they lose physical and mental capacities. Aging in America is particularly difficult, where youth is almost revered, and images of youthful effervescence are everywhere. Elderly people need to be respected for who they are rather than for economic accomplishment, physical prowess, or other forms of productivity. But in a culture in which youth is prized and the traditional teaching functions of the elderly have been transferred to the computer, the elderly are frequently the victims of ageism.

Ageism is especially directed toward elderly people with dementia who are clearly unable to live up to cultural standards of productivity and hypercognitive values. A stable marriage in old age can function as a buffer against ageism, providing a social context for dependence and care, without which many elderly people would be lost. In fact, this context is often critical to survival: many older husbands and wives die soon after their spouses.

For many people with dementia, quality of life is dependent upon spouses who remain committed to them. Gerontologist Lori K. Wright interviewed forty-seven couples; among thirty of them, one of the spouses was in the early to middle stages of AD. All of the couples lived in and had meaningful ties to the community. Most couples expressed commitment to their marriages. Caregiver spouses "valued the mate as a unique person despite cognitive impairment and sometimes difficult

160

behaviors in the afflicted spouse."[16] Spousal caregivers tended to exhibit faithfulness and gratitude, and when they relinquished care, they did so largely because of their own physical limitations.

The following case illustrates the issues. Mrs. A. cared for her husband, Joseph, until he died of AD at age seventy-two. The early symptoms began when he was sixty and they were living in Cleveland. Mrs. A. reported that each evening Joseph would ask to go back to New York — not an obviously pointless request for a man from Brooklyn. She would say that they had to wait for something to arrive in the mail. She would never argue with him or say they wouldn't return in the future. This settled Joseph down — emotionally but not physically. He was a constant wanderer, and at night he wouldn't sleep; he would move about continually. He liked to move furniture around until the early morning hours. This meant that Mrs. A. could seldom rest. As time went on and Joseph's memory worsened, Mrs. A. had to explain things to him repeatedly. But she would do so in a soft, patient voice, and this would calm him.

Eventually, however, he became combative and belligerent. Mrs. A. was asked how Joseph, who used to be happy and outgoing, could have become so combative. She claims haloperidol, a drug frequently prescribed for individuals with AD, was the culprit. Another medication hadn't been much better: it had made Joseph more animated and aggressive in his wandering, and once he had thrown rocks and stones at Mrs. A. and refused to enter the house.

Finally, following an episode of violent behavior, Joseph was brought to the hospital and then to a nursing home, where he was not allowed to stay because he was threatening to residents, patients, and staff. Three more nursing homes refused him until he was finally placed successfully. In the nursing home that finally took Joseph, he was tied into a geriatric chair. He was also tied to the bed hand and foot because he simply wouldn't lie down. One nurse's aide told Mrs. A. that the staff was able to untie him when she visited because he seemed to calm down in her presence. No doubt that happened because Mrs. A. continued to

16. Lori K. Wright, *Alzheimer's Disease and Marriage: An Intimate Account* (Newbury Park, Calif.: Sage, 1993), p. 101.

talk to her husband without yelling or getting angry with him, and because she touched him reassuringly. She thought that one particular aide was good at calming Joseph and could leave him untied "because of her tone of voice and attentiveness."

AD continued to take its toll on Joseph. "He eventually didn't know my name," said Mrs. A, "but he knew I was someone who took care of him." One day he asked, "Where's Marian [Mrs. A.]?" At that point he no longer remembered forty years of marriage to his wife. The memories of most of a lifetime were gone. Still, Marian continued to visit him faithfully until he died.

*   *   *

Two centuries ago, when the average life span in the West was under forty years, it was uncommon that a husband or wife would end up caring for a spouse with dementia. Now it is very common.

The direction in which conjugal stewardship points, even in difficult cases, is illustrated by Gabriel Marcel, a French existentialist and philosopher of solicitude. Marcel reacted against Jean-Paul Sartre's assumption that every human being is the enemy of the other, which interprets all human encounters as forms of conflict. Sartre believed that freedom and fidelity are opposed: freedom of self demands an individualism unhampered by the bonds of love and promise. Marcel preferred the ideals of mutual self-giving and faithfulness to others; he rejected self-absorbed individualism for an authentic existence of commitment to others. "Creative fidelity," argued Marcel, satisfies human longings for certainty and steadfast love; it liberates people from chaos and unpredictability.[17] Marcel was himself a model of conjugal fidelity: he cared for his terminally ill wife over a period of years. It was the creative act of caregiving that Marcel esteemed.

As society ages, there is increasing pressure on conjugal caregiving. Good husbands and wives with little sympathy for the contractual interpretation of the ends of marriage will nevertheless question how much

17. Gabriel Marcel, *The Philosophy of Existentialism,* trans. M. Harari (Secaucus, N.J.: Citadel Press, 1956).

can be expected of them. They do not doubt that they are custodians of one another, and they are prepared to serve one another at considerable cost to themselves — emotional, physical, and financial. But they can give care only insofar as they are able. Still, as the examples here illustrate, it is amazing and truly heartening to see what challenges people surmount to express marital love and commitment to their ailing spouses.

Filial Care

There is likewise nothing easy about filial caregiving for people with dementia. Here is a case in point, as told by a daughter caring for her mother.

Her mother was born in 1920, and in 1985 she was diagnosed with dementia. Her paranoia was directed at her daughter. She always thought her daughter was stealing from her. In addition, this woman had arguments with some people she "saw" in the mirror and would become very agitated. To calm her, her daughter chased these imaginary people out of the house by yelling at them and waving a cloth at them. This seemed to help. (Had this intervention not worked, it would have been appropriate to give her major tranquilizers to reduce these symptoms.) But her mother also had friends in the mirror and a little doll collection that she would show them. So her daughter used mirrors and other visual aids to make her more comfortable. In her house she repainted rooms with much brighter colors, improved the light wherever she could, and put lots of mirrors all over. Her mother would wander from mirror to mirror, talking with her friends and her baby dolls. If the women were in the car, her daughter would put down the mirror above her mother's seat, and she would again start talking with her friends, which seemed to keep her content. She also enjoyed listening to Pavarotti several times a day; she pretended to conduct. When her daughter bought a motor home for traveling, she would sometimes bring along her mother. On these occasions she would put lots of mirrors around and bring her mother's dolls and music disks. She could even leave her mother in the motor home for short periods and she would be happy. She realized that the keys to keeping her mother happy and calm were stimulation, safety, and security. How she treated her mother had a powerful effect on her behavior.

This woman was fortunate to have help with her mother's caretaking. Sometimes her aunt and her sister would step in and lend a hand. A friend also started taking her mother to a day-care center, which was wonderful.

Her mother eventually got to the point where she became more difficult and belligerent. She didn't want to bathe at all — she would kick and scream and try to rip down the shower curtain when her daughter tried to put her in the tub — and she didn't want to brush her teeth. Drugs controlled her behavior somewhat, and her daughter's treatment of her also had a calming effect.

This account of a remarkably caring daughter indicates the importance of personal care based on a loyal relationship of love.

* * *

As the proportion of elderly people in Western societies grows larger, adult children are increasingly bound by obligations to chronically ill elderly parents. Classical moral systems emphasize filial duties because it is tempting to set them aside. A century ago the British moralist Henry Sidgwick wrote that the obligation of children to parents is based on gratitude, that "truly universal intuition." That children have a moral duty to requite benefits is so clearly agreed upon, argued Sidgwick, that it is open to no dispute "except of the sweeping and abstract kind."[18] He allowed that filial obligation might be limited in cases in which parents had been irresponsible in fulfilling their duties, although he hoped that such cases would be rare.

Certain contemporary philosophers do not believe that filial obligations exist because, after all, no one chooses to be born. But not all modern philosophers are ready to jettison the concept of loving stewardship for the aging parent. Philosopher Christina Hoff Sommers, most notably, writes about filial morality in a manner consistent with reli-

18. Henry Sidgwick, *The Methods of Ethics* (1907; reprint, Indianapolis: Hackett Publishers, 1981), pp. 259-60.

gious tradition. Sommers warns against the consequences of the modern hostility toward the moral practices and institutions "that define the traditional ties binding the members of a family or community." Before this century, she notes, "there was no question that a filial relationship defined a natural obligation."[19]

I myself call upon the example of the ordinary person who attests to commitments in the sphere of filial morality, generally based on reciprocity for past parental care. Everett Hall, the philosopher of "common sense realism," takes much the same approach. He writes that our knowledge of values must "find its test in the main forms of everyday thought about everyday matters in so far as these reveal commitment in some tacit way to a view or perhaps several views about how the world is made up, about its basic dimensions."[20] That people tend to take filial morality seriously and that it is so firmly ensconced in so many varied traditions indicates that it is not to be lightly dismissed by novel ethical theory.

By and large, then, the Western heritage of ethical ideas has underscored the importance of caring for elderly parents, despite the challenges involved, so long as parents have themselves been responsible (as culturally defined). Gratitude for parental love and respect for aging parents as fully dignified human beings are deeply inscribed in our moral consciousness.

In our aging society, however, many adult children of elderly ill parents are faced with caretaking responsibilities of unprecedented magnitude. Given the proportions of the demographic transition to an aging society, we may well be at the crossroads between stewardship and the disregard of the aged. I would argue that despite the serious pressures created by technologically expanded care, the tradition of filial caregiving needs to be sustained. Here a verse from Psalm 71 is helpful: "When our strength fails us, . . . do not forsake us."

Those whose parents have never been even minimally responsible or who have been cruel and abusive should not be expected to fulfill filial obligations. For example, a woman in her fifties brought her father

19. Christina Hoff Sommers, "Filial Morality," *Journal of Philosophy* 83, no. 8 (1986): 439.
20. Everett Hall, *Our Knowledge of Fact and Values* (Chapel Hill, N.C.: University of North Carolina Press, 1961), p. 6.

into a dementia clinic (where I frequently visit) for evaluation. She said she would never care for him because he had sexually molested her as a child. She felt that, as a daughter, she owed him nothing. She told me that she had brought him in for diagnosis not because he was her father but because he was "still a human being." This woman deserves immense credit for maintaining this ethical attitude.

Everyone has legitimate physical, psychological, and spiritual self-concerns that influence their readiness and ability to serve others. Certainly all of us know someone who has been able to make tremendous sacrifices in order to fulfill the responsibilities of caring for a chronically ill parent. But the circumstances that allow for such sacrifice can vary greatly from person to person, and from family to family, and thus affect the point at which an individual with dementia might be placed in a nursing home. Clearly, more individuals and families with certain limitations might be able to provide their loved ones with longer sustained care if society stepped in to help. Indeed, society has much to gain by assisting the family that would, if it could, continue to provide care. The caregiver who feels unsupported can make valid appeals on the basis of integrity of self and proper self-concern — and such appeals should be heard.

It has rightly been pointed out that, historically, a crucial problem for women has been selflessness and self-abnegation at the expense of a healthy self-love. Today it is not unusual for women to express the fear that the technological extension of the lives of chronically ill parents will put them in a position of sustained caretaking for so long that they will succumb to the "experience of nothingness" — that is, the surrendering of their individual concerns to serve the immediate needs of others to the extent that they do not have the opportunity to develop as independent persons. It is right to caution against having too much of the caretaking burden fall on women. As sociologist Elaine Brody points out in *Women in the Middle,* the extension of the human life span means that "contemporary adult children provide more care and more difficult care to more parents and parents-in-law over much longer periods of time than ever has been the case before."[21] And studies indicate that

21. Brody, *Women in the Middle,* p. 13.

daughters and daughters-in-law outnumber men as the caregivers for severely disabled parents by a ratio of four to one.[22] Although results vary somewhat from study to study, about half of these women caregivers experience stress in the form of depression, sleeplessness, anger, and emotional exhaustion. Indeed, significant numbers of women are harmed by the gender expectation that they — and not men — should embrace caregiving as their vocation in life. This is why the traditional patriarchal ethic of family care is unacceptable.

What is required is described by philosopher Susan Moller Okin as "equal sharing between the sexes of family responsibilities," the "great revolution that has not happened."[23] She makes a persuasive case for the equal sharing of roles of direct care and an end to gendered family institutions — that is, "deeply entrenched institutionalization of sexual difference" with respect to familial and social-professional roles. It is morally unacceptable to encourage family caregiving and self-denial without strongly asserting that direct caregiving is a task that should fall equally to men and women.

While the ethics of familial caregiving are deeply complicated by gender injustice, it is important to point out that some women may find caregiving roles to be profoundly meaningful and even inspiring. Furthermore, adult sons who have parents suffering from dementia frequently care directly for them, not just indirectly by handling finances and other arrangements. Indeed, Judaism specifically enjoins the son to be personally engaged in the everyday emotional care of the feeble parent, although actual practice may not always live up to this ideal.[24]

Finally, it is also important to note that caregivers should not be co-opted by a culture that seems to devalue caring. In an article entitled "I Want to Burden My Loved Ones," theologian Gilbert Meilaender argues that caregiving responsibilities enable family members to establish

22. Brody, *Women in the Middle,* p. 35.

23. Susan Moller Okin, *Justice, Gender, and the Family* (New York: Basic Books, 1989), p. 4.

24. Harlan J. Weschler, "The View of Rabbinic Literature," in *Justice across Generations: What Does It Mean?* ed. Lee M. Cohen (Washington, D.C.: American Association of Retired Persons, 1993), pp. 19-34.

a countercultural ethos of self-giving.[25] Our laissez-faire society is rooted in the Lockean myth of an individual in a state of nature before society with no essential connections to others or any innate social sympathies. But in fact we are shaped by essential connections and dependencies.

A Theological Comment on Personhood

In our culture of independence and economic productivity, which so values intellect, memory, and self-control, the perils of forgetfulness are especially evident. On the one hand, AD is a quantifiable neurological atrophy that objectively assaults normal human functioning;[26] on the other hand, as medical anthropologists highlight, AD is also viewed within the context of socially constructed images of the human self and its fulfillment.[27] A longitudinal study carried out in urban China, for example, indicates that dementia does not evoke the same level of dread there as it does in the United States.[28] Thus, the stigma associated with the mental incapacitation of dementia varies according to culture.[29]

The stigma of dementia varies as concepts of personhood vary. I have grown increasingly critical of personhood theories of ethics because these bestow a higher moral status on human beings envisioned as self-legislating moral agents. In fairness, however, I must point out that those philosophers who emphasize the superior moral status of the cognitively intact have not all excluded the person with severe dementia from moral

25. Gilbert Meilaender, "I Want to Burden My Loved Ones," *First Things* 16 (October 1991): 12-16.

26. S. Gilman, "Alzheimer's Disease," *Perspectives in Biology and Medicine* 40, no. 2 (1997): 230-43; and N. C. Fox, P. A. Freeborough, and M. N. Rossor, "Visualization and Quantification of Rates of Atrophy in Alzheimer's Disease," *The Lancet* 348, no. 9020 (1996): 94-97.

27. E. Herskovits, "Struggling over Subjectivity: Debates about the 'Self' and Alzheimer's Disease," *Medical Anthropology Quarterly* 9, no. 2 (1995): 146-64.

28. Charlotte Ikels, "The Experience of Dementia in China," *Culture, Medicine and Psychiatry* 22 (1998): 257-83.

29. See *Ethnicity and the Dementias,* ed. G. Yeo and D. Gallagher-Thompson (Bristol, Pa.: Taylor & Francis, 1996).

consideration. H. Tristram Engelhardt Jr. has argued that while people with severe AD are objectively nonpersons (in the strict sense of no longer being able to function as moral agents), they may still be persons in a "social sense" within a particular community, and thus would be protected.[30] But David H. Smith writes that even such a "conferred" or "social" sense of personhood means that "at some point someone entering into a dementia begins to count less than, or have a different status than, the rest of us." He describes caring for his AD-affected mother-in-law and contends that personhood theories can diminish our sensitivity to the well-being of those with AD: "Used as an engine of *exclusion,* the personhood theory easily leads to insensitivity, if not to great wickedness."[31]

In *The Moral Challenge of Alzheimer Disease,* I warn against the tendencies of a "hypercognitive culture" to exclude the deeply forgetful by reducing their moral status or by neglecting the emotional, relational, aesthetic, and spiritual aspects of well-being that are open to them, even in the severe stage of the disease.[32] I reject categorizing people with dementia as nonpersons because this fails to affirm the capacities that remain.

In contrast to personhood theorists, I believe that persons who lack certain empowering cognitive capacities are not nonpersons; rather, they have become the weakest among us and thus the most worthy of care. The hypercognitivist value system that shapes personhood theories of ethics is merely an example of how our culture's criteria of rationality and productivity blind us to other ways of thinking about the meaning of our humanity and the nature of humane care. I remain impressed with the work of anthropologist Charlotte Ikels, who points out that in Chinese culture, "the cognitive domain is not taken to be the total sum of the person," nor is the self conceptualized as essentially independent and autonomous.[33] Thus in the eyes of the Chinese family, the person

30. H. Tristram Engelhardt, Jr., *The Foundations of Bioethics,* 2nd ed. (New York: Oxford University Press, 1996), p. 150.

31. David H. Smith, "Seeing and Knowing Dementia," in *Dementia and Aging: Ethics, Values, and Policy Choices,* ed. R. H. Binstock, S. G. Post, and P. J. Whitehouse (Baltimore, Md.: The Johns Hopkins University Press, 1992), p. 47.

32. Post, *The Moral Challenge of Alzheimer Disease.*

33. Ikels, "The Experience of Dementia in China."

with dementia is still "there." Fortunately, not everyone in the world kowtows before the exclusionary phrase of the error-prone Descartes: "I think; therefore I am." In Japanese culture, there are some who see dementia as providing a release from the fetters of everyday cares and occupations.[34]

People with AD and their caregivers have convinced me that they do not need the arrogant hypercognitive ideology of human worth; they do need more sympathetic people who are ready to lend a hand in the world of the forgetful. For nine years, I have devoted most of my professional life to people with AD through service, community dialogue, and work with national associations. I work in the context of the Judeo-Christian tradition of a prophetic ethics, which chiefly asserts the moral principle of protecting the most vulnerable and the "least" among us.[35] A basic moral problem in AD care is that many people want to separate themselves from those with dementia. But love (synonymous with "care," "chesed," or "agape"), a basic solicitude, can overcome the tendency to exclude the forgetful.[36] This care is often best expressed in "being with" the forgetful rather than by the "doing to" of invasive medical technologies.

For care to succeed, we must struggle to overcome the stigma against AD. Around the country, people with mild AD point to this problem in the context of my workshop panels. One of the finest autobiographical accounts of living with the diagnosis and initial decline of AD is *My Journey into Alzheimer's Disease* by Reverend Robert Davis. Davis admits that he "mourned the loss of old abilities," but he nevertheless focuses on the positive, struggling to find a degree of peace through his religious faith: "I choose to take things moment by mo-

34. See S. Ariyoshi, *The Twilight Years* (New York: Kodansha International, 1984).

35. See W. Harrelson, "Prophetic Ethics," in *The Westminster Dictionary of Christian Ethics,* ed. J. F. Childress and J. Macquarrie (Philadelphia: Westminster Press, 1986), 508-12.

36. R. J. Martin and Stephen G. Post, "Human Dignity, Dementia, and the Moral Basis of Caregiving," in *Dementia and Aging: Ethics, Values, and Policy Choices,* ed. R. H. Binstock, S. G. Post, and P. J. Whitehouse (Baltimore, Md.: The Johns Hopkins University Press, 1992), pp. 55-68.

ment, thankful for everything that I have, instead of raging wildly at the things that I have lost."[37] Even as he struggles for this self-acceptance, he is also keenly aware of people who "simply cannot handle being around someone who is mentally and emotionally impaired."[38]

Stories like this one remind us that we must not separate "them" from "us." Instead, we must support the remaining capacities of those with AD and enhance their well-being by using information that indicates which interventions are most helpful.[39]

But an appreciation for the quality of life still available to the person with dementia does not justify the protraction of morbidity, especially in the advanced stage of the disease. Generally speaking, no caregiver should feel that the technological extension of the life of someone suffering from severe AD is necessary or beneficent. One clear marker of the severe stage is the loss of the capacity to swallow. Artificial nutrition and hydration can be employed, but they are usually quite uncomfortable for the sufferer and should be thought of as protracting morbidity rather than extending life.[40] Assisted oral feeding sustains life as long as or longer than tube feeding.

The clinician should proactively clarify for caregivers the burdens of invasive treatments in order to spare them the sense of guilt associated with not doing everything to prolong "life" in its narrowest sense. Chaplains should advise caregivers that their love is better expressed through compassion, commitment, and humble entry into the culture of dementia rather than through the imposition of technology.[41]

37. Robert Davis (with help from his wife, Betty Davis), *My Journey into Alzheimer's Disease: Helpful Insights for Family and Friends* (Wheaton, Ill.: Tyndale House, 1989), p. 57.

38. Davis, *My Journey into Alzheimer's Disease,* p. 115.

39. S. R. Sabat, "Recognizing and Working with Remaining Abilities: Toward Improving the Care of Alzheimer's Disease Sufferers," *The American Journal of Alzheimer's Care and Related Disorders and Research* 9, no. 3 (1994): 8-16.

40. Stephen G. Post and Peter J. Whitehouse, "Fairhill Guidelines on Ethics of the Care of People with Alzheimer Disease: A Clinician's Summary," *Journal of the American Geriatrics Society* 43, no. 12 (1995): 1423-29.

41. G. D. Weaver, "Senile Dementia and a Resurrection Theology," *Theology Today* 43, no. 4 (1986): 444-56.

How Sensitive Care Can Enhance the Quality of Life

It is possible for people with progressive dementia to experience — to varying degrees — emotional, relational, aesthetic, and spiritual well-being. Informed and sensitive caregivers can find ways to encourage and enhance this well-being.

Emotional and Relational Well-Being

Tom Kitwood and Kathleen Bredin developed a description of the "culture of dementia" that is useful in appreciating the emotional and relational aspects of well-being for AD sufferers. The following behaviors are indicators of well-being in people with advanced dementia: the assertion of will or desire, usually in the form of dissent despite various coaxings; the ability to express a range of emotions; the initiation of social contact (for instance, a person with dementia who has a small toy dog that he treasures will place it in front of another person with dementia to attract attention); affectional warmth (for instance, a woman who wanders back and forth in a caretaking facility without much socializing may respond when people say hello to her by giving them a kiss on the cheek, then continue her wandering).[42]

Many a person with dementia has been badgered by those who wish to impose reality long past the point when that is realistically possible. If a person is in the mild stage of AD, there is much to be said for trying to orient him or her to reality; if the person is at some point in moderate to severe AD, however, it is merely oppressive if others are constantly trying to impose reality on him or her.

Aesthetic and Spiritual Well-Being

The aesthetic well-being possible for people with AD is obvious to anyone who has watched them in art or music therapy sessions. In some

42. Tom Kitwood and Kathleen Bredin, "Towards a Theory of Dementia Care: Personhood and Well-Being," *Ageing and Society* 12 (1992): 269-97.

172

cases, a person with advanced AD may still draw a long-valued symbol, as though through art a sense of self is retained.[43] The abstract expressionist Willem de Kooning painted his way through much of his struggle with AD. Various art critics commented that his work, while not what it had been, was nevertheless impressive. Kay Larson, former art critic for *New York Magazine,* offered this observation:

> It would be cruel to suggest that de Kooning needed his disease to free himself. Nonetheless, the erosions of Alzheimer's could not eliminate the effects of a lifetime of discipline and love of craft. When infirmity struck, the artist was prepared. If he didn't know what he was doing, maybe it didn't matter — to him. He knew what he loved best, and it sustained him.[44]

A review of de Kooning's late art indicates, on the one hand, a loss of the sweeping power and command of brush typical of his work in the 1950s; but his later work also has a beauty that should not be diminished.

As for spiritual well-being, chaplains can engage people with AD and their caregivers in a clinically relevant ministry. Chaplain Debbie Everett of Edmonton explains how developing this kind of ministry taught her new things about spirituality:

> If a deeper experience of life could be realized by myself through a greater awareness of touch, music, human presence, love, smell, color, play, laughter, nature, and so on, what could this mean in the lives of those with Alzheimer's disease? In discovering how better to meet the spiritual needs of these people, in essence I found what spirituality means in a wider context beyond intellect, in the realm of our bodies and emotions.

Everett adds that if part of spirituality in Eastern and Western religions includes an awareness of the present moment and its potential, there

---

43. See A. A. Clair, *Therapeutic Uses of Music with Older Adults* (Baltimore: Health Professions Press, 1996). See also A. D. Firlik, "Margo's Logo," *Journal of the American Medical Association* 265 (1991): 201.

44. K. Larson, "Willem de Kooning and Alzheimer's," *The World & I* 12, no. 7 (1997): 297-299.

may even be something to learn from people with AD. She writes, "The paradigm shift that I advocate in the care of those affected by AD is to discover and appreciate a wider range of communication possibilities."[45]

Spirituality may also play an important role in the experience of some caregivers. In a recent study of variables in relation to perceived caregiver rewards, S. J. Picot and her co-authors found that religiosity indicators (i.e., "prayer, comfort from religion, self-rated religiosity, attendance at religious services") are especially significant as coping resources in African-American women caregivers.[46] Because it is a clear stress deterrent, religiosity also impacts depression rates, which are extraordinarily high in AD caregivers. "If religiosity indicators are shown to enhance a caregiver's perceived rewards," these authors suggest, "health care professionals could encourage caregivers to use their religiosity to reduce the negative consequences and increase the rewards of caregiving."[47]

Conclusion

Caregivers today are faced with the problem of having to provide extended care for loved ones when they themselves are largely "uncared for" in specifically relevant ways by larger social institutions. Besides scarce support services, families providing home care also face the difficult problem of "competing obligations." The needs of one family member can, in conditions of scarcity, compete so seriously with those of another that the caretaker must relinquish some responsibility. Can there be a moral ordering of responsibilities? Should care for children take priority over care for the elderly because the young have had less

45. Debbie Everett, "Forget Me Not: The Spiritual Care of People with Alzheimer's," *Proceedings of the Sixth National Alzheimer's Disease Education Conference* (Chicago: Alzheimer's Disease and Related Disorders Association, 1997), p. A4.

46. S. J. Picot et al., "Religiosity and Perceived Rewards of Black and White Caregivers," *The Gerontologist* 37, no. 1 (1997): 89-101.

47. S. J. Picot et al., "Religiosity and Perceived Rewards of Black and White Caregivers," p. 89.

opportunity to explore their potential? If choices must be made, does one care first for one's children, then one's spouse, then one's parents, and finally one's siblings? These questions are difficult and distasteful, even for scholars: I know of no moral theologian or philosopher who has attempted an ordering of family responsibilities.

In an aging society and a technological culture that can prolong the lives of infants and others who not long ago would have passed away according to a more "natural" science, stewardship becomes more complicated; choices may have to be made concerning who can receive care. I make no attempt here to develop a moral calculus or ordering of family responsibilities, and it may not be a good idea for anyone to do so. A great deal of individual heterogeneity in priorities and interpersonal proximities is inevitable. In light of the technological expansion of care, the ordering issue must be resolved by individual consciences.

This is just one of the many issues and challenges that now confront marriage and the family. These unions are important not only for the proper rearing of children but also for the care of those children who may never be able to establish independence due to serious physical or mental impairments. Marriage and family are equally important for the care of elderly parents who invariably lose certain of their capacities and may even lose their very selves to dementia. And marriage and family are vital for those, young or old, who suffer from major disabilities caused by such traumas as spinal cord injuries, strokes, and limb amputation. It is in these circumstances that the reassuring expectations and routines of life's journey break down. On a deep existential level, the family is thrown into crisis and attempts to adjust to previously unthinkable conditions.

Spirituality often becomes very central to these families as they cope in a world that has become very different from the one they knew before. In times of caregiving crisis, families can and do achieve a certain degree of piety and faith in the future that seems to be encouraged by the shattering of easy routines. Having a newborn child in the neonatal intensive care unit, a spouse paralyzed in an accident, or a parent diagnosed with dementia are all terrible tragedies — as well as doors to the sacred.

Love is the affective affirmation of the other. Love therefore implies care. The expression "tender loving care" captures a feature of human experience that will always be expected in the family, and hopefully will extend beyond it.

7

Familial Bonds and Love for All of Humanity

A ll that Jesus taught regarding marriage, permanence, and the love of children (see Chapter Two) must be viewed in light of the gospel message to take a personal interest in the neediest and most imperiled neighbor. But how does a Christian do this? How does he or she, as a moral agent, balance the powerful responsibilities of family life with important commitments to the Christian ideal of universal *agape*? Perhaps the most difficult moral challenge in everyday life is balancing moral commitments across various spheres of responsibility. Choices must be made because human beings are finite creatures with limited time and resources. But what choices must a Christian make in the "order of love"?

In a useful analysis of the ethics of Christian priorities, Garth L. Hallett, S. J., focuses on a classic case of a father's choice between using his financial resources to provide his son with a college education or directing these considerable resources toward saving many people perishing in a famine. Both these needs are significant. Moreover, for a Christian, these needs should really be in tension or even in conflict. Hallett has drawn on specifically Christian ethics as well as moral philosophy to conclude that "to the extent that he can, the father should give preference to the starving."[1] He rightly points out that Christian ethics looks

1. Garth L. Hallett, *Priorities and Christian Ethics* (Cambridge, U.K.: Cambridge University Press, 1998), p. 112.

toward the neighbor (who represents all of humanity) and values human life as a gift of God. He praises people such as Suzie Valadez, known in south Texas as "Queen of the Dump" for all the work she has done to feed, clothe, and care for thousands of impoverished Mexicans living in the Ciudad Juarez garbage dump. Her own children, Hallett explains, "were required to make real sacrifices in the interests of their mother's cause and grew up with little beyond the mere necessities."[2] This remains the Christian ideal, Hallett argues, even for those who cannot implement it. I take no issue with his point.

Hallett's argument on behalf of the neediest human beings is in accord with Scripture and Christian tradition. But on the more routine level of day-to-day family living, I would be interested in more details about the lives of Suzie Valadez's children. Exactly what needs and wants are these children being told to sacrifice? How are they responding? Do they help their mother in her work? Do they feel that she gives them sufficient spiritual and emotional support?

Let me briefly discuss a personal situation that enables me to existentially appreciate the complexity of these questions. As I indicated in the previous chapter, my particular inclination has been to work with and for the most deeply forgetful, who are surely needy and often oppressed in a hypercognitive culture. Over a three-year period (from 1997 to 1999), I devoted about three days a week to this work. I developed and led more than sixty major weekend workshops on the ethical issues of dementia for chapters of the Alzheimer's Association from coast to coast. This was important work to do, and the Association greatly appreciated it: in 1998 I received recognition for "Distinguished Service." But every time I left home to get on yet another airplane, my young son, who was a preschooler during this period, would cry out resentfully, "Daddy, please don't go away from me!" No matter how sensitive the rest of the family and I tried to be, this was very painful for Andrew. From his perspective, he really needed to have his dad around more. As for my teenage daughter, Emma — well, I'm not sure that daughters her age want their fathers around all that much. Still, I wasn't able to be much of an adviser to her at times. Complicating all of this were some

2. Hallett, *Priorities and Christian Ethics,* p. 94.

filial issues: my father died, and afterward my mother moved from New York to the Cleveland area, near me and my family. Meanwhile, demands at the major academic medical center where I work were more intense than ever.

I use this personal example partly to make the point that the problem of the order of love and ethical priorities is very complex — physically, financially, emotionally, psychologically, and spiritually. I could tell my wife and my daughter that the work I was doing with family caregivers was my limited expression of Christian love for all of humanity, and they could understand — but my son simply couldn't at the time. Hallett would fully endorse this pedagogy, for he thinks that our children can learn much about ethics by seeing this sort of behavior and having to make certain sacrifices as a consequence of it.[3] Hallett reassures the troubled reader with a complex family life that we are right to struggle, that such struggle is consistent with the New Testament, the church fathers, Thomism, and good moral theory.[4] Evangelical writer Rodney Clapp is similarly reassuring when he contrasts the privatized and secularized middle-class family with the truly Christian family and its not-so-private household — which he describes as a "mission base," consistent with the New Testament, the early church, and the wider Christian tradition.[5] Every Christian family, parents and even young children, must avoid the familial narcissism that focuses on constant emotional gratification and dyadic intimacy, consumerism, and material comfort; instead, the Christian family must accept the moral authority of the Christian tradition in its command to "love thy neighbor as thyself" — the neighbor who is everyone, but especially the one most in need.

3. Hallett, *Priorities and Christian Ethics,* p. 95.

4. Insofar as Hallett refers to my previous writings, suffice it to say that if my review of his past work in any way encouraged his recent attention to "priorities" in Christian ethics, then I am honored. See Stephen G. Post, "Garth A. Hallett's *Christian Neighbor-Love: An Assessment of Six Rival Versions," Journal of Religious Ethics* 19 (1991): 196.

5. See Rodney Clapp, *Families at the Crossroads: Beyond Traditional and Modern Options* (Downers Grove, Ill.: InterVarsity Press, 1993), especially Chapter Eight, "No Christian Home Is a Haven."

The distinctive and justifying elements of the Christian family are imperiled without active engagement in the community of faith and its service to the world. Perhaps a focus on service to the neediest would lower the levels of low-conflict divorce in the Christian community; spouses would realize that their ideal of perfect emotional intimacy, consistent with the psychology of self-realization, should be replaced by an ethos of service to the world, which brings its own kind of more lasting union. Ultimately, Christian spouses and their children must be brought into greatest intimacy through the spiritual harmony of purpose that emerges from the challenges of serving the world. In Henri Nouwen's phrase, spouses and children should become "wounded healers" to one another and to the world.[6] But it must never be forgotten that we do have special obligations to those who are nearest by virtue of family ties.

The Order of Love

The moral issue of ordering loyalties to biological family members, the church community, and all of humanity remains central to Christian ethics and to all moral thought. It was addressed by both Augustine and Thomas Aquinas under the rubric of *ordo caritatis,* and it has been restated recently by the Catholic ethicist Louis Janssens: "At every moment our particular action can only benefit some, e.g., ourselves, a neighbor, a certain group. Why do we act for the well-being of this person or this group rather than for the advantage of others (the classical problem of the *ordo caritatis*)?"[7] Catholic theologian Stephen J. Pope has even criticized the Catholic tradition, which was perennially nuanced in its response to this question, for recent neglect of the *ordo caritatis.*[8] I suspect this neglect is related to the fact that so much of con-

6. See Henri J. M. Nouwen, *The Wounded Healer* (1979; reprint, London: Darton, Longman & Todd, 1997).

7. Louis Janssens, "Norms and Priorities in a Love Ethics," *Louvain Studies* 6 (1977): 212.

8. See Stephen J. Pope, "The Order of Love, and Recent Catholic Ethics: A Constructive Proposal," *Theological Studies* 52, no. 2 (June 1991): 255-88. This is an

temporary Catholic ethics focuses on issues of social justice and liberation that the earlier attention to the familial sphere has appeared to be of little significance. But as Hallett contends, in response to both Pope's work and my own, this focus makes a great deal of sense in the light of the emerging prosperity of many American families and the absolute poverty rampant throughout many parts of the world.[9] The lively debate over priorities will continue, since a certain amount of tension will always exist between the sphere of the near and dear and the sphere of the stranger. And the debate will also be fueled by those who focus so much on one sphere that they neglect the other.

There are people, for example, who do good for near and dear ones too exclusively, giving insufficient attention to strangers. They make an idol of their closed social system and express no solicitude for those outside of it; they deny the universal loyalty that is grounded in the Christian assumption that no one is outside God's solicitude. This is why the family *needs* the community of faith, which is open and dedicated to all people — what philosopher Josiah Royce calls "the Beloved Community" that saves us from limited loyalties and enmity.[10] Western monotheism is radical in requiring religious and moral suspicion of narrow loyalties; it takes the family images of mother, father, brother, and sister and extends them metaphorically to the family of all humanity, thus creating an important new universal ethics. Herein lies the greatness of Christianity.

A Concern

Suspicions of the narcissistic and self-indulgent family must not hide the equally significant reverse problem — loving the neediest stranger

---

excellent criticism of recent Catholic ethics for failing to attend sufficiently to the ordering of love. Pope develops his recovery of Aquinas through the insights of certain aspects of sociobiology. See also Pope's book entitled *Love, Human Nature, and Christian Ethics* (Washington, D.C.: Georgetown University Press, 1994).

9. See Hallett, *Priorities and Christian Ethics*, p. 7.

10. Josiah Royce, *The Problem of Christianity* (New York: Macmillan, 1931), pp. 172-213.

(who is also the neighbor) while ignoring the truly legitimate emotional and physical needs of near and dear ones, especially children. I surmise that this problem is actually exceedingly rare; after all, people who fail to meet the essential needs of their own children are probably not much concerned with the neediest on the other side of the world, or even just down the street. Perhaps a married saintly figure with a daughter, such as Gandhi, could be criticized for being such a harsh taskmaster — alhough Gandhi's daughter did ultimately learn from him and rise to become India's prime minister. Suzie Valadez could be criticized (by non-Christians) for having her children do without certain amenities, but I agree with Hallett that she is probably teaching them a valuable moral lesson.

The problem that I'm addressing here is, however, different than Hallett's; at least the relatively well-to-do parents who are sending their children to universities when they could be using that tuition money to save innumerable starving people *do* care for their sons and daughters, even if they may be morally myopic. But what of the parent who has no ample solicitude or sense of obligation to the children he or she has brought into the world, and who, given this absence of solicitude, is unlikely to have any concern whatsoever for the unknown neediest neighbor? What of my undergraduate students who work thirty hours a week in a coffeeshop to make ends meet because their fathers, now divorced from their mothers, are unwilling to provide educational support — let alone provide for starving people around the world?

When Albert Camus describes the condition of modern moral consciousness in *The Fall,* he does so through the confessions of Clamence, an expatriate Frenchman in a seedy Amsterdam bar.[11] Clamence recalls his past life as a highly respected lawyer and champion of noble causes. On the streets, Clamence helped the blind along crosswalks, lent a hand "pushing a stranded car," and supported the Salvation Army (*TF,* p. 22). This sounds impressive. But Clamence confesses that he is a libertine who manipulated woman after woman, ad-

11. Albert Camus, *The Fall,* trans. Justin O'Brien (1957; reprint, New York: Vintage Books, 1991). All subsequent references to this volume will be made parenthetically in the text.

mitting that "I never loved any of them" (*TF,* p. 57). He laments that genuine love entirely escaped him and that he has a "congenital inability to see in love anything but the physical" (*TF,* p. 59). As for friends, Clamence has none — and he has compensated for that accordingly: "To make up for this, their number has increased; they are the whole human race" (*TF,* p. 73). Having failed in friendships and all other special relationships, he saw love of humanity as the easier alternative. But such love was only a thin veneer over the "selfishness wound up in my generosities." Though renowned for his generosity, Clamence confesses "how much a part of my soul loathed" invalids and the "lousy proletarian" (*TF,* p. 91). Yet he greatly enjoyed the social recognition that his reputation for beneficence ensured.

The Fall teaches, among other things, that it is easy to "love" people who are fleeting presences in our lives because we do not have to remain with them long enough to begin to detest them for their inevitable human imperfections. Tossing a coin in the poor man's box or speaking eloquently of all humanity does not require that any particular person be continuously present with us. It is hard to steadfastly love the near and dear ones whom we see and know, for we become aware of their faults. Hence the adage, "I love humanity; it's people I can't stand."

Charles Dickens approached this form of moral failure through the character of Mrs. Jellyby in his novel *Bleak House.*[12] Though he was greatly concerned about the suffering of the working class during England's industrial revolution, Dickens was a harsh critic of people who took up social causes to the neglect of their children and immediate neighbors — people like Mrs. Jellyby. Dickens describes her as having "a curious habit of seeming to look a long way off," as though she could see "nothing nearer than Africa" (*BH,* p. 36). She would utter "beautiful sentiments" about "the Brotherhood of Humanity," but was neither emotionally present for her children nor particularly interested in them (*BH,* p. 41). Her daughters were deeply harmed by her inattentiveness. Similarly, she neglected her neighbors. Mrs. Jellyby "swept the horizon

---

12. Charles Dickens, *Bleak House* (1853; reprint, New York: Oxford University Press, 1987). All subsequent references to this volume will be made in the text.

with a telescope in search of others" while failing in "her own natural duties and obligations" (*BH,* p. 537).

People like Clamence who have no solicitude for those near to them also have no genuine solicitude for the needy neighbor — even if their philanthropic actions are laudable and important to all of humanity. No matter how we might wish to diminish the moral significance of motives, Clamence does not strike us as a moral individual; rather, we consider him pitiable and morally disordered. Like Clamence, Mrs. Jellyby strikes us as morally disordered and inauthentic, because she seems singularly unconcerned about her daughters, who genuinely need her emotional support and attentive presence. These characters stand in sharp contrast to people like Gandhi and Suzie Valadez, people who, we can safely assume, genuinely struggle with the ordering of their loves because they do in fact love their children. Christian tradition surely wants us all to struggle in this way — but not at the expense of failing to meet the needs of those near and dear to us.

A Brief Comment on Christian Moral Tradition

Christianity points toward love of neighbor in a manner consistent with impartiality, for all persons are children of the same heavenly Father. True to the spirit of Christianity, Augustine emphasized that all people are to be loved, but he also noted that "since you cannot be good to all, you are to pay special attention to those who, by the accidents of time, or place, or circumstance, are brought into closer connection with you." As though by "a sort of lot," wrote Augustine, some people happen to be nearer to us than others. Because we are embodied and temporal creatures, we are simply unable to love all humanity, except in intention.[13] In this, Augustine followed the Stoics, as did Aquinas, who provided an account of the order of love in question 26 of his *Summa Theologiae (secunda secundae)* that consists of no fewer than 13 articles. Aquinas argued that we should love those who are connected by "natural origin"

---

13. Augustine, *On Christian Doctrine,* in *Augustine,* trans. J. F. Shaw, Great Books of the Western World series (Chicago: Encyclopedia Britannica, 1952), p. 632.

most, except when they are "an obstacle between us and God." We might well take issue with his conclusion that we should love our parents more than our children, and our fathers more than our mothers because men provide the "active principle" in conception (II-II, q. 26, a. 10). Nevertheless, Aquinas took seriously the notion that, due to human finitude, an ordering of love is essential to the moral life.

Garth Hallett emphasizes that while innumerable Christian theologians of antiquity and the medieval period recognized an order of love (with some interesting variations in detail), we cannot simply take their endorsement of special duties to the near and dear as an endorsement of familial insularity. Citing an array of sources, Hallett focuses on their appeals to our common humanity (as members of one family all sprung from Adam), that we might fulfill Christ's mandate (especially Matt. 25:31-46) to serve the poor, limit the rightful accumulation of property, value simplicity as an antidote to greed, and forgo inordinate family affections.[14] Still, we must not neglect those near and dear in the process.

My point is that Augustine, Aquinas, and others realized that some rough ordering of love must allow for special considerations (based on significant needs but not what amount to frivolous wants) with respect to the family. As Henry Sidgwick noted, we should not resolve "all virtue into universal and impartial Benevolence," as though the well-being of any one person is "equally important with the equal happiness of any other, as an element of the total."[15] Ethical theory should never swing too far from thinkers such as Thomas Aquinas, Bishop Butler, Adam Ferguson, Adam Smith, and Sidgwick, all of whom believed in "the Order in which Individuals are recommended by Nature to our care and attention."[16] It is reasonable to first meet the genuine needs of those closest to us for whom we are particularly responsible — for example, as parents.

Even theories that dictate strict impartiality would seldom go so far as to diminish the beneficial role of highly personal altruism that is

14. Hallett, *Priorities and Christian Ethics,* pp. 55-60.
15. Henry Sidgwick, *The Methods of Ethics* (1906; reprint, Indianapolis: Hackett Publishing, 1981), p. 241.
16. Adam Smith, *The Theory of Moral Sentiments,* ed. D. D. Raphael and A. L. Macfie (1759; reprint, Indianapolis: Liberty Classics, 1982), p. 216.

rooted in a history of ongoing relationships. To some extent we must leave the greatest happiness of the greatest number to God. But to what extent? Adam Smith suggested that "the care of the universal happiness of all rational and sensible beings, is the business of God and not of man."[17] But Smith's statement seems to go too far. As Christians, we certainly should be much concerned with "the care of the universal happiness of all rational and sensible beings." Even if we cannot tend to these concerns in every case, we should always pray that someone else will and make whatever contribution we can.

Simple moral formulas will not suffice. Other than to point strongly toward the ideal of serving all humanity and the problem of familial solipsism, I cannot say exactly how much the physician should sacrifice the well-being of spouse and children in order to serve until midnight in an overcrowded clinic day after day. There is inevitable variation in the particular loves and correlative commitments that individuals develop within their sphere of proximity. As a general rule, this proximate sphere is acceptably emphasized so long as (1) overindulgence and demonic consumerism are avoided and (2) the neediest neighbor remains of great concern.

Ethical theory over the last decade has started to take up the order of beneficence, although it has been recast as the partiality/impartiality debate. According to Marilyn Friedman, impartialists have clustered ethical theory around some "fictional images," such as Rodrick Firth's "ideal observer," which she characterizes as omnipercipient, omniscient, dispassionate, uncreaturely, but "otherwise normal."[18] Of course, the position of the impartial spectator or the ideal observer is useful in encouraging us to strive for a view of the whole picture of human need far and near, and is especially relevant in some ethical areas, such as in a court of law. "But this is hardly a way to treat loved ones," writes Friedman.[19] I am not questioning the ideal of impartiality; I am simply saying that it is not the whole of ethics. I would agree with Lawrence C. Becker, who points out that while morality "requires (at least some-

17. Smith, *The Theory of Moral Sentiments,* p. 237.
18. Marilyn Friedman, "The Social Self and the Partiality Debates," in *Feminist Ethics,* ed. Claudia Card (Lawrence: University Press of Kansas, 1991), p. 163.
19. Friedman, "The Social Self and the Partiality Debates," p. 163.

times) that we not play favorites, or manipulate rules to our personal advantage, or make ad hoc exceptions for ourselves," there are other times when impartiality is inappropriate: "What makes this problematic is the evident foolishness of following this logic to its apparent conclusion — that is, to the conclusion that we must act with perfect Godwinian impartiality in every aspect of our lives and with perfect Kantian attention to universalizable principles."[20]

As human beings we are finite creatures who are often immersed in and emotionally exhausted by the routines of daily family living, which are even more tiring if they involve caring for a parent with dementia or a child with severe retardation. If this is our immediate situation, often the best we can do toward meeting the needs of all humanity is to heroically struggle to meet the overwhelming needs of a single debilitated person living under the same roof with us. Our duties of beneficence are equal only in a most abstract way; in real life, duties are often laid down in a hierarchy and are to be fulfilled accordingly.

To ignore proximity and the difficulty of being overcommitted is to ignore most of the everyday moral dilemmas that weigh heavily on the conscience of most of us. In his discussion of neighbor love, the eighteenth-century Anglican moralist Joseph Butler emphasized the importance of removing "prejudices against public spirit." Butler was as suspicious of "private self-interest" as any impartialist. Yet, following both Stoic and Christian precedent (*philanthropia* and *agape*), he considered beneficence not a "blind propension" but one "directed by reason." He states that "the care of some persons, suppose children and families, is particularly committed to our charge by nature and Providence; as also that there are other circumstances, such as friendship or former obligations, which require that we do good to some, preferably to others."[21] A society ought not to forget these special commitments in determining public policies.

20. Lawrence C. Becker, "Impartiality and Ethical Theory," *Ethics: An International Journal of Social and Legal Philosophy (Symposium on Impartiality and Ethical Theory),* vol. 101, no. 4 (July 1991): 698.

21. Joseph Butler, "Fifteen Sermons," in *British Moralists, 1650-1800,* ed. D. D. Raphael (Oxford: Clarendon Press, 1969), pp. 373-74.

Justice and Special Relations

What Christianity rejects is providing for those near and dear in ways that go beyond essential needs while the neighbor suffers from injustice, insofar as his or her minimal human needs are ignored. But the justice of redistribution can become unfair — for example, when it forces parents to pay taxes on behalf of some morally legitimate cause, and the burdens of that payment will make it impossible for them to care adequately for their own children's genuine needs. Modern theories of distributive justice, like theories of beneficence, tend to ignore the family as a mediating structure between the individual and society. Predicated on an atomistic view of the self, these theories bury the social fact that there are morally meaningful relationships between the individual and society.

It is remarkable that this dimension of human social experience is so little discussed in contemporary philosophical writings. This may be because family loyalties have been interpreted by some as detracting from the public good. As Lawrence C. Becker writes, "Philosophers have long been divided about whether or not familial relationships are subversive of other social structures, especially those in the 'public' sphere." The priority sometimes afforded family relations has been associated with the perpetuation of "unjust property arrangements, and deeply entrenched, self-perpetuating inequality of opportunity."[22] Becker is right about philosophers' long-standing suspicion of the family. Indeed, in his *Republic,* Plato argued for the elimination of family relations altogether; in his later dialogue, the *Laws,* he still advocated severe regulation of the family. But it is important to bear in mind that Plato was talking about an ideal polis that never existed. And Aristotle, once Plato's student, developed an opposite viewpoint. In the first two books of his *Politics,* Aristotle retrieved family life as a good, and the Romans followed suit. Cicero referred to the family as the "seedbed of the state."[23]

22. Lawrence C. Becker, *Reciprocity* (London: Routledge & Kegan Paul, 1986), p. 392.

23. For a brief summary of historical material, see Jeffrey Blustein, *Parents and Children: The Ethics of the Family* (New York: Oxford, 1982), section 1.

Following Aristotle, Cicero, and Thomas Aquinas,[24] one philosophical position takes seriously the social value of family relations and obligations with respect to meeting needs. Its philosophy of the self takes into account biologically based roles and relations, and views the uniquely powerful duties that correlate with these roles as socially beneficial. Families often provide a uniquely loving environment for their members, and can also provide economic support that would otherwise come from the state. These are both individual and social goods.

Family relations and feelings do detract from social and distributive justice when they become ideologically absolutistic, thereby diminishing tolerance for that necessary redistribution of wealth which provides basic goods for those persons who clearly are unable to care for themselves. But those who, like Plato or Marx, would dismantle the family in order to ensure the common good have always discovered that the significance of the family has been re-embraced as enthusiasm for their idealistic theories has faded. Utopian efforts to ignore and even destroy the family inevitably result in dystopian tyranny. "After all," Josiah Royce writes, "fidelity and family devotion are amongst the most precious opportunities and instances of loyalty."[25]

No theory of justice that fails to strike a reasoned balance between the family and the common good or total utility is adequate; moreover, respect for familial loyalties contributes to the common good in most cases. An adequate theory of justice requires a principle of *subsidiarity* — that is, the notion, characteristic of Catholic social thought, that it is a disturbance of right social order to assign to a greater and higher association (the state) what a lesser and subordinate organization (the family) can do, or to seriously compromise the economic autonomy of the family through excessive redistribution. As John Paul II writes,

> The family is the primary institution at the base of our existence as human beings. It forms part of the large society which it constantly helps to create, but it also has its own distinct existence, its own char-

24. Thomas Aquinas, *Summa Theologiae,* trans. D. J. Sullivan (Chicago: Encyclopedia Britannica Press, 1952), II-II, Q. 26, A. 8.
25. Josiah Royce, *The Philosophy of Loyalty* (New York: Macmillan, 1908), p. 221.

acter and ends. Both these characteristics — its imminence in society on the one hand, its peculiar autonomy and inviolability on the other — must find reflection in legislation. The point of departure must be the law of nature; legislation concerning the family must objectively express the order implicit in its nature.[26]

Public policy should not undermine the rights of the family as an independent entity.

But many modern theorists writing about justice have lost touch with the principle of subsidiarity. They want to begin the theory of justice at some fictional zero point rather than build on and harness the realities and strengths of familial ties. The philosopher John Rawls has articulated the most respected modern theory of justice in his substantial work entitled *A Theory of Justice*. He places his hypothetical decision-makers in the "original position," and allows that "each person in the original position should care about the well-being of some of those in the next generation."[27] Only toward the end of this massive work do we discover the bias that prevents Rawls from having a more substantial view of the self and its relation to the family: "Of course, in a broader inquiry the institution of the family might be questioned, and other arrangements might indeed prove preferable."[28]

Despite their individualism, the libertarians do acknowledge the social nature of the self with respect to family relations. Friedrich A. Hayek, for instance, argues that justice must make good use of "the natural partiality of parents for their children." Moreover, he comments, "once we agree that it is desirable to harness the natural instincts of parents to equip the new generation as well as they can, there seems no sensible ground for limiting this to non-material benefits."[29] Robert Nozick, who, like Hayek, rejects all "patterned" theories of distribution, observes that those with non-libertarian views have great difficulty ac-

---

26. Karol Wojtyla (Pope John Paul II), *Love and Responsibility,* trans. H. T. Willetts (San Francisco: Ignatius Press, 1981), p. 217.

27. John Rawls, *A Theory of Justice* (Cambridge: Harvard University Press, 1971), p. 128.

28. Rawls, *A Theory of Justice,* p. 463.

29. Friedrich A. Hayek, *The Constitution of Liberty* (Chicago: University of Chicago Press, 1960), p. 91.

knowledging the social importance of families: "To [them], families are disturbing; for within a family occur transfers that upset the favored distributional pattern."[30]

But the libertarian view is not, in the end, Christian, because libertarians such as Nozick and Hayek reject all of the careful qualifications on family accumulation and connectedness that are characteristic of the Christian tradition (proscriptions against greed, excessive accumulation well beyond reasonable present and future need, inattentiveness to the neediest people outside the biological family). In seeing responsibilities to all humanity consistently eclipsed by responsibilities to the family, the libertarian simply refuses to take the struggle of the order of love seriously.

Yet, as moral philosopher Owen Flanagan points out, a degree of partialism seems human and acceptable, unless our moral theories are to violate what can be understood as psychologically possible in many (but not all) cases.[31] Michael Walzer, a political philosopher, would agree. In *Spheres of Justice,* he begins by describing the empirical particularities of distinctive spheres of justice, of which the domestic sphere is one. He notes that Plato set out to abolish "special affections," and the family in particular, for the purpose of the common good. However, Walzer rejects Plato and the wider historical tradition of anti-familialism that Plato set in motion. I quote Walzer's impressive passage in full:

> What we might think of as the highest form of communal life — universal brotherhood and sisterhood — is probably incompatible with any process of popular decision making. The case is the same in moral philosophy. A number of writers have argued that the highest form of ethical life is one where the "rule of prescriptive altruism" applies universally and there are no special obligations to kinfolk (or friends). Faced with a choice between saving my own child or someone else's from an imminent and terrible danger, I would adopt a random decision procedure. It would be much easier, obviously, if I were not able to recognize my own children, or if I had no children of my

30. Robert Nozick, *Anarchy, State, and Utopia* (New York: Basic Books, 1974), p. 167.

31. Owen Flanagan, *Varieties of Moral Personality: Ethics and Psychological Realism* (Cambridge: Harvard University Press, 1991).

own. But this highest form of ethical life is available only to a few strong-minded philosophers or to monks, hermits, and platonic guardians. The rest of us must settle for something less, which we are likely to think of as something better: we draw the best line that we can between the family and the community and live with the unequal intensities of love.[32]

Walzer reminds us that however much the philosophers and hermits choose to ignore the moral importance of familial affections and obligations as they develop an ethic for the neediest alone, most of us reject such reductive views of our duties. However much deductive theorists spin out theories of strict impartiality with regard to duties, Walzer points out, human beings do establish priorities that take the family into account.

Theories of justice might take the Scottish Enlightenment as a starting point, for it stressed the moral value of family affections and of affections in general. Since it is through the affections that family relations are generally expressed, it comes as no surprise that the strict rationalism of the Kantian and utilitarian schools would view these relations as obstacles to be overcome in the name of reason alone, and as hindrances to the realization of the universal community of rational beings. But the Scottish did, in fact, have a view of the human moral agent that properly takes into account the biological and emotional connections of common human experience. Thus, in 1792, Scottish philosopher Adam Ferguson wrote that moral theory must consider "the scenes in which we find ourselves destined to act." Ferguson underscored the moral value of "natural affections," "instinctive attachments," and the "relations of consanguinity." This moral value stems from the benefits that familial attachments and duties have for society: "Families may be considered as the elementary forms of society, or establishments the most indispensably necessary to the existence and preservation of the kind."[33]

Consistent with Scottish tradition, Alasdair MacIntyre has com-

---

32. Michael Walzer, *Spheres of Justice: A Defense of Pluralism and Equality* (New York: Basic Books, 1983), pp. 230-31.

33. Adam Ferguson, *Principles of Moral and Political Science,* in *The Scottish Moralists: On Human Nature and Society,* ed. Louis Schneider (Chicago: University of Chicago Press, 1967), p. 82.

plained about the "abstract and ghostly" theory of the self characteristic of Kant and of the Enlightenment in general. He writes, "I am brother, cousin and grandson, member of this household, that village, this tribe. These are not characteristics that belong to human beings accidentally, to be stripped away in order to discover the 'real me.' They are part of my substance, defining partially at least and sometimes wholly my obligations and duties."[34] The self is, phenomenologically considered, essentially immersed and morally bound by particular relations; moreover, these relations should not be overlooked, as though from the moral point of view only universal benevolence counts for goodness.

Ethics is more than what occurs between us and strangers, people we see once and will likely never see again. To take away all distinctions of preference based on family relations or loyalties resulting from relationships over time is to strip the moral domain of those areas that are especially valuable. Max Scheler, writing in 1915, warned of the social philosophers of his time: "Looking away from oneself is here mistaken for love!" He commented pointedly that "all love for a part of mankind — nation, family, individual — now appears as an unjust *deprivation* of what we owe only to the totality."[35] Scheler contrasted "love of mankind" with "love of one's neighbor," which is directed personally at those who are near and dear. He criticized Jeremy Bentham's simplistic notion that "each individual should count for one," as though ethics could be adequately grasped by a form of beneficence "only interested in the *sum total* of human individuals." Scheler concluded that modern ethics makes concern with proximate persons appear "*a priori* as a *deprivation* of the rights due to the wider circle."[36] His criticisms stand up well over time. I will add only that the inverse problem of deprivation is equally serious from a Christian perspective — that is, the concern with a narrow circle which makes concern with distant persons appear as an *a priori* deprivation.

34. Alasdair MacIntyre, *After Virtue: A Study in Moral Theory* (Notre Dame: University of Notre Dame Press, 1981), p. 32.

35. Max Scheler, *Ressentiment,* ed. Lewis A. Coser, trans. William W. Holdheim (1915; New York: Free Press, 1961), pp. 96, 115 (emphasis in original).

36. Scheler, *Ressentiment,* p. 116 (emphasis in original).

A Subpoint: Freud and Ethics

Interest in the order of love is not the sole purview of philosophers. Indeed, inattention to the order of love with respect to both beneficence and justice greatly concerned Sigmund Freud. Ernest Wallwork's *Psychoanalysis and Ethics* is a splendid study of Freud as an ethicist. Wallwork draws his interpretation of Freud chiefly from *Civilization and Its Discontents,* but also from *Group Psychology and the Analysis of the Ego.* At one point he concentrates on Freud's criticism of the love commandment for ignoring the complexity of competing moral demands. It is perceptive of Wallwork to include at the beginning of this discussion a footnote with the following qualification: "Because Freud's target is the common understanding among lay Christians, it is thus not surprising that the ethical writings of at least some theological ethicists generally escape his criticisms: for example, Aquinas recognizes that neighbor love should include the self, and that universal love of humankind is impossible if it is interpreted as requiring the same kind of affection for everyone (*Summa Theologica,* II-II, Q. 25, art. iv. and viii). Additionally, Aquinas maintains, as does Freud, that we ought to love our near ones more than others (*Summa Theologica,* II-II, Q. 26, art. vi)."[37] Freud's criticism of the love commandment would convincingly apply to the writings of Søren Kierkegaard and Anders Nygren, among others, who pay scant attention to so-called "special relations," and for whom the embeddedness of the moral agent in biological ordering, inevitably partial relationships, and in time itself seems to be irrelevant.

Of Freud's suspicions of the love commandment, I will concentrate on what Wallwork calls "The Unfairness of Equal Universal Love." Wallwork points out that Freud's objection to the love commandment "is the predominantly ethical claim that even if we could manage to love a complete stranger equally with an intimate, it would be 'wrong to do so' (SE 21 [1930]: 109)." Wallwork notes that Freud took seriously the duties imposed by special relationships and by the norm of reciprocity. Familial relationships and friendships have a cer-

37. Ernest Wallwork, *Psychoanalysis and Ethics* (New Haven: Yale University Press, 1991), p. 195, ft. 4.

tain priority within the domain of love, and they require no apologetics. But, Wallwork adds, the love commandment, as Freud understood it, "counsels promiscuity."[38] It is true, as Freud suggests, that if special relations are afforded their proper position in an order of love, then neighbor love becomes less morally simplistic and abstract. Yet as Garth Hallett would correctly inject, for the Christian, an intentional love for all of humanity, even while complex in its implementation, is a valid ideal that ought not to be reduced to moral "promiscuity."

Freud rejected the view that human beings lead a shadow-like existence amid principles, as though the moral life is by definition impersonal. His inductive and realist approach to beneficence seriously grapples with the boundaries between the near and distant domains. The fact is that most people struggle to balance obligations to strangers with obligations to family members and friends, as Wallwork suggests Freud himself did. Moreover, they confront difficult moral choices between obligations to self, spouse, children, aging parents, and siblings. Theories of ethics need to say more about how these competing obligations should be morally resolved.

Don S. Browning is among those who are working to deepen and flesh out an ethic that will inform the order of love. Partly influenced by Freud, Browning asserts that "equal-regard does not mean that we should sacrifice the needs of our own children or spouse in an effort ourselves to meet immediately and directly the needs of all other children and all other spouses." Browning argues that the order of beneficence is grounded in commitments and relations that are "necessities of life."[39] He develops a recovery of the *ordo caritatis* through the social sciences, and psychology in particular, while noting that the question of order has not been of interest to most modern ethicists.

38. Wallwork, *Psychoanalysis and Ethics*, p. 199.
39. Don S. Browning, *Religious Thought and the Modern Psychologies* (Philadelphia: Fortress Press, 1987), pp. 153, 154.

A Final Conclusion

The challenge facing the family is to nurture familial bonds in loyalty while simultaneously caring for the neediest neighbors. The consumer culture of material indulgence threatens to turn the family in upon itself so that it becomes morally distorted. In this context the outward-looking vision of neighbor love must distinguish the Christian family from the insular family that ignores the neediest and indulges the excessive wants of the nearest. It is perhaps in reaction to such excess that Christianity, with its prophetic ethic of neighbor love for all humanity, has sometimes neglected to fully appreciate the immense God-given value of the family as an institution upon which the well-being of society rests.

In this book I have underscored that immense value in a variety of ways consistent with the Prophets, with the teachings of Jesus of Nazareth, and with the history of Christian thought and culture. More lasting unions in marriage are the necessary foundation for the care of children and for the well-being of husbands and wives in relationships that develop and sustain deep spiritual, intellectual, and physical equality and respect. And as each of us grows old, no longer able to sustain the pace of earlier years, we hope that we have a caring spouse, faithful children, and the joy of grandchildren. This seems to be the pattern of creation and procreation to which most of us are called. The God who intends this good for us shows parental love toward everyone, and makes brothers and sisters of us in sibling solicitude. This divine model can inform and inspire us as we seek to build and nourish the family in society.

Selected Bibliography

Amato, Paul R., and Alan Booth. *A Generation at Risk: Growing Up in an Era of Family Upheaval.* Cambridge: Harvard University Press, 1991.

Atkinson, Clarissa W. *The Oldest Vocation: Christian Motherhood in the Middle Ages.* Ithaca, N.Y.: Cornell University Press, 1994.

Blankenhorn, David. *Fatherless America: Confronting Our Most Urgent Social Problem.* New York: Basic Books, 1995.

Browning, Don S., et al. *From Culture Wars to Common Ground: Religion and the American Family Debate.* Louisville, Ky.: Westminster/John Knox Press, 1997.

Burguire, Andre, et al., eds. *A History of the Family.* 2 vols. Cambridge: Harvard University Press, 1996.

Cherlin, Andrew J. *Marriage, Divorce, and Remarriage.* Cambridge: Harvard University Press, 1992.

Clapp, Rodney. *Families at the Crossroads: Beyond Traditional and Modern Options.* Downers Grove, Ill.: InterVarsity Press, 1993.

Feldman, David M. *Marital Relations, Birth Control, and Abortion in Jewish Law.* New York: Schocken, 1968.

Gies, Francis, and Joseph Gies. *Marriage and the Family in the Middle Ages.* New York: Harper & Row, 1987.

Glendon, Mary Ann. *Abortion and Divorce in Western Law.* Cambridge: Harvard University Press, 1987.

Hallett, Garth L. *Priorities and Christian Ethics.* New York: Cambridge University Press, 1997.

Hsu, Al. *The Single Issue*. Downers Grove, Ill.: InterVarsity Press, 1997.

Jewett, Paul K. *Man as Male and Female: A Study in Sexual Relations from a Theological Point of View*. Grand Rapids, Mich.: Wm. B. Eerdmans, 1975.

Lasch, Christopher. *Haven in a Heartless World: The Family Besieged*. New York: W. W. Norton, 1977.

McLanahan, Sara, and Gary Sandefur. *Growing Up with a Single Parent: What Hurts, What Helps*. Cambridge: Harvard University Press, 1994.

Morgan, Edmund S. *The Puritan Family: Religion and Domestic Relations in Seventeenth-Century New England*. New York: Harper & Row, 1944.

Phillips, Roderick. *Untying the Knot: A Short History of Divorce*. New York: Cambridge University Press, 1991.

Popenoe, David. *Disturbing the Nest: Family Change and Decline in Modern Societies*. New York: Aldine de Gruyter, 1988.

————. *Life without Father: Compelling New Evidence That Fatherhood and Marriage Are Indispensable for the Good of Children and Society*. New York: Free Press, 1996.

Post, Stephen G. *The Moral Challenge of Alzheimer Disease*. 2nd ed., rev. Baltimore, Md.: The Johns Hopkins University Press, 2000.

————. *Spheres of Love: Toward a New Ethics of the Family*. Dallas: Southern Methodist University Press, 1994.

Schillebeeckx, E. *Marriage: Human Reality and Saving Mystery*. Trans. N. D. Smith. New York: Sheed & Ward, 1965.

Stackhouse, Max L. *Covenant and Community: Faith, Family, and Economic Life*. Louisville, Ky.: Westminster/John Knox Press, 1997.

Van Leeuwen, Mary Stewart. *Gender and Grace: Love, Work, and Parenting in a Changing World*. Downers Grove, Ill.: InterVarsity Press, 1990.

Waite, Linda L., and M. Gallagher. *The Case for Marriage*. Cambridge: Harvard University Press, forthcoming.

Whitehead, Barbara Dafoe. *The Divorce Culture: Rethinking Our Commitments to Marriage and Family*. New York: Vintage Books, 1996.

Witte, John, Jr. *From Sacrament to Contract: Marriage, Religion, and Law in the Western Tradition*. Louisville, Ky.: Westminster/John Knox Press, 1997.

Index

abortion, 134

Abraham, 51, 57, 115

adoption: as agapic act, 119-20; and birth mothers, 133-36; birth parent reunions, 122-23; Christian views of, 130-33, 140; and genealogical mimicry, 121-22; history of, 125-29, 137; transracial, 142, 147-49

Adoptions and Assistance Act, 144-45

Adoptive Rights Movement, 122

adultery, 78, 84-85, 100

African Americans: and adoption, 147; as caregivers, 174; and foster care, 143; stereotypes of, 10-11

agape: and adoption, 119-20; and families, 66; and humanity, 3-4; and parental solicitude, 61-63; and self-sacrifice, 17. *See also* love

aging, 3, 153, 160. *See also* Alzheimer Disease; filial obligations

Albigensians, 71

Alexander III, 72

Althaus, Paul, 77

Alzheimer disease: and societal trends, 153-55; symptoms of, 155-57, 172. *See also* patients

Amato, Paul R., 14-15, 99

Anglicanism, 82-83

annulment, 84

Aquinas, Thomas: on love of humanity, 194; on marriage holiness, 71, 73, 75; on *ordo caritatis,* 180, 184-85

Aristotle, 80, 188

Atkinson, Clarissa W., 67, 73-74

Augustine, 180, 184, 185

Bainton, Roland, 77

Bakan, David, 105

Balch, David, 55, 57, 68

baptism, 88-89, 127-28. *See also* christening

Barth, Karl, 132, 140

Barth, R. P., 147

Bartholet, Elizabeth, 141

batchelorhood. *See* singleness

Becker, Lawrence C., 186-87, 188

Bentham, Jeremy, 193

Bernard, Jessie, 98

Betz, Hans Dieter, 88-89

Blankenhorn, David, 106-7

Booth, Alan, 14-15, 99

Boswell, John, 69, 127-29, 137

DiIulio, John J., 31-32

divorce: and children, 12-15; in covenant marriage law, 103; in Deuteronomy, 51, 53; historical grounds for, 78, 84-85; in Judaism, 54; in Lutheranism, 78; in Malachi, 51; in Mark, 45; and modern contributing factors, 13, 21; and men, 14, 27-28; in New Testament, 56; no-fault, 21, 103; Puritan view of, 79

divorce rate, 6-7

Dobson, James, 35-36

domestic partners, 39-40

Dominicans, 71, 74

Donagan, Alan, 130-31

dualism, 68, 72, 89-91

Eastern Orthodox Church, 70

Elshtain, Jean Bethke, 150

Engelhardt, H. Tristram, Jr., 169

Enlightenment, 91, 102-3; Scottish, 192-93

Epstein, Daniel Mark, 115

Erasmus, 84

ethics: and Freud, 194-95; natural-law, 30; and personhood, 168-71; prophetic, 29-36; Scheler's view of, 193. *See also* Christian ethics; prophetic ethics

Eugenius, 84

Everett, Debbie, 173

Familiaris Consortio, 75

family: caregiving role of, 157-60; versus common good, 188-93; definitions of, 5-6, 95-99, 97; diverse patterns of, 34; and equal regard, 35-36; genealogical, 120-24; and holiness, 66, 69; and Jesus Christ, 44, 55-59; Luther's view of, 76-77; mainline Protestant view of, 96; as metaphor, 60-62, 70; mission-based,

178-80; and preservationism, 143-45; Puritan view of, 80; as social institution, 94-95; transracial, 142

Farley, Margaret, 17

fatherhood, 104-8; and commitment, 19; and discipline, 81; evolutionary inclination toward, 26-27; Marcel's view of, 105; Puritan view of, 79. *See also* patriarchy

Feldman, David, 53

feminism, 98-99, 107, 108-9, 112

Ferguson, Adam, 192

filial obligations, 3, 50-51, 164-66

Finnis, John, 30

Fiorenza, Elisabeth Schüssler, 88-89

Firth, Rodrick, 186

Flanagan, Owen, 191

foster care, 143-45

Franciscans, 74

Frankel, Tamar, 53

Freud, Sigmund, 194-95

Friedman, Marilyn, 186

Gager, Kristin, 125

Garrett, William R., 96

Gaylin, Willard, 114-15

gender identity, 11-12, 167

genes, 16, 26, 28, 123

Genesis: Jesus' quoting of, 55-56; Lutheran view of, 76; and monogamy, 50-52; and "one flesh," 50-51, 75, 86; in Paul, 59-60

God: and holiness, 66; and maleness and femaleness, 111, 117; as parent metaphor, 60-61, 70; and Prodigal Son parable, 116-17

Gomer, 52

Goody, J., 71, 72

Great Awakening, 81

Great Britain: and adoption, 125; and divorce rate, 6-7; and no-fault divorce, 21; and stepfamilies, 17-18